Ready To Fi

How India and I Survived The ISRO Spy Case

CW00766468

Ready To Fire

How India and I Survived The ISRO Spy Case

S Nambi Narayanan, Arun Ram

BLOOMSBURY

NEW DELHI • LONDON • OXFORD • NEW YORK • SYDNEY

BLOOMSBURY INDIA
Bloomsbury Publishing India Pvt. Ltd
Second Floor, LSC Building No. 4, DDA Complex, Pocket C – 6 & 7,
Vasant Kunj, New Delhi, 110070

BLOOMSBURY, BLOOMSBURY INDIA and the Diana logo
are trademarks of Bloomsbury Publishing Plc

First Published in India 2018
This edition published 2022

ISBN: PB: 978-93-56400-65-8; eBook: 978-93-86826-27-5
6 8 10 9 7 5

Typeset in Bembo by Manipal Technologies Limited
Printed and bound in India Gopsons Papers Pvt. Ltd., Noida.

To find out more about our authors and books visit www.bloomsbury.com and sign
up for our newsletters

DEDICATION

I was neither a good husband nor an ideal father. I dedicate this book to my wife Meena and children Sankar and Geetha.

—Nambi Narayanan

ACKNOWLEDGEMENTS

Writing this book has been virtually reliving the incidents mentioned in it. Hence whoever helped me survive the ISRO spy case has helped me write this book, directly or indirectly.

I place on record my gratitude for these lawyers who helped me fight many a protracted legal battle:

K L Narasimhan, K Parasaran, K K Venugopal, Harish Salve, M N Sukumaran Nair, S Vijayakumar, B Raman Pillai, T S Arunachalam, S Muralidhar, Umapathy, P Surendran Nair, V G Govindan Nair, V Bhasurendran Nair, K P Dandapani, Thottathil B Radhakrishnan, V Giri, C Unnikrishnan, V Venugopalan Nair, V Selvaraj, Ponnappa Pillai, D Jayakrishnan, R Praveen Kumar, Suresh Kumar. V G Govindan Nair's clerk Krishnan Kutty was as efficient as a lawyer.

When a majority of Malayalam newspapers eagerly bought half-baked police stories and cooked up their own, an army of journalists, most of them from the English media, stood by the fundamentals of journalism. While all of them refused to be swayed by sensationalism, some exposed holes in the conspiracy theories.

They include T N Gopakumar, K M Roy, Zacharia, Madhu Nair, Ramanan, Narayana Pillai, Gopal Raj, KS Jayaraman, T S Subramanian, Ramachandran, Sekhar Gupta, Ritu Sarin, M G Radhakrishnan, Anand Parthasarathy and J Rajasekharan Nair.

Maithreyan, a social worker, The last one had also been a pillar of personal support to me. He also spent long hours giving me courage to fight on.

Several of my friends and colleagues have remained my pillars of support; they find mention in the book. I remember with gratitude Prof S Chandrasekhar, my long-time colleague in ISRO, who flew down to Kerala amidst his busy schedule to depose in a case I had filed for compensation.

Acknowledgements

I also salute two former CBI officers, M L Sharma and P M Nair, who were part of the spy case investigation team and later became my well-wishers.

AUTHOR'S NOTE

This book is not just an account of the ISRO spy case in which I was an accused. The case that broke out in the late 1994 as a potboiler of sex, spies and rocket science before dying down as a police misadventure that eventually fed an international conspiracy, however, forms the fulcrum of this book.

The spy case became such a defining incident that everything that happened in my life and in the development of India's space programme so far falls into either of the two periods: Before Spy Case and After Spy Case.

When the Kerala Police arrested me on November 30, 1994, I was 53. India's space programme, put to shape by Vikram Sarabhai as the Indian National Committee for Space Research (INCOSPAR) in 1962, was 31.

I, having taken over as the cryogenic project director and in the process of getting the technology from Russia, was scaling a peak of my career. The Indian Space Research Organisation (ISRO), which had just registered the nation's first successful launch of a Polar Satellite Launch Vehicle (PSLV) only the previous month, was at the cusp of a great leap in space.

This book seeks to tell you how an 'incident' involving an allegedly amorous police inspector's attempt to corner a Maldivian woman soon snowballed into an espionage case; how a faction in the Congress party used it to bring down a government; and how India's Intelligence Bureau (IB) played into some foreign hands to halt India's march in space.

As time proved, the grand design failed. The Central Bureau of Investigation (CBI) exonerated all the six accused and found the case to be 'false.' The premier investigating agency went to the extent of sending confidential reports to the Government of India and the Government of Kerala, naming officers of the IB and Kerala Police who fabricated the case, and seeking appropriate action against them.

Twenty-three years after I was implicated in the case, my family has been able to regain much of our pride; my son and daughter no longer have to live as a traitor's children; the media considers me a phoenix. But some of the damages the conspirators and their foot soldiers inflicted are irreparable. Like my career and my wife's mental peace.

A nation rebounds faster than a family. India's PSLV is today one of the most reliable and sought after rockets for satellite launches. India has developed its own cryogenic rocket engine to take heavier satellites to the geosynchronous orbit and send probes to the unexplored corners of the solar system.

But the ISRO spy case was able to delay India's cryogenic engine by at least 15 years. What does one gain from that? For one, a lot of money. India today offers to launch a satellite at a fraction of the price that NASA charges. A 2015 report of the Colorado-based Space Foundation pegged the global space economy of 2014 at $330 billion, with a 9% growth over the previous year. Satellite launches and related commercial activities constitute 75% of it.

It is in public domain how the US applied sanctions on India and Russia in 1992, a year after the two countries signed a contract for transfer of cryogenic technology. Piece together the timing of the ISRO spy case and a few later incidents, including a top IB man being given marching orders for supping with the CIA, and you see the plot.

There was a time when I wanted to end it all, but I had to live to tell the tale. And see my tormentors get their comeuppance. This book is not an effort in revenge. This is an experiment in something more powerful: truth.

— *S Nambi Narayanan*

PROLOGUE

On 20 October 1994, *Thaniniram*, a Malayalam eveninger, broke a story of a woman spy being arrested in Trivandrum. It spoke about a woman called Mariam Rasheeda, 38, a Maldivian spy on a mission to Trivandrum to get secret drawings of Indian rocket engines.

CPM mouthpiece *Desabhimani* followed up the story the next morning. Two days after the Maldivian woman's arrest, *Kerala Kaumudi*, another Malayalam daily, dropped a bombshell: Inspector General of Police Raman Srivastava, an officer considered a favourite of Chief Minister K Karunakaran, has links with the spy ring.

On 13 November 1994, the local police arrested another Maldivian woman, a friend of Mariam, called Fauziyya Hassan. Soon, virtually every vernacular newspaper in Kerala was reporting the spy case. Mariam, the reports said, served as a honey trap with Indian Space Research Organisation (ISRO) scientists to cart away drawings and documents of the cryogenic engine to her masters in Pakistan. Though Mariam Rasheeda, said to be a contract employee of the Maldives Government on a primary mission to gather information about a possible coup being planned against Maldives President Maumoon Abdul Gayoom, was first booked under the Foreigners Act for overstay, another case was filed under the Official Secrets Act.

The Kerala Police made more arrests by the end of the month and the list of accused included K Chandrasekhar, a Bangalore-based Indian representative of Russian space agency Glavkosmos; D Sasikumaran, deputy director, cryogenic project, ISRO; S Nambi Narayanan, director, cryogenic project, ISRO and S K Sharma, a Bangalore-based labour contractor. The Kerala Police formed a Special Investigation Team (SIT) headed by Siby Mathews, a deputy inspector general of police to investigate the case.

On 30 November 1994, the day Nambi Narayanan was arrested, Siby Mathews wrote to the Kerala DGP recommending that the case be handed over to the Central Bureau of Investigation (CBI). On 2 December 1994, the state government made this request to the Centre. By now, the Intelligence Bureau (IB) had already moved in and started interrogating the accused in Trivandrum. In a few days, the IB had sent reports to the higher ups including the Prime Minister's Office confirming espionage and implicating Raman Srivastava, though the Kerala Police had not named him as an accused.

On 13 January 1995, hearing a public interest litigation (PIL) by an NGO called Niyamavedi, a division bench of the Kerala High Court headed by Justice Sreedharan made some adverse comments on the CBI investigation, which did not find any evidence to link Srivastava with the case. This led to the IPS officer's suspension on the same day.

The CBI moved the Supreme Court bench of Justice Sujatha Manohar and got the remarks expunged. But by then, K Karunakaran was forced to step down as the Chief Minister after the opposition and a faction of the Congress accused him of shielding Srivastava and aiding the spy ring.

When the CBI started its investigation on 4 December 1994, the IB had readied a grand theory of espionage that included names of some businessmen in India, a few woman conduits in Sri Lanka and a few Pakistanis based out of Sri Lanka who were alleged to be the financiers of the deal. It said Nambi Narayanan and Sasikumaran passed on drawings and flight details of India's Polar Satellite Launch Vehicle (PSLV) and a cryogenic rocket engine to Pakistan through the Maldivian women and some other contacts in Colombo. It spoke about meetings in a few hotels in Chennai and Trivandrum where tens of thousands of dollars changed hands.

It also mentioned the names of Aleksandr Dunayev, the chairman of Russian agency Glavkosmos and its administrative officer in charge of cryogenic technology Aleksey V Vasin, while propounding the theory that the Russian Ural Airlines was used to smuggle out drawings and flight details of the rockets. The accused were booked under several laws, including the Official Secrets Act, 1923.

Much before the CBI refer report, on 14 November 1995, the Chief Judicial Magistrate (CJM), Ernakulam had acquitted Mariam Rasheeda in the case of overstaying. The court said inspector Vijayan was 'chasing the victim' and 'obstructing her from leaving India.'

The two ISRO scientists and the two other men were released on bail as early as in January 1995, but Mariam and Fauziya remained in jail as they were slapped with cases under the National Security Act and did not get sureties for bail. Mariam, in media interviews, said she was implicated in the case because she did not yield to inspector Vijayan's sexual advances.

The CBI, after custodial interrogation of the accused for more than fifteen days and another sixteen months of investigation, submitted a 'refer report' before the CJM, Ernakulam on 28 April 1996, saying the spy case was false.

Examining every point raised by the Kerala Police and the IB, the CBI report said there was no evidence to substantiate the charges. The ISRO scientists were not found to have passed on any drawings or documents to anyone. No significant document from ISRO was missing. Many of the foreigners named by the IB were found to have not been in India, some of the alleged conspirators had neither known each other nor met.

The meetings, where the documents were allegedly exchanged for money at hotels in Trivandrum and Chennai, were found to have not happened. Neither any incriminating document nor money – Indian or foreign – was recovered from the accused. A scrutiny of their bank accounts did not indicate anything suspicious. There was no mention of any spy activity in Mariam Rasheeda's diaries. The report also noted that some of the accused where tortured in the custody of the IB.

'To sum up,' the CBI report said, 'in view of the evidence on record, oral as well as documentary, as discussed above, the allegations of espionage are not proved and have been found to be false. It is therefore, prayed that the report may kindly be accepted and the accused discharged and permission be accorded to return the seized documents to the concerned.'

The CBI report also mentioned in passing about 'certain lapses' on the part of the Kerala Police and the IB. On this, the investigating agency send separate confidential reports, one on the IB investigation to the Union Government and the other on the Special Investigation Team to the Kerala Government.

In the former, the CBI said the interrogation reports as recorded by the IB officers were incoherent and full of contradictions. It said the IB officers acted in an unprofessional manner. The report specifically mentioned the names of joint director Mathew John and deputy director R B Sreekumar for having 'failed' in their duty to conduct the inquiry in an objective and fair manner.

In its report on the Kerala Police officers, the CBI named S Vijayan, special branch inspector; K K Joshwa, DSP, Crime Branch CID; Siby Mathews, DIG, Crime. On Siby Mathews, the CBI report said: "It was unprofessional on his part to have ordered indiscriminate arrests of top ISRO scientists who played a key role in the successful launching of satellites … thereby caused avoidable mental and physical agony to them."

On 2 May 1996, the CJM, Ernakulam passed an order accepting the CBI report and discharging all the accused in the spy case. That was not the end of the case. E K Nayanar, who was sworn in as the Chief Minister on 20 May 1996, under pressure from state police officers Siby Mathews, K K Joshwa and S Vijayan, ordered further investigation. When the accused and the CBI challenged this, the Kerala High Court bench headed by Justice K G Balakrishnan gave a peculiar order that said it cannot quash the government order, but the state had no jurisdiction to file a chargesheet under the Official Secrets Act.

This meant that whatever the further investigation found would not hold good in a court. The accused and the CBI challenged this order in the Supreme Court. The ISRO spy case finally came to a logical end on 29 April 1998 when the Supreme Court quashed the Kerala Government's notification for further investigation.

Justices M K Mukherjee and Syed Shah Mohammed Quadri of the Supreme Court noted in their order: 'If before taking up further investigation an opinion has already been formed regarding the guilt of the accused and, that too, at a stage when the commission of the offence itself is yet to be proved, it is obvious that the investigation cannot and will not be fair—and its outcome appears to be a foregone conclusion.'

All the accused in the spy case have disappeared from media glare, but not accused no. 5 Nambi Narayanan who has taken the battle to the enemy. The National Human Rights Commission ordered an 'immediate' interim compensation of Rs 10 lakh to Nambi Narayanan in 2001. It, however, took another eleven years and a Kerala High Court order for the Kerala Government to release the compensation.

He continues the battle with two goals: bring to book the officers of IB and Kerala Police who foisted the ISRO spy case. Expose the master conspirators of the case that affected the morale of Indian Space scientists and slowed down the nation's leap in space.

FOREWORD

This book is an autobiographical account of Nambi Narayanan, who is Nambi for his friends at the Indian Space Research Organisation (ISRO). From his early days in ISRO I knew him as an intelligent, hardworking and dedicated scientist with unquestionable integrity.

By watching him from a distance, I could see the potential of Nambi and I started closely associating with him on different occasions. As a director at ISRO headquarters, I had the opportunity to understand his eagerness to develop liquid propulsion technology for India. Nambi studied liquid propulsion technology in Princeton University, USA, with a NASA Fellowship. He secured his Master's degree in a record time of less than a year.

Prof Satish Dhawan gave all his support to Nambi to jointly develop the Vikas engine with a French company called SEP. I happened to closely associate with Nambi during this period. His excellent performance with very limited manpower under stringent financial constraints enabled India to master the Vikas engine technology.

This highly reliable engine was flight-tested in PSLV and, ever since 1994, continues to perform without a single failure. Nambi is much like this engine that came out of several trials by fire. He was falsely implicated in the ISRO spy case and arrested in November 1994. A CBI inquiry later found the case to be false – something which everyone who knew Nambi closely was sure about – and found fault with some officers of the Intelligence Bureau and the Kerala Police who investigated the case.

Besides documenting his trials, Nambi elaborates in this book the evolution of ISRO from its inception to the present. ISRO is a great achiever with an envious success rate compared to other departments of the Government of India.

This book also throws light on some internal politics and inflated egos that stood in the way of India's great leaps. Many of the anecdotes in this book are not known to the outside world. Some of them are interesting, even hilarious, some others are shocking. Some incidents narrated here give a peep into many personalities who rose to high levels in the organisation.

I am sure this book will be of great interest as much to the old generation that looked at a rocket with awe as to the young generation raring to go on interplanetary explorations.

T N SESHAN

CONTENTS

Contents

INTRODUCTION

By Parisian standards, it was an unusually bright morning when I stepped into the Paris–Le Bourget airport to see the Aerospace Exhibition, 1975. The rocket engines on display glistened in the light that streamed through the glass panes and bounced off the sobre white walls. I walked past the array of items on display—a liquid propulsion engine here, a prototype of a dual-frequency radar there—with my colleague P Mohana Prasad in tow.

We often travelled together on such assignments. We enjoyed each other's company, partly because of our shared passion to make India a space superpower, and partly because of our differences that helped fill the gaps between our common goal and our varying perceptions on how to achieve it.

Prasad, who went on to develop India's Vikas engine with me, would brood over scientific puzzles for days. He would run multiple tests and cross-check results before commenting on something scientific. I, on the other hand, would sometimes be impulsive, even on scientific matters. I might look at a microscopic groove in an intricate engine, and, before scientific validation, instinctively say that the depth is two microns, and not one micron as planned. We all knew very well that the unaided human eye couldn't see the difference; nevertheless I 'saw' something that impelled me to comment. Indeed, we would run it through tests to ascertain the depth of the groove—and my instant, scientifically unaided, observation would be correct, nine out of ten times.

That morning at the Paris-Le Bourget Airport presented me with one such moment of instant cognition—a 'Blink' moment, as Malcolm Gladwell called it. It was a moment that would eventually lead me to a series of incidents—apparently normal, some even unconnected—that would change my life and, to a great degree, alter the pace of India's space research, some nineteen years later.

As we walked past a few charts on display, between a heat shield of a rocket and a model of an improvised payload, there sat a rocket engine from the USSR. It was grey, and it had everything the texts said about such an engine. There was nothing apparently remarkable about it, but I found myself staring at it longer than I wanted to.

Then I realised it: The engine wasn't what its label read—RD-100. 'They've got the label wrong,' I told Prasad, as we were about to move on to the payload on display. But Prasad stopped to take closer look. We seemed to be having a difference of opinion here; so the first thing to do was to ask a Russian scientist for clarification. But there was none nearby. At a distance sat a seventy-five-something man, his clothes as wrinkled as his skin. He appeared to be a helper of some sort, one of those who understood little English and no science.

No sooner had we moved on than someone called out, 'Now, gentleman, what makes you think it's not an RD-100?'

It was the Russian, now his face even more wrinkled because of a frown. I walked up to him and, trying to be polite to the point of being apologetic (not for the comment I made about the engine, but for the assessment I made of him), said, 'Because it doesn't look like one.'

He insisted it was an RD-100, but I stuck to my guns. 'An RD-100 has a different type of a cooling passage,' I said, and went on rattling out whatever I knew about the engine and its inconsistencies with the piece on display.

The frown on the Russian's face was now a scowl. He looked at me for a few seconds in silence and, as if ironing out those folds on his forehead, ran his palm over his eyebrows, and assumed the calmness of a disturbed saint. 'Can we discuss this over dinner?' he asked.

Later that evening, over delicious French soup and bread, the Russian explained to us the specifications of the engine on display. 'And yes,' he said after a noisy sip of tourin, 'it is not what it's labelled.' It was another engine, the specifications of which the USSR did not want to divulge. There were several such pieces of secret pride in the Soviet storerooms, he said, one such was the KVD-1 cryogenic engine.

'What's the specific impulse of this KVD–1 engine?' I asked, unable to hide my curiosity at the mention of the word 'cryogenic'.

'The specific impulse is,' the Russian paused, '461 seconds'.

We all knew that the Americans and the Russians were in a space race, the latest being in the development of cryogenic engines. Cryogenics, the science of extreme low temperatures, has been a tricky thing to master, and the two countries had achieved quite a few breakthroughs. Like the space-faring giants the US and the USSR, India—which had just put its first satellite Aryabhatta in space with Russia's help—had realised that only cryogenic engines could power rockets to take heavier satellites and make farther explorations in space. The specific impulse of an engine, broadly speaking, defines its strength. The Americans had developed engines with lesser specific impulse. Russians were great engineers—and much more amiable towards Indians than the Americans were—but they having developed anything better than the Amercan cryogenic engine sounded farfetched.

'You must be joking,' I told him, trying to make it sound more like banter than an argument. The Russian wasn't amused. He gulped down the soup, looked me in the eye with the same calmness he had the moment before he invited me for dinner, and said, 'Come to Russia, and I will show you.'

It was a new beginning of a friendship between two countries that later fired India's cryogenic dreams. Eighteen years later, when the Kerala police came knocking at my door in Thiruvananthapuram, that dream was threatened. I was to be branded a spy who sold rocket engine secrets to Pakistan through women spies from the Maldives—a conspiracy that would be eventually defeated, but not before dampening India's space dreams and virtually demolishing my life.

But India's space ambitions, fuelled by such greats as Vikram Sarabhai and Satish Dhawan, would overcome the *agnipariksha*, as time proved. Curiously enough, it took another eighteen years for me to prove my innocence—and for others to accept that the sordid drama of the ISRO spy case was but a fallout of a reckless police sub-inspector's misadventure with a Maldivian woman; a drama that a foreign agency was only too eager to prolong and propel, penetrating into such agencies as the Indian Intelligence Bureau, and taking some of its officials as pawns, to scuttle India's inevitable march to space.

This is the story of that conspiracy against my country. This is my story.

CHAPTER 1

I SPY

'Whoever is tapping our phones should have some fun.'

They came early in the afternoon. Jogesh, the inspector of Vanchiyoor police station, Trivandrum, Thambidurga Dutt, the sub-inspector, and the two constables were cordial.

'Sir, the DIG wants to talk to you,' said Jogesh.

'Am I under arrest?' I asked.

'No, sir' the inspector said, 'The DIG wants to talk to you.'

I put on a shirt and trousers and walked out with them to the waiting police jeep.

'Should I take the backseat or should I sit in the front?' I asked.

In Kerala, criminals are dumped between the back seats that constables occupy to land blows on the back of the accused. Usually the police inspector or the sub-inspector sat in the front seat. Jogesh was considerate. He ushered me to the front seat.

This arrest, as it turned out, was not totally unexpected. The date was 30 November 1994.

More than a month earlier, on 20 October to be precise, a Maldivian woman named Mariam Rasheeda was arrested on charges of overstaying in Trivandrum. In the subsequent days, Malayalam newspapers had reported her alleged role as a spy and a conduit in carting away India's rocket secrets to Pakistan by using some contacts in Indian Space Research Organisation (ISRO). On 13 November, the local police arrested another Maldivian woman named Fauziyya

Hassan, a friend of Mariam, in connection with what was now called the espionage case.

The first ISRO scientist whose name was dragged into the story was that of D Sasikumaran, my deputy in the cryogenic engine project, which I was heading. I was also the project director in charge of liquid propulsion systems.

As the ISRO spy story got raunchier by the day, we, a few close friends in the organisation, started discussing whether Sasikumaran actually had something to do with Mariam. But we all laughed at the espionage part of it. The reason was simple: India just did not have the know-how to make a cryogenic engine. There were of course several drawings and blueprints of the Vikas engine which we had developed over five years working with French space scientists, and those were routinely shared with Indian manufacturers. There was nothing classified which had to be smuggled. Anyone with a basic understanding of rocket science knows even if the drawings are given, an engine cannot be made without long years of development, guidance and extensive tests. In other words, you can't make a rocket engine based on know-how—you need the 'know-why'. If rockets were built merely with drawings, there is no reason why every space-faring nation is making rockets its own way and not copying from others.

My colleagues Mohana Prasad, M K Gopinathan Nair and I frequently spoke about the absurdities in the spy story the police and the newspapers were cooking up. Often we spoke on the phone. During one such conversation, I felt that my phone was being tapped, and immediately told Gopi, who was at the other end.

'How do you know?' he asked.

I told him there was a 'click' noise after which the volume dipped slightly—tell-tale signs of unsophisticated telephone tapping.

'Anyway, whoever is tapping, let him have fun. We have no secrets,' I said.

We carried on with our conversation. The more the stories of spying came out, the more convinced we were of the stupidity of the perpetrators, whoever they may be. But it ceased to be a laughing matter as police arrested Sasikumaran on 14 November. The police had found in Mariam's diary the telephone numbers of Sasikumaran's residence and office.

It later turned out that Sasikumaran did know Mariam through a common friend called Chandrasekhar, with whom ISRO had a business in connection with the cryogenic project. Chandrasekhar, who met Mariam at the Trivandrum airport, had put her on to Sasikumaran for a consultation with his wife who was a doctor. Some admissible evidence of their meeting with Mariam was to become clear to me only much later.

A fortnight after Sasikumaran's arrest, on 30 November morning, Gopi, Mohana Prasad and Isaac Mathew, an industrialist friend close to my family, came to my place. It was unusual for the trio to be there without notice. They looked glum. Having seated them in the drawing room, I asked what was wrong. They looked at each other.

'Is someone unwell?' I prodded. After a minute of silence, Isaac spoke.

'Nambi, you will be arrested today.'

I said he must be joking. He explained that he had come to know the previous night from an IB officer called Mathew John that I would be arrested. The three friends discussed the matter and debated whether to tell me the previous night, but decided to come personally this morning to break the news.

Now that the possibility had sunk in, I called my son Sankara Kumar. 'See, I don't know if it is true, but I may be arrested,' I told him. As we were talking my wife Meena passed by and we fell silent. We did not want her to know anything now. I told my son that my bank balance was poor, maybe a few thousands of rupees there, but don't worry about money since he can ask Isaac or Mohana Prasad. Sankar went out to find out if the news was authentic. He got back early afternoon. One look at his face and I knew it. He started crying.

'They're coming for you, Appa,' he sobbed.

At the Vanchiyoor Police Station I was asked to sit on a bench. Policemen kept passing by, some throwing nasty glances at me, some others just curious. A constable stared at me with an expression that reflected utter contempt. I couldn't stand it and shouted, 'Why are you staring at me?' Before he could get near me, someone took him away. There was no sign of DIG Siby Mathews. Whenever I asked for the officer, policemen said he was on the way. In the evening, a policeman came and asked me what food I wanted. I said nothing. I felt like having a smoke. I had quit smoking in 1991, before which I used to smoke about forty cigarettes a day. 'I need a packet of cigarettes,' I said.

'Which brand?'

'Get me a pack of Wills.'

The policeman came with the cigarettes and I started chain-smoking. I could hear in bits and pieces policemen discussing the ISRO spy case. I heard the names Mariam Rasheeda and Sasikumaran. Then I heard someone mentioning my name. Someone brought a biryani which I refused to eat. I had water. I smoked. I felt like asking for a drink, but decided against it. Nobody came till nightfall, and I slept on the bench. I dreamt of my father.

KAMARAJ AND KINETICS

A giant comes to campus, a teacher shows anything is possible.

Mathematicians think they can solve any problem. And then, life intervenes with its absurd equations and cruel calculations. Being good at mathematics made me think I can anticipate, encounter and solve any problem. As for the unsolvable ones, I knew why there can't be an absolute solution, and hence should seek alternatives. This had kept me in good stead as a student, as a sugar factory employee, and later as a rocket scientist.

But fate did intervene in different ways; sometimes taking me to levels of confidence that bordered on arrogance, at others to black holes of emotions where suicide was a logical end, and then to a state of measured optimism, courageous fight back and composed indifference. Some call it the survival kit of a spy who never was. I call it life.

I was born when my father, a well-to-do businessman who traded in copra, coir and oil in Trivandrum, suddenly realised that he either miscalculated his life or never bothered to calculate at all. He had partnered with his elder brother, and together they had made quite a fortune when his brother died. Suddenly, the brother's wife, my aunt, said my father had no right over the capital, savings or profit. He fought a case for eleven years.

It was at the end of my father's eleven-year legal battle that I was born on 12 December 1941. The first boy in the family after four girls, my arrival was considered a lucky omen as within a month the court settled the business dispute in my father's favour. He got his fair share of the business, but was still in no mood to rejoice as he felt sad about having got into a duel with the family of his brother who he so adored.

Adding to father's misery, his brother's wife committed suicide, probably because she could not take the outcome of the long drawn court case. My father could well have continued his business in Trivandrum, but so heartbroken he was that he decided to pack his things and move the family to Nagercoil, where he would start an oil business, with modest results. I was a few months old then.

I have no memories of my father struggling; he kept us happy. We lived in a decent house that had electricity and water supply, which were not common in the early 1940s in that southern tip of India. As for school uniforms, books and other facilities, I did not have to ask. And I loved mathematics.

But my initiation to schooling was not easy—at least for my mom. When admitted to the first standard at the Parakkamadai Government School in Nagercoil, I just refused to go. The reason was simple: I wanted to be with my mother. When she offered to come along to the school, she did not know what she was getting into.

I agreed to go to school under the condition that mother stood outside my class, in my field of vision. She must have thought she could slip away back home after a couple of days of this torture, but every time she disappeared from my sight, I would make a hell out of it forcing the teacher to stop the class and bring back my mother to stand outside the classroom. This continued till the third standard before I let her go home. After fifth standard, I shifted school.

Schooling at Desiya Vinayaka Devasthanam was a breeze, and I topped in the tenth standard. In the pre-university course at South Travancore Hindu College, too, the feat repeated. When my close friend and academic competitor Kaliyampillai chose to study medicine, I thought for a moment and decided that applications of Pythagoras won't help much in treating cholera or removing an appendix. So engineering it was for me.

Just when I was to apply for an engineering seat, I fell ill with typhoid, pneumonia and pleurisy. It was a deadly combination, and my mother was paranoid that something might happen to me. And she had her reason; my eldest sister had died at the age of eighteen. All I was told was that she had a 'bone problem.'

Down for several weeks, I missed the admission that year and joined Scott Christian College, Nagercoil as a BSc Maths student. It was only an interregnum, and I resolved to apply for engineering the following year.

Tamil Nadu had just six engineering colleges then, two government colleges and four in the private sector. The government colleges were in Chennai and Coimbatore. The others were Thyagaraja College of Engineering, Madurai; Alagappa Chettiar College of Technology, Karaikudi; PSG College of Technology, Coimbatore; and College of Engineering & Technology, Coimbatore. Though a year late, my grades in the pre-university course still kept me in good stead.

I chose Thyagarajar College of Engineering, Madurai, a 500-acre hilly campus where peacocks roamed. Thyagaraja Chettiar, the founder, was not an academician, but he made sure that the college had the best of faculty and facilities to produce a bright crop of engineers that the nation badly needed.

I joined the college in June 1960. It was one of the most poignant moments in my life, when I realised the depth of my emotional bond with my father—and vice versa. So far, father had been a figure of respect and fear for me; he rarely interacted with us children. He would leave early for his oil shop and by the time he got back home, we would be fast asleep.

So I was surprised when father insisted on accompanying me to the college on the first day. The college buildings were still under construction and outstation students were given some rented houses on the outskirts as hostels. After the first-day formalities at the college, father came with me to the hostel—a small house with the number 'A31' at Thiru Nagar about three kilometer from the campus. After depositing me and the bags, father held my hand and started crying.

It was the second time I was seeing him in tears—the first was when his mother, my grandmother, died. I could not fathom the emotional turmoil I was going through. I felt myself choking while trying to stop myself from crying. I never thought my father and I shared such a bond. I suddenly felt I would be too lonely without my father's silent presence.

'Take care of your health, study well,' he said, and walked away.

I stood there at the gate even after he disappeared around the bend of the road. I felt a vacuum within. Five months later, I would be standing here again, on a rainy night, to receive a telegram from home.

On that November night, when the rain came down in sheets, I lay awake as if expecting the bad news. When the postman clanked the gate around 3.30 am, I opened the door as if it was all pre-progammed. I walked up to the gate as if in a trance and took the telegram. Before opening it I knew the content. The telegram read: FATHER SERIOUS. START IMMEDIATELY. The crumpled paper with the black telegraphic letters was wet. It must have been the rain. Or my tears.

I do not remember packing anything, I just walked out of the hostel with whatever little money I had. A goods truck took me to Tirunelveli from where I took a bus to Nagercoil. My house was still some distance away. I walked to the place of Shanmugham, a news agent I knew in Nagercoil. He was not there. I took his bicycle and pedalled home.

A cousin saw me coming and took me inside the house. My father was lying unconscious. The cousin briefed me that father had suffered a heart attack the previous day and the family had taken him to Dr Seetharaman in Trivandrum. Father had slipped into a coma, and that is when they sent me the telegram. On the doctor's advice, they had brought him home. Father died on the third day.

It was only now that I realised I hailed from a financially mediocre family, and its prime breadwinner was no more. By providing us everything we needed, father had shielded us from the financial constraints of bringing up five children with his sole income. Now, that shield was gone.

Two of my elder sisters were married, and there were two more to be taken care of. Mother looked up to me, and I looked inward. There was a discussion whether I should continue my studies or take over father's business. My two brothers-in-law, who were prospective successors to father's business, backed out.

Suddenly, I was a responsible person. And that can be tough at the age of nineteen, when you dream of getting an engineering degree and probably going abroad for higher studies. Fortunately for me, two of my sisters put their foot down: 'Nambi will continue to study.'

Another blessing—and a big one at that—was the merit-cum-means national scholarship my academic record had ensured. The money— Rs 1,400 a year—was enough to meet my study-related expenses. As for my occasional visit from the campus in Madurai to the family in Nagercoil, the sisters chipped in. I was back in college. While I mingled with a large number of students who had come to the campus from far and wide, three of us from Nagercoil—A Chandran, Lawrence and I—remained as 'the gang'. We would go to our native place together during holidays, and were like an extended family. Lawrence's father, a retired army man, was entangled in a false case and the burden of running the family fell on his mother. She did this gracefully, and the pleasant woman remained a source of motherly love for all of us.

Chandran's father Mr N A Appan was a jovial man. Having retired as a labour commissioner in Singapore and returned to Nagercoil, he welcomed, mockingly, the devaluation of the Indian rupee at that time. He would joke that now his pension, when converted to Indian currency, was more than his salary. Lawrence later became a Colonel in the Indian Army; Chandran became my ISRO colleague and succeeded me in heading the Vikas engine project team in France in the late 1970s.

Outside 'the gang', a classmate called K Kalanidhi attracted my attention for his calmness. Those were turbulent times of the anti-Hindi agitation, and Kalanidhi showed great balance of opinion and action. After being elected the joint secretary of the student's union in my third year, I worked to make Kalanidhi the secretary in the fourth year, but he lost the election by a few votes. He died in a bus crash in 2014 while travelling from Chennai to Madurai.

K S Mani, another college mate, who I respected for his unflinching loyalty to fairness beyond caste and creed, came to be known as Avro Mani, after he miraculously survived an Avro aircraft crash in 1971. Mani, then with ISRO, was on his maiden flight, from Trivandrum to Chennai, when the plane crashed into the Meghamalai tea plantation. Mani survived with a broken angle and a few bruises.

The rigour of the course then was such that only twelve of the 120 students passed out of the campus with a first class. I owe it to a handful of great teachers for being one of the high-fliers of Thyagarajar College of Engineering. Amidst the hectic schedule of classes, exams and some wonderful projects, I found time to take part in student activities and got elected as joint secretary of the student union.

It was the peak of the Dravidian movement in Tamil Nadu, but K Kamaraj remained the Chief Minister—and the undisputed king of many hearts. Thyagaraja Chettiar, the founder of our college was keen on bringing Kamaraj to the campus for an interaction with the students, but a section affiliated to the Dravida Munnetra Kazhagam (DMK) laughed at the idea. Their logic was simple: Kamaraj was neither a scholar nor an orator—both perceived prerequisites for a college guest at a time when DMK leaders like C N Annadurai were the faces of intellectualism.

I took upon myself the mission of bringing Kamaraj to the campus. After much effort when I finally met him, Kamaraj gave the same reason as the Dravidian sympathizers had for not having the Chief Minister on the campus. 'What do I, a school dropout, talk to you brilliant students?' he said. 'All I have to tell you youngsters is to study well and serve the country.'

I did not give up. After much persuasion, when the great man finally agreed to address the Thyagaraja College students, Chettiar was happy. And I was proud.

Kamaraj won over even his detractors with his simplicity and clarity of thought. What attracted me more to the Congress leader was his sense of empathy, which was at the root of every decision he took as the Chief Minister. For what he had not learned from books—as Annadurai and some other Dravidian party leaders did—Kamaraj imbibed from life experiences.

The now famous mid-day meal scheme in schools was one such initiative. The British had introduced the programme to feed poor children in primary schools of Madras Presidency as early as in 1925, but after Independence thousands of children were out of school because they had to work to support their parents to earn. It was not a sense of history that prompted Kamaraj to reintroduce the scheme in 1962. It was a life event of a school boy called Valluvan that moved Kamaraj to feed the children and keep them in schools.

Providence—some call it coincidence—has played a key role in the making and unmaking of history. Here, it so happened that Valluvan was a sympathetic boy and the son of N D Sundaravadivelu, who was then the director of public instruction and Kamaraj's advisor on education. Valluvan often went home hungry and sad. When Sundaravadivelu asked him the reason, the boy said he was giving away his lunch to students who could not afford a morsel and hence were irregular to school. Sundaravadivelu reported this to Kamaraj who immediately ordered the mid-day meal scheme. It became a benchmark for several other Indian states and a reference point for international agencies dealing with nutrition and education.

While student activities on the campus instilled in us a sense of societal commitment, a crop of outstanding teachers made academics gruelling and rewarding. I owe much more than my engineering skills to six professors—V Subbaraman, C Kothandaraman, P L Meiyappan, Krishnan, Maria Loius and M V Ramamurthy. Professor Kothandaraman taught heat transfer, and was in charge of the laboratory which went on to become the workshop of many great beginnings.

Prof. V Subbaraman, head of the department of mechanical engineering who taught me applied thermodynamics, was a man of fairness. When another professor, who had an unexplained dislike for me, gave me very low marks in an internal, it was Prof. Subbaraman who intervened and set right the anomaly. While facing problems at my first job, I had contacted Prof. Subbaraman who asked me to stay put. Engineering college projects are usually done piece meal: one student does the design, another fabricates, and a third tests. Prof. Kothandaraman wanted each student to do a complete project, from scrap to functional testing. Prof. Kothandaraman taught me to say 'it's possible'. And that was something I repeatedly said as a rocket scientist years later, while developing the Vikas rocket engine, and later as the head of the cryogenics project.

Prof. Meiyappan, who taught applied mechanics, and Prof. Maria Loius who handled electrical engineering were equally brilliant, but contrasting in their decibels. Prof. Meiyappan would have the class in rapt attention with his thundering voice; Prof. Louis virtually whispered, making us strain our ears to get the equations right. At the end of the year, the teacher surprised us speaking loud. 'You know, I have a loud voice,' he said. 'But I kept talking in a low tone because I wanted you to concentrate more on what I was saying.'

Prof. Krishnan was a no-nonsense teacher of mathematics. Having taken the day's attendance, he would say, 'Now, whoever wants to leave may please do so; only those who want to learn, stay here'. And towards the end of the year, he would tell those few students who had the courage to leave his class, 'You have bunked enough to flunk the exams, but I assure you if you attend the class at least from now, you will go out of this campus with an engineering degree.' None left the class thereafter.

Prof. M V Ramamurthy approached the most convoluted of problems in the jolliest manner possible—and made learning a pleasure for us. Prof. Kothandaraman took all kinds of questions—including those on unsolvable problems—with ease. He was a genius who was never afraid of problems. Later in my life, when a rocket project either failed or got delayed, I thought of Prof. Kothandaraman and took the problem head on. But life is not always rocket science, as the spy case would teach me more than thirty years later. However, when the universe appeared to be conspiring against me, I conjured up images of my gurus, and when everyone said I may not be able to make it to sanity, I told myself: It's possible.

Because of the Chinese aggression of 1964, the course was accelerated to be completed in January 1965, a couple of months ahead of schedule. Before the course ended, I had started dreaming bigger. Royal Naval Engineering College in Southampton, UK, was offering a course in naval engineering; I applied. I also sent in my application to Princeton University and California Institute of Technology (Caltech). There was no reply from Southampton. With offers of admission from both Princeton and Caltech came a dilemma: My mother was ailing; do I chase my dream or be with her? Mother did not say anything, but I could sense what she wanted. 'Be near me,' appeared to be telling me. 'The nearer the better.'

CHAPTER 2

IN THE DOCK

'What's the charge?'

In the morning, I went to a dirty loo attached to the Vanchiyoor Police Station, and was on my way back to the bench when I heard the commotion. Newspaper reporters and photographers were thronging the police station to get a glimpse of Nambi Narayanan, the traitor who sold state secrets to Pakistan through two Maldivian women who acted as honey traps. Then I saw the four-column news below the fold of the day's *Malayala Manorama*: ISRO spy case mastermind arrested. An enterprising journalist had managed to get an old photograph of mine from somewhere to go with the text. Since I could not read much Malayalam, and since it did not matter what they wrote about me, I left the newspaper there and sat on the bench as photographers clicked away.

Among the journalists was a man in a kurta with a sling bag—the trademark of many journalists of Kerala then. He spoke only Hindi, and appeared to be at a loss as the other journalists and policemen chatted away in Malayalam. It would only be days later that I would see this man again, this time as a CBI officer. P M Nair, the officer, was in disguise to glean what the buzz about the spy case was all about.

Nair, a Deputy Inspector General with the CBI, was in Trivandrum on another assignment. He was to return two days later when his boss asked him to stay back: The Kerala Government had sent a requisition for a CBI probe into what was turning out to be the ISRO spy case. The CBI top brass wanted Nair to nose around a bit before returning to

Delhi. Nair, a Malayalee, was pretending to be a Hindi-speaking man to eavesdrop on policemen. Later Nair told me he had to struggle not be biased against the Kerala police, as the conversations at the police station were about 'fixing' rather than finding the truth.

The Vanchiyoor Police took me to Additional Chief Judicial Magistrate Anil Kumar.

'Do you plead guilty?' were his first words.

'What's the charge?' I asked.

A court clerk brought a plain white paper and asked me to sign. I asked what it was for, and he said some formalities. I did not want to sign on a blank paper, but I had to. So I signed on the top end of the paper so that they wouldn't write something above it and hold me responsible for having endorsed it. I looked around the courtroom. There was a crowd outside, but I couldn't find any friend or acquaintance. Another round of scanning and I saw a familiar face—that of Raj Chengappa, a journalist who had been in touch with me while doing stories on ISRO. I called out to him and he said something sympathetic. The Additional Chief Judicial Magistrate remanded me in police custody for eleven days. Now I was officially an accused in the ISRO spy case.

When I came out of the courtroom there was a huge, swelling crowd. Press photographers jostled with each other to get a good shot of mine. A policeman offered a towel and told me I could use is to cover my face. I refused. Among the crowd were two or three familiar faces, including that of Gopinath, a clerk in the medical section of ISRO. Later, I was told that many friends and colleagues had come there.

I was still in shock, then a trance. At one instance it appeared to me that I was watching a movie—with me as the central character. Here I was watching at myself from a distance, being arrested and taken to prison for having sold India's rocket science secrets to an enemy country. In the brief and intermittent moments of my return from the trance, such questions bolted through my mind: Why did this happen? Who is behind this treachery? What wrong did I do? Why me? There were no answers; and I did not try too hard to find them. At least not now.

I got into the police jeep. Just when the vehicle was to move forward, a group of photographers rushed in, clicking furiously. I requested the driver to stop the vehicle.

'Let everyone get a good photograph of mine. Everyone should be satisfied,' I said.

Among the photographers was Babu, a friend of mine. His click made it to the cover page of *India Today* magazine. And I became the iconic face of the ISRO spy case. Babu came to me after my release, and apologised profusely.

'You were just doing your job,' I told him. 'And you did it quite well.'

I was in police custody now, which meant they were going to interrogate me. I did not know where they were taking me, but the route was familiar to me as I had lived most of my life in Trivandrum. From Vanchiyoor Police Station, the van moved to Pattoor, took a turn to the right, up to the General Hospital junction and then to Vazhuthakaud. Finally we arrived at the Latex Guest House in Poojapura. This place would be my residence for four days when I would be tortured by a group of Intelligence Bureau officials with a fictitious story outline they had no idea how to fill in.

INTO THE BAGASSE PIT

Without the right partner, a game of bridge and rocket science can end with some very bad blood.

Friends told me in half jest that I had the sweetest job offer when Parry & Co. advertised for a trainee assistant engineer for its facility, Deccan Sugars & Abkari Company in Trichy. I applied, and the job was mine. The company made a deal: I will be designated trainee assistant engineer for three years with a monthly stipend of Rs 300 for the first year, Rs 400 for the second and Rs 500 for the third, before the job will be confirmed and the 'trainee' tag will be sent to the crushing mill. I said yes.

I needed not more than Rs 100 to meet my expenses, and sent the rest home. It wasn't a job I wanted to do, but it wasn't bad in the beginning. I had to oversee everything from cutting and crushing of sugarcane, till the juice was turned into sugar crystals through a series of simple processes. Sugarcane came from the fields, fresh—the sugar yield can be as high as

10% of the cane weight if they reach the factory within a couple of hours; the longer it took, the poorer the yield. From the yard where truckloads arrived, sugarcane was moved on a rail-like system to the mill where it was shredded and crushed before the juice was sent to an evaporator, pan and a centrifuge where sugar crystallized. Bagasse and molasses were the by-products. While molasses went to distillers, the sugar factory used bagasse to fire a boiler that generated steam which in turn went into the power system that ran the plant.

A stationery maker, Seshasayee Paper Boards, found better use for bagasse—to make a fine variety of paper—and entered into a deal with the sugar factory. The paper mill would take bagasse from the sugar factory, and install an oil-fired boiler to produce steam for the factory. Witnessing this barter was to contribute much to my striking a deal with the French, several years later, for the development of the liquid propulsion Vikas engine which remains at the core of every successful PSLV launch by the Indian Space Research Organisation (ISRO).

The technology used at the sugar factory was so simple that I learned every bit of the operation in a couple of weeks. Anyone with a basic knowledge of fluid dynamics, heat transfer, steam engines and applied mechanics could master the working of a sugar factory easily. Work became less challenging and more boring, but I laboured on. To keep myself occupied, I explored all nooks of the workplace, including the smelly bagasse pit where engineers feared to tread. And there came a turning point of my job.

Karuppan, a man so true to his name dark, was in the pit when I sauntered in well ahead of my duty time. Karuppan was strenuously digging at the outlets in the bagasse pit to keep the flow, but he wasn't doing enough. Bored as I was, I asked him to get out and took his place in the pit. Getting a feel of what the lowest grade worker does gives you an idea of wholesomeness. It works in a bagasse pit; it works in a rocket assembly clean room.

So, here I was, sweating it out in the bagasse pit, when I felt someone towering over me. It was the general manager, a genial Scot who loved to pay surprise visits to the work floor after a couple of sun-downers. He did not utter a word, though he was surprised that an engineer was doing the job of a menial worker. I was to be surprised soon with a letter cutting short my three-year training period to six months.

Parthasarathy, a diploma holder and my immediate boss with an innate sense of ridicule for youngsters with an engineering degree and not experience, was not impressed when I gave him the news of my promotion. Curiously enough, my immediate boss appeared to be in the dark about it.

'Six months?' he said. 'You mean they are reducing your training period by six months?' I explained, 'No, the total training period would now be only six months.'

'So you think now you know the entire operations of the factory?'

That was the truth, but I did not reply.

He tried his best to make life difficult for me, but with little success, as the general manager liked me. Call it my luck, the super bosses having a soft corner for me continued when I was with ISRO, where I always had the ears of Vikram Sarabhai, Satish Dhawan and U R Rao, the three greatest chairmen of ISRO.

The promotion as assistant engineer of the sugar factory came with loads of money—Rs 500 a month—and some other perks like a membership in the officer's club which was open only to officer-grade employees and their families. My entry did not go well with some club members who were not amused by my 'out of turn' promotion, but soon many of them turned to be my friends, thanks to my skills in the games of bridge and billiards. Parthasarathy, my prime adversary at work became my favourite partner at the bridge table. The reason was simple: There was just not anyone who was half as good as Parthasarathy and me when it came to a game of cards.

In bridge, not having the right partner—as is the case with space science—can be irritating, and the game can end with some very bad blood. It happened to me when my bridge partner was the wife of a senior employee. In the game, one needs to give enough hints to the partner about his deck of cards without exposing anything to the rivals. This woman knew nothing about this trick, and remained tight-lipped through the game, thereby not allowing me to win though I had a great set of cards.

Parthasarathy, who was not playing but was looking at my cards, said, 'Nambi, you have a great set, why don't you close the deal.' I could have, but for the partner's inability. I retorted: 'I can close, but she is not opening her mouth.'

It was a straight forward comment which the woman mistook, probably for a double entendre, and made a big issue out of it. 'You don't know how to speak in the presence of a woman,' she screamed. I was stunned. I politely asked Parthasarathy what wrong had I done. Knowing the woman's temper, Parthasarathy patted me. 'Don't bother, let's leave the place,' he said.

This camaraderie did not reflect in Parthasarathy's attitude towards me at work where he continued to discourage me. Eighteen months after I joined the sugar factory, sometime in August 1966, I got a telegram from home: MOTHER SERIOUS. START IMMEDIATELY. Bored as I was with the routine, and this was a valid reason to apply for leave, but Parthasarathy would not grant me leave. I explained that my mother was unwell, I pleaded, but the boss would have none of it. I walked out of his room, got a paper from his personal assistant sitting outside his office, and wrote my resignation letter. I re-entered the room and gave the folded paper to Parthasarathy.

'I said you are not going,' he continued shouting. 'Now take back that leave letter.' I told him it was not a leave letter, it was my resignation. Parthasarathy sat frozen. My leaving the job would be a double whammy for him: He would lose a qualified engineer on the floor; if I mention to the general manager that I was leaving because of Parthasarathy, it would be worse.

Now it was his turn to virtually plead. I quietly packed my single bag and took the first bus out of the beautiful village. It was the beginning of a journey that would take me to great heights of rocketry in India.

CHAPTER 3

THE PLOT THICKENS

'You sold the drawings of our rocket engines to Pakistan.'

The Hindustan Latex Guest House at Poojappura, Trivandrum, was a nice place where Intelligence Bureau guys had great fun interrogating the dodgiest of suspects. I was given a spacious, air-conditioned room on the first floor, with a bed in a corner and a small teapoy in the middle. Great comfort for an accused, I thought. But something seemed amiss: usually the telephone in guest houses, as in hotels, is kept by the bed. Here it was on the teapoy in the middle of the room.

A constable, supposed to be my guard, walked in. I asked him what was going on. He kept mum. He put a finger across his mouth, gesturing me not to speak. When I again asked him, he repeated the gesture, this time with a 'shhh …'.

Through gestures he told me that the place was bugged. Now the telephone in the middle of the room made sense. There was a microphone under it. The constable, who later identified himself as Anil, was courteous.

Half an hour later he took me downstairs. It was the customary photo session for the accused. They clicked four photographs—two from the front and one from each side. One of the profile shots soon appeared in some Malayalam dailies. After the photo session, I was made to sit in a room on the ground floor.

A circle inspector whose name I later learnt was Charles, an acquaintance of my ISRO colleague John George, appeared briefly. He seemed to be eager to talk to me, but decided against it and exited. I heard 'click' noises of tape recorders. Police constable Anil remained silent. Now I was asked to get back to the room on the first floor.

As I was entering the room, an official was leaving it. He reminded me of my old classmate K Shanmugham. The officer, who appeared to be in his forties, was tall (maybe 5'11") and of medium built. Against his wheatish complexion, a burn mark stood out below the left cheek, around the neck and shoulders. He might have had a fire accident. Later, when he interrogated me, he asked me to call him by the same name— Shanmugham—after I told him about the resemblance.

Someone brought some rice and *sambar* on a plate. I tried to eat, but could not. I left most of the food on the plate and washed my hands. And then, the first team of interrogators arrived.

The interrogators looked so different from each other that, for a moment, I thought the stark contrast was by design. One was short, small built, fair and appeared to be in his mid-30s. The other was about six foot, had a flat nose and a round face. He must have weighed 80 kg on the scale we used to measure hardware in the lab, and had the arrogance of the fiftees. During interrogation, when I asked these men their names, they said they, as a matter of the IB's policy, never revealed their names to the accused. After a minute of what they thought was creative thinking, one said his name was *Satya* (truth); and the other *Dharma* (duty). 'Nice names,' I said, resisting the temptation to say that my name is 'Neeti' (justice).

Soon their actions made me think that they should be named after two *asuras* of the Indian *puranas*. By the way one of them spoke I inferred that he was a Keralite; he quoted from the Bible. He said he had more than twenty-five years of experience in interrogation. He continuously smoked Panama cigarettes. I learned he was a subordinate of State IB deputy director R B Sreekumar, and hence an IB man. He mockingly tried to talk very sweetly, and hence I nicknamed him Sweety.

Sweety was often accompanied by a subordinate who stopped taking notes only occasionally to abuse me. Around 5'8", he was dark, had grey hair. His nose was certainly sharper than his intellect. He, too, made

Biblical references. At least ten other officials came and went during the next few days of interrogation. A couple of them, whom I understood were from R&AW, were more matter of fact and reassuring that the truth will come out sooner than later. The R&AW men did not torture me.

The first to interrogate me were the ones who called themselves *Satya* and *Dharma*; two other men in vests and shorts stood behind me. It did not take long before I realised the two men had taken positions behind me to land blows on the small of my neck.

The senior began thus: 'You are a brilliant scientist, an excellent manager, a national asset. So why did you do this?'

'What did I do?'

'Espionage.'

'What espionage?'

He cleared his throat. 'Mr Nambi … sorry, Dr Nambi …'

'No, I am not Dr Nambi, mister suits me fine.'

'That's okay, you are as good as a doctor,' the man assumed a satirical tone. 'Now tell me why did you do this crime?'

'Please understand,' I replied. 'I have done no crime. What is it that you really want?'

'Don't bullshit. If you confess, your life will be easy; otherwise we know how to make you confess.'

That was the first sign of a threat.

'What is my crime?'

'You don't know?' Now he stood up and sat down again. 'We have proof that you sold the nation's secrets, rocket technology to Pakistan. Now we want to hear that from your mouth. Tell us how did you do it? How much filthy money did you get?'

At this point, three others walked into the room. One wore a grey safari suit and was introduced by a thin, short person as 'the biggest man in IB'.

Then suddenly, the thin man with a poke-marked face shouted at me.

'You bastard, do you know what the charges against you are?'

When I replied in the negative, he pulled out a paper from his file and started reading out the charges. I had sold sensitive rocket technology to Pakistan. This is an offence under the Official Secrets Act, punishable with a fourteen-year sentence.

Then, pointing to the 'biggest man in IB,' he continued: 'This great man has come all the way to hear it from your mouth. He reports directly to the most powerful person in the country. He has to return to Delhi soon, so you better confess everything now.'

It would occur to me only much later that the 'biggest man in IB' was not really one, it was M K Dhar, the joint director of IB.

Now, I replied calmly: 'I have nothing to tell you than the fact that I am innocent. This must be a misunderstanding.'

'No,' he barked. 'We understand everything clearly. Now, tell us when did you first meet Mariam Rasheeda?'

'I never met her.'

'How dare you lie? She has told us everything. Come on, tell us the truth before we turn brutal. Accept everything or else you are gone.'

'Please believe me,' I said in a matter of fact tone. 'I have never met these Maldivian women you are talking about. I don't even know how they look. How can they say I met them?'

'If you continue to deny, I will bring Fauziyya here and make her slipper you. And that photograph will appear in all the newspapers.'

My mind was racing. What would be their motive? Why would the Maldivian women say they had met me?

The 'biggest man in IB' and his associates soon left, and the prime interrogator continued.

'It is not just those two ladies who have confessed; your subordinate Sasikumaran also has. Now don't try to hide anything.'

'What did you say?' I almost jumped from my chair. 'Sasi has confessed? What is it that he has confessed?'

'So you are worried, Mr Nambi …' he smirked. 'Sasi has told me everything … details of the drawings and documents of rocket science that you passed on to Pakistan through him, the several meetings you all had in Madras and Trivandrum, and how many millions of dollars you received.'

'See,' I assumed my calm posture again, 'I don't know what Sasi has told you and why. I am not worried about that. The point is that I have done no crime. I just don't understand what you are talking about.'

It must have been night by then. A boy brought me some rice and sambar. I did not touch the food. Now, the two men left the room; another duo took over.

'Tell us, why did you do this?'

This set of interrogators were fresh, but the questions were as tired as me.

'You sold drawings of India's Vikas engine and cryogenic engine to Pakistan,' said one.

'You clearly don't understand rocket science. There are no classified drawings and no drawing has gone out of ISRO. Even if some get the drawings, they can't make such an engine without active collaboration with us for several years. If you don't know, India doesn't have a cryogenic engine; we are still struggling to make one.'

'So you agree that you gave some drawings and documents?'

'No, I said nobody will buy your drawings and documents because nobody can make a rocket out of those papers. Do you know how we acquired the technology of the Viking/Vikas engine you are talking about? We spent 150 man years with French scientists at their facility in Vernon, France under a legal contract. We had hands-on training in everything including fabrication, assembly, testing and result analysis. In spite of all this we took more than sixteen years to make a Vikas engine. It is just not possible to transfer rocket technology by selling drawings and documents. Nobody will buy that.'

'Why not?' Now my interrogator was sounding not just absurd, but impervious to scientific explanation. 'If Pakistan wants to duplicate Viking engine, can't they do it using the drawings you gave?'

'Believe me,' I tried one last time to drive sense into this man who I was not sure was genuinely dull or just acting stupid, 'drawings are not sufficient to make rockets.'

'You mean drawings are useless? Then why do you have them?'

'No, I said they are not sufficient. In the development of a rocket or an engine, drawings are but a minor part. Conceptual drawings are available in textbooks and journals. Nobody will pay money to buy them.'

At this point, the second man asked a few questions which made me think that he was interested in knowing about the technology—and perhaps the truth.

✱ ✱ ✱

I asked for Siby Mathews. They wanted to know why I need to meet him. I told them that I had heard of Siby Mathews as the police officer who handled a mark list case in Kerala, and that I felt he was an upright officer.

'I can convince him of my innocence,' I said.

They said it was Siby who is convinced of my involvement in the ISRO spy case. When I insisted on meeting them, they left the room. Soon, the first set of officers came back. One of them lit another Panama cigarette and offered me a smoke. I took one, lit it and inhaled deep. The interrogation resumed.

'Your subordinate Sasi has told us that you all met at Hotel Madras International on 24 January 1994 to finalise the deal. Now tell me what the deal was,' he said.

'I don't know of any deal.'

'Where were you on 24 January 1994?'

'I don't remember.'

'You try, you will remember. You cannot forget that day so easily. When your subordinate Sasi remembers everything so vividly, how can you forget? You are known for your memory power.'

I was getting irritated.

'Can you please tell me where you were last Friday?' I shot back.

The prime interrogator was now furious. 'Don't ask me questions. Just answer mine.'

'I will answer your questions, but be reasonable. You are asking me to remember what I was doing on a particular day ten months ago. See, you cannot remember where you were last Friday. Unless a date is important or special to you, say, like a birthday or a wedding anniversary, you don't remember it, right?'

Even as I was speaking, it struck me: 25 January 1994 was the first birthday of my granddaughter Shurthi. I also remembered that two days earlier, on 23 January a colleague and a close friend, Manikandan, had died. I had attended his funeral on 23 January.

My interrogators had noticed my sudden silence. I continued.

'Ah, yes, I remember. It was the day after my colleague Manikandan passed away. On 24 January I was back at work. The next day was my granddaughter's first birthday.'

The men exchanged glances. I went on: 'More than 500 people would vouch for my presence at the burial ground on 23 January. Another 100 people had seen me at my granddaughter's birthday on 25 January. On 24 January I was in my office in Trivandrum. You may check my official vehicle log book. You may also find that I had signed some purchase files on the same day.'

They again exchanged glances. I was wondering why these men who claim to be experienced interrogators did not even check these basic things before trying to implicate me in a fictitious conspiracy meeting in a hotel in Madras on 24 January.

'Okay, okay, we agree that you were not in Madras on 24 January, but you see that the others were there. And you were aware of that meeting. Your subordinate Sasi has told us that he took orders from you over the phone from Madras.'

Now I was thinking why these men were stressing that Sasi was my subordinate. Technically speaking he was my junior in ISRO, but there seems to be something fishy about the repeated use of the term 'subordinate'. Could they be charting an easy route to fix me by extracting a statement from Sasi under duress and link me to him by saying he acted on my orders?

I spoke. 'See, Sasi is not my subordinate. He need not take any orders from me. Please also understand that he does not report to me administratively. In ISRO we have a matrix management system where there is a general hierarchy of seniors and juniors, but people are deputed under different projects and they report to different bosses. In one such project, the cryogenic project, Sasi is the deputy project director and I the project director. That does not make him my subordinate in ISRO.'

'Are you saying Sasi is not your junior?'

'He is. And it does not mean he is my subordinate.'

The next question shocked me, not because of its ingenuity, but as it related to a top secret operation ISRO was running with the knowledge of only a few people in the organisation and the Ministry of External Affairs. 'Didn't you bring the drawings and components of a cryogenic engine by Ural Aviation flights from Russia?'

It convinced me that my interrogators had been supplied with half-baked information by an external agency. This was to be a vital clue for me to understand later how the agency bought over a few Indian intelligence officers to fabricate the ISRO spy case and scuttle India's efforts to develop a cryogenic engine. This was a crucial programme that would make India capable of not just interplanetary exploration, but also developing geosynchronous launch vehicles with higher capability. How I managed to bring some components and blueprints of a cryogenic engine when the US arm-twisted Russia into going back on a technology transfer deal is another tale of determination.

We chose Ural Aviation to do this since the Russians were more than willing to give the drawings and parts before the Americans did something more nasty, but our own Air India chickened out when asked to bring the consignment, since the national carrier feared the US would stop its trans-Atlantic operations to New York and Washington, and thus take away a big chunk of its revenue. Ural Aviation flew four times carrying in its belly hardware, components, valves and design drawings of a cryogenic engine from Moscow to Trivandrum.

The IB men asked how many times I had been to Pakistan. I said I have travelled to virtually every country, but not Pakistan. That was the truth. Making it evident that their foreign masters either did not have full information about my Ural Aviation adventure or did not give the full picture to these men, they said, 'We know the Ural Aviation flight that took off from Moscow landed in Karachi before coming to India.' I did not question the stupidity of the idea that I would escort a cargo flight carrying the cryogenic parts to India.

Further questions exposed their pre-determined plot to link me to Pakistan.

'Who is your best friend?'

'Prasad.'

'No, no. We want the name of a Muslim friend.'

I started seeing the plot.

'A P J Abdul Kalam.'

The first blow from one of the men standing behind me caught me off guard. I struggled to keep my balance, and braced for more torture.

'Now don't be too smart,' barked one of the interrogators, 'Give us another Muslim name.'

'Mohammed Yousuf Khan, my childhood friend.'

'Where is he now?'

'I don't know.'

'Then give us another name, a Muslim name, with whom we can inquire about you.'

After a minute of thinking, I named Abubaker, a friend from Palayamkottai in Tamil Nadu. Soon I realised that I could be unnecessarily putting him in danger. Later I realised that the IB had prepared stock names of ISI agents and they wanted similar sounding names to be linked to me.

Now blows showered on me. Enduring a sense of disorientation after the first few hits, I resolved to stand my ground, and challenged my tormentors to do whatever, but I would not endorse their fabricated story of spying. They were about to leave, saying the interrogation would continue the next day, when I told them:

'Why don't you keep that microphone out in the open? Why do you hide it under a telephone when I know the room is bugged?'

With a good measure of courage, I added:

'I knew my phone was tapped when I was talking to my friends before I was implicated in the case.'

The men were now offended.

'So you are a daredevil,' mocked the man who has been asking for the Muslim name and went on to shower abuses on me. I noted him especially for his insults and cuss words and later figured out he was IB officer Jai Prakash.

Now I calmly replied that I had nothing to hide and hence I can dare them.

I kept asking for Special Investigation Branch DIG Siby Mathews, on whose instructions I was told I was taken for questioning. The interrogators asked me if I would tell the truth only if Siby Mathews met me. I said I just want to meet him since he is a senior officer who may understand me better. The DIG came on the third day for a meeting that lasted less than two minutes. The six-footer of an officer with thick lips and a moustache walked in and sat on the table top. I was seated on a chair.

'Mr Nambi, why did you do this?' he asked.

I looked him in the eye, but he evaded my gaze. 'Do you think I would have done such a thing, Mr Siby?'

The officer murmured something and left me to the old set of interrogators who took turns to torture me till the next morning.

DOGS, GOATS AND OTHER SPACE SCIENTISTS

'I am APJ Abdul Kalam, rocket engineer.'

When I chucked the sugar factory job and came home empty-handed, mother was happy. She was proud of me for getting an engineering degree and a job, but she wanted her only son to be with her. And here I was, to take care of her, but unsure for how long. I took her to Trivandrum-based Dr Narayana Pai, the biggest name in cardiology in that part of the world then. I knew I had to find a job, but leaving my mother to work far away did not sound good. And then came the monthly groceries from AT Ganapathiya Pillai's shop in Chaalai Bazaar that was to solve my problem.

One of the items was wrapped in a newspaper which I was about to throw into the bin when a two-column advertisement on it caught my eye. Thumba Equatorial Rocket Launching Station (TERLS) in Trivandrum was inviting applications for the post of Technical Assistant (Design). The qualification: a degree in mechanical engineering. The candidate should have graduated with a first class. I fitted the bill, but had no idea what the fledgling TERLS was, and what was expected of the technical assistant. Then I saw the ad again: the last day for applying was the previous day. It was 3 September 1966.

I knew TERLS was a government set-up, and they would not entertain applications beyond the deadline, as bureaucratic strictures do not make allowances of flexibility even if it is for the better. Nevertheless, I decided to make an attempt. I took my cousin R Subbiah's Fiat and drove to the seaside TERLS, which was then but an old church and the bishop's house converted into a working space for India's space programme. The genesis, as I later learned, was in 1962 when Prime Minister Jawaharlal Nehru set up Indian National Committee for Space Research (INCOSPAR) under

Vikram Sarabhai to formulate India's space programme. It was to later grow into the Indian Space Research Organisation (ISRO). Sarabhai had taken over from Homi J Bhabha as the head of Department of Atomic Energy. Incidentally, on 24 January 1966, the day Bhabha died in a plane crash over Mont Blanc, Indira Gandhi took over as the Prime Minister. Sarabhai enjoyed a fine rapport with Indira, which kept ISRO in good stead.

Sarabhai set up TERLS and made HGS Murthy its first director.

I walked up to the desk of P A Kurien, administration assistant with my application form. 'It's all over,' said Kurien, 'but you can try your luck with the director.' Murthy turned out to be a considerate person, and TERLS—for years to come—remained outside the stupidities of typical bureaucracy, as Sarabhai had given the powers to Murthy to take decisions that went beyond the confines of red tape. Murthy inquired about my experience, and I told him about my eighteen months in the sugar factory. I explained that I may not be able to produce an experience certificate from my previous employer since I had quit against his wishes.

Murthy asked me why I left the job, and I told him it was boring. 'Go ahead and apply,' said Murthy.

'And if you get this job and find it as boring as the sugar factory one, you are free to walk out any time.'

I did not have the Rs 5/- postal order which was mandatory for the application. I ran out to a nearby post office and got one. Three days later, I got a call letter for an interview.

I wanted to know more about the nature of the job, but nobody seemed to know what this bunch of young people were doing in a coastal town under the spire of Mary Magdalene Church. Even today, not many know that Thumba—where the Vikram Sarabhai Space Centre (VSSC) now stands—is an enviable location for anyone interested in atmospheric and space sciences for the simple reason that it is close to the magnetic equator of the earth. This strategic location came with the advantage of firing sounding rockets above the equator to conduct a series of experiments on upper atmospheric conditions.

All that was to dawn on me much later, but now I was keen on understanding what was in store for me if I landed the job. My brother-in-law came with the news that some of the scientists involved in TERLS were staying in a lodge. As I was entering the lodge, one of the residents, a man in a pale blue shirt and dark trousers was coming down the stairs. I thought he must be involved in the Thumba project and introduced myself as an applicant.

'I am A P J Abdul Kalam, rocket engineer,' he said.

When I told him my intention to know more about TERLS, he asked me to meet his colleague Aravamudan, who was also staying at Indira Bhavan. Aravamudan, who was called Dan by his colleagues, explained that the idea was to launch sounding rockets.

'Just sending up rockets, is it?' I said.

'Maybe a bit of research and development too,' he said.

I was impressed, but the job wasn't mine yet.

The interview panel comprised TERLS chairman Murthy, Kalam, D Eswar Das and M R Kurup. After the usual questions to test my knowledge on engineering, Kalam asked if I had done any project. I mentioned the axial flow compressor I had designed, fabricated and tested under the guidance of Prof Kothandaraman while in college.

'You mean you did it all alone?' said Kalam.

I nodded.

Kalam was impressed, and I knew I would get the job. But they did not tell me if I had cleared the interview. I waited outside, and when Murthy came out, I went up to him.

'When can you join us?' Murthy said.

'Tomorrow.'

On 12 September 1966, nine days after a soiled newspaper from Ganapathiya Pillai's grocery shop landed in my hand, I was offered a job with India's first space science team for a monthly salary of Rs 650.

CHAPTER 4

GETTING BITTER

'Get up, you bastard!'

A new team that came after the DIG's lightning visit was more brutal. One of them shouted, 'Get up, you bastard! You don't deserve to sit anymore.' I stood up. I'd had no food all day. I had kept asking for water, which they gave. Now they stopped giving me water. They threatened to take me to a torture cell somewhere in Pathankot or Kashmir, where they said I could be killed and my body thrown away, without anyone asking any questions. 'We would say that you escaped from our custody,' one of them said.

I visualized being killed and my body being thrown into snow-covered wilderness. And then, images of my father crossed my mind. I remembered his advice. If you face a crisis, he had told me as a child, be prepared for the worst. That night's questioning by teams that came in shifts, not allowing me to sit or sleep for more than thirty hours, drained me. At one point, I felt a sense of coldness seeping into my body from the cement floor.

I felt dizzy, and thought it must be approaching death. It was easy to yield to it, end it all. For a moment I thought I should let myself go. But I fought back. I summoned that last warmth leaving my body, took deep breaths and stood my ground.

I spoke.

'You guys are committing a big crime, and you will be punished for this.'

Having bounced back from a point of ultimate submission to fate to a state of inevitable fight-back, I continued, 'I will not leave you. Remember, you too have families.'

Suddenly I found myself threatening my torturers. Was that a flash of fear that crossed one of the faces?

'But you don't know who we are, even if you do get out alive,' said one of them.

I said I would make sketches of each one of them, identify them, and hunt them down one by one.

Then one of them said in a tone of mock politeness, 'Sir, we are doing our duty. If what you think is the truth and you stay vindicated, you can slap us with your slippers.'

Twenty-two years later, I have kept my slippers for them.

* * *

When did you first meet Mohammed Aslam of Pakistan?'

Now, what was this, I wondered.

'Who is Mohammed Aslam?'

'Don't act. We know you are good at acting.'

'Honestly, I don't know any Aslam.'

'Ok, let me help you.' The interrogator moved his chair forward, leaned a bit, and cleared his throat, and continued. 'Mohammed Aslam is a well-known nuclear scientist from Pakistan. He came to India and struck a deal with you for rocket technology in 1985. Now accept it.'

I shook my head.

'I don't know any Mohammed Aslam. But I want to know why Pakistan would send a nuclear scientist to get rocket technology. What's the connection here? If India wants to do espionage on Pakistan, would it send APJ Abdul Kalam or U R Rao for that? Wouldn't it be safer to send an unknown person? Does your story make sense to yourself?

The two men were by now appearing to be comical. They looked at each other, nodded their heads and continued. 'You are right. We were only trying to see your reaction to such a statement. So you say it must be an unknown person. Who was that?'

It was now getting clear to me that these intelligence bureau men with visibly low intelligence had woven a story or an imaginary case of spying, but it was riddled with holes. They were seeking information to add muscle to that weak skeleton, with basic information about our working style and contacts. They wanted names, incidents and connections between them. They were constantly amending their story of fiction, and, in fact, I was inadvertently helping them make these changes to make their version a slightly less absurd one. I decided to stop clarifying and educating these morons, and stick to bare answers.

They kept asking for the name of the 'unknown person', I repeated that I had met no such person.

'Mr Nambi, you think you are smart,' he said. 'But you should understand that we are smarter. We have more than twenty-five years of experience in interrogation. We have cracked tougher nuts than you. We pray for our daily bread while you bastards sell national secrets to enemies to amass wealth.'

The scene here was deteriorating rapidly—and violently.

Now two others entered the room. One, a short dark man in spectacles, came straight to me and started hitting me on the face. I stood still, receiving the blows. Nobody, not even my father had ever hit me. My mind was drifting in a sea of humiliation, confusion and sadness. I felt no physical pain.

The man who hit me shouted if I am afraid of anyone. The other officer sprang up with an answer: 'Yes'.

I looked into his eyes and corrected him: 'No'.

The man in spectacles looked bewildered, stared me for a moment and walked away with his associate.

The Panama smoker came near me and whispered: 'Why are you getting bashed up? Why don't you tell us the truth and be spared?'

'Because I don't know any such person or any such deal.'

Now he was feigning to be helpful. 'Don't worry. You just give us any name. Give us a Muslim name.'

There, I thought, he was letting me in to the layers of his imaginary spy story. When I stood my ground, the officer said if I don't go by their story line I would be handed over to some other team which would take me to Pathankot in Punjab. There, he threatened, I would be shot dead and the media will be told that I was killed in an encounter while trying to escape from the investigating team.

I asked for water.

'Unless you confess you are not going to get a drop of water,' he said.

'You third rate criminal,' now shouted the subordinate officer, 'you want water?'

My tormentors have taken out third–degree measures, I realised. I had a choice: To stand by my innocence or yield to their designs. I was helpless, I may even be shot dead in Pathankot. But how can I tell myself, leave alone this bunch of goons who masqueraded as IB officials, that I could do anything against my mother land? After all, it was Vikram Sarabhai's dreams and convictions that I followed to serve my country. I cannot let down Sarabhai, my father, my gurus and myself. I resolved to die if that was the way out of this mess.

The subordinate was holding a glass of water a couple of feet away from me, as if to lure me into parroting their cock–and–bull story. I got up from my chair.

'I don't want water. I don't want to sit any longer. I will stand here, without food or water, till you agree that I have done nothing wrong.'

Now the interrogators appeared to have been tired of making me tell things that went with their story line; so they decided to give a gist of their story so that I merely agreed. Having decided not to question or correct them, I listened as they gave me an outline of their creation:

The six accused in the ISRO spy case – Mariam Rasheeda, Fauziyya Hassan, D Chandrasekhar, D Sasikumaran, S Nambi Narayanan and SK Sharma – worked as a group and transferred rocket technology to Pakistan. Raman Srivastava was the leader of the gang that met on 24 January 1994 at Hotel Madras International and struck a deal with Zuheira, a Sri Lankan woman who acted as a conduit. Mariam and Fauziyya were funded by a Maldivian banker.

On 24 September 1994, money changed hands at Hotel Luciya, Trivandrum. Nambi Narayanan's son Sankara Kumar received the money and handed it over to Sasikumaran at his house. This money was meant for floating a company to produce bullet-proof materials for export by Srivastava. Thomas

Kurisinkal, an industrialist based out of Cochin, was financing the operations. Aleksey Vasin, an officer of the Russian space agency Glavskosmos was involved in the transfer of technology. The plan was to use the drawings and produce Viking engine in North Korea with the help of Russian scientists. A company, a joint venture, was to be floated by Pakistan and Germany. These rockets were to be taken to Pakistan. Indonesia and Brazil were also involved in the deal.

When they summarised the story, I was not sure if I had to laugh or cry. Probably sensing that I was silently ridiculing the lack of logic in their concocted tale, the senior officer became blunt.

'Mr Nambi, we know nothing of this sort happened, but we want this story corroborated by you. All you have to do is mention the name of a Muslim friend.'

The cycle continued, with me naming Abdul Kalam and then Abubaker, my childhood friend who years later had come to me for help to get a job for his son in ISRO. I had told him that I would try if he qualified the written test. The boy did not.

All the while I was on my foot, refusing to take a chair, food or water. The two principal tormentors left and another man, who I reckoned as a Research and Analysis Wing (R&AW) officer, came in.

'You need not lie, just tell what you know. Also remember that we (R&AW and IB) submit different, independent reports to the higher ups. So be bold and tell the truth.'

I told him I have so far said nothing but the truth. After he left, however, I felt reassured. Also, sad that my organisation, ISRO, had not officially condemned our arrest. I wondered what Vikram Sarabhai would have done in these circumstances.

MEETING VIKRAM SARABHAI

'They call me Vikram.'

I was attached to the rocket engineering division headed by Abdul Kalam, who had joined Sarabhai's group of 'space men' in 1963 from DRDO. It was a team of just five of us—Kalam, V Sudhakar, M K Abdul Majeed, C R Satya and me. Closely associated with us for payload integration were a bunch of scientists Sarabhai had selected from

Physical Research Laboratory, Ahmedabad, including O P N Calla, Satyaprakash, E V Chitnis and P D Bhavsar.

The five-member rocket engineering division comprised four tables joined, around which we sat the most informal way imaginable in a government office. There was no designated desk for anyone, including Kalam, though we all had a drawer or two to keep stationery. I might look for a design paper and find it where Majeed was sitting; Kalam would lean over to borrow a pen from me. We had two draftsmen, Alex and Achari, who worked in another room of the church. Then we had Thankappan Nair, Kalam's personal assistant who ended up being an assistant for all the five of us. Thankappan Nair was called a walking dictionary, and often people called out to him with such questions: 'Thankappan Nair, how do you spell euphoria?' Director Murthy's office was in the nearby Bishop House.

India was into something big, as Indira Gandhi and Vikram Sarabhai saw it, but it was not clear even to them on how we were to go about it. Sarabhai, who was a terror at the Department of Atomic Energy, adopted a totally different approach here. He thought since there was no systemic plan—though he was clear that applications of space science would one day turn India into a super power—it was best to let things be fluid, let people do what they want, and take progress one step at a time. This he could do because of the immense talent he found in his men, the individual integrity of the members and the cohesion of the team. Hierarchy was there for basic administrative reasons; but Sarabhai and Murthy did not allow the typical Indian bureaucracy to interfere with work.

This I realised at my first day at work. I walked in and Kalam asked me, 'What are you interested in doing?'

I said I will do anything he wants me to, provided it was engineering. Kalam suggested I create some devices on pyrotechnics, the science of explosives.

'Why don't you develop an explosive bolt?' he said.

I knew little about that, but the sound of the term made it clear to me that it was a bolt that would explode. I did some reading and found that an explosive bolt is primarily used by test pilots to snap their seat belts in case of an emergency ejection. A small explosion goes off inside a bolt that holds the seat belt and, poof, he is ejected. Our application of the device would be for an adaptation called cable cutter. This chute has to be deployed at high altitudes after a payload is taken into the upper atmosphere by a sounding rocket. The payload has to be recovered without damage, and hence the parachute.

I started drawing the plan for a 0.5-inch diameter bolt. The idea was to create a cavity in which there would be an explosive charge and a squib. When given an electric charge, the squib—which is a narrow 'U' shaped thread-like structure with a small quantity of an explosive— sparks and triggers a slightly bigger explosion in the bolt, snapping it. Two weeks later, I was making calculations for the thickness of the cavity and the kind of charge to be used when a shadow fell on the floor a few metres ahead of my desk.

Seated as I was with the drawing board resting on the chair, the paraphernalia virtually having nailed me to the seat, I looked up and saw a handsome man in a white kurta-pajama walking in. The man had grace and radiated energy. Behind him, Kalam and a couple of others had emerged, trying to tell me something I could not understand. I remained seated and was about to return to the drawing when the man spoke.

'May I know what you are doing?'

I was a bit irritated at being disturbed by a stranger, and my impulse was to retort, 'Who are you?'

Better sense prevailed and I said, 'I am designing an explosive bolt.'

The next question: 'How much time would you take to make the bolt? Now I was irked. I said, 'Who are you?'

By now Kalam was furiously gesticulating, and I realised this man was someone big. He smiled and said, 'They call me Vikram.'

Even then I didn't realise that the smiling intruder was Vikram Sarabhai. After he left, Kalam came running.

'Do you know who he is?' he said. 'He is Vikram Sarabhai, the space programme chairman. Why didn't you get up?'

I said I did not know who he was, plus it was difficult to spring up with the drawing board and set squares around me. That was the truth. Sarabhai became the person I admired most with his uncanny ability to foster the spirit of commitment in his men, encourage healthy competition, and give India a direction to become a space super power.

Later, after I realised the stature of Sarabhai, I thought I should have stood up and saluted him even if I was hanging upside down. In our internal parlance, my grade meant just that—hanging upside down. I was Scientist B (SB); and 'B' stood for bat. The other grades—in the ascending order of seniority were SC, SD, SE, SF, SG, then a plain 'G' before 'H'. Above all these was the chairman post.

Each alphabet was assigned—unofficially of course—the name of an animal. 'C' stood for cat, meaning someone who stealthily moves around and often has nine lives, 'D' signified dog for the barks and sometimes the loyalty. Dogs graduated to become elephants that walk with a thud before turning into cunning foxes. Then, we joked, the scientists became goats of the sacrificial kind. The plain 'G' stood for 'absolute goat'. If the goats survive long enough, they become horses that walk majestically and gallop. Kalam was Scientist D, two notches above me the bat, who fluttered around at night and hung upside down during the day.

These virtual designations of the animal kind became famous within the organisation only much later, so in the late 1960s and early 1970s, cats and dogs worked hand in hand with bats. Since we had no blueprint to work on, everything from the explosive bolt I made to the dart at the tip of the sounding rockets was a result of trial and error. Trials we had in abundance, and so were the errors. Some of the trials gave us confidence; a few made us realise how scientifically naïve we were. We laughed at our own comedy of errors, but we learned in the process. So much so that today India is capable of launching satellites into the geosynchronous transfer orbit and send spacecraft to Mars and beyond using rockets of our own.

CHAPTER 5

THIRTY HOURS

Now I realised how wrong I was, and how potent this truth-driven non-violent, non-cooperation was!

It was 3 December 1994. By now I had been standing for more than thirty hours, without food or water. Just when I thought that the last of the devils had gone, a bald man walked in. He looked dignified, but by now I was wary of anyone who came to me.

'Take your seat,' he said.

'I don't deserve a seat.'

'So you admit you are guilty?'

'I don't deserve a seat—that's what your guys say.'

He offered me water, but I refused.

'Are you on a *satyagraha*?' he said. That is when I realised that what I am doing was indeed *satyagraha*. Sensing how my refusal of water and a seat after a day and night of torture scared some of them, I felt the power of *satyagraha*. Till then I was never a fan of Mahatma Gandhi, I have even felt how useless non-violent defiance was in the face of the high and mighty. Now I realised how wrong I was, and how potent this truth-driven, non-violent, non-cooperation was.

'How long will you stand?'

'As long as my legs permit me.'

Something told me that this man was not from IB, and could probably be from R&AW, the external intelligence agency. He turned to one of the IB men who had accompanied him, and said something in Hindi, which I deciphered thus: 'You are playing with fire.' (*agni* is the word he used).

After thirty hours of standing sleepless, I collapsed. Someone took me to the bed where I lay semiconscious, but they thought I had passed out. The rest was all a mental haze, names floating in a stream of incoherent voices in and out of my bruised mind. That's when I first heard the name Sreekumar, who I later identified as that of a deputy director of the Kerala unit of IB.

'See these officers have vanished and now we are in trouble. What if something happens to this man,' a voice wafted in. 'None of the senior officers will own responsibility if he dies. That's why they never showed up after giving us orders to torture him.' In the depths of my semi-consciousness, someone's conspiracy was slowly unfolding.

I am not sure how much time elapsed before I opened my eyes to see just one person in the room. His outline was blurred, and it took a while for my eyes to adjust. As I lay there trying to remember what had happened, a bald portly man who appeared to be in his fifties approached my bed. I could make out that he was a doctor (Later I came to know he was Dr P Sukumaran from Krishna Clinic; he was called to revive me). He inspected me and found my legs swollen, the skin at the knees bruised and virtually bursting. I was bleeding. This was not from the beating—that was all on the head, neck and torso—but because of the thirty hours of standing.

The doctor then turned to the IB men who had entered the room, and said, 'Do you know this man is walking on a razor's edge. He may fall either side.'

I felt happy that someone was finally scolding my interrogators. The doctor gave me two tablets and left, saying, 'Let him sleep.' I slept like never before, so deep that there was no memory of falling into that abyss, no dreams, no pain, no concern of what would happen when I wake up.

I woke up when the door creaked open, letting in the harsh daylight.

TRIAL, ERROR AND TRIUMPH

'See, it fired.'

Some of the early errors at TERLS spoke of our childishness. Once while working on the Judi-Dart project, Kalam was discussing with me how to test the dart. Rocket Judi came from France and I was in charge of developing the dart, which is the pointed portion on the top that holds a bundle of needle-like copper chaff that has to be dispersed in the upper atmosphere through a controlled explosion by opening of the bottom part of the dart at high altitudes. Radars would then pick up the movement of the copper chaff which would float and swim in the upper atmosphere, to understand wind patterns and more.

We had no facilities for simulations or ground-testing. And TERLS director Murthy had given strict instructions not to fool around with explosives on the church campus in Thumba. But somehow we had to do it. When neither Kalam nor I could come up with a method, our draftsman, Alex, casually suggested that we keep the sharp edge of the dart in the beach sand in our backyard and fire it, so that the base facing upward would give way and throw the copper chaff into the air.

Primitive as it may sound now, but we decided to do that. Alex felt proud that the scientists approved his brilliant idea, and off we went with the dart to the beach. We buried the sharp end in the sand and fired. As expected, the copper chaff was ejected into the air. What we didn't know was that the chaff would fly in a trajectory and fall across the road on which Murthy was passing by in his car. I haven't asked him till now whether he felt something falling on his car. When we came back to see the success of the experiment, the dart was missing. In the recoil, it had penetrated the sand. Kalam and I frantically tried to dig and search, but it was nowhere to be found. So, another secret of the Indian space programme lies buried somewhere deep in the sands off the Arabian Sea—the sharp end of a Judi rocket dart.

More dramatic was the testing of an igniter to be used for the Centaure sounding rocket for a sodium vapour experiment. The year was 1967. The French rocket was designed to fly to an altitude of about 100 km where the payload would disperse sodium vapour in the atmosphere. This would be photographed from several locations around the globe. My job was to make the igniter work. This was to be done by using a squib with a small measure of an explosive at the tip, which would in turn ignite gunpowder (G20) to open the payload and send the sodium vapour out.

Four rockets were to be launched from Thumba, at an interval of four hours. Ground observation stations across the globe were kept ready and the world was looking eagerly at what this space toddler called India could do. Murthy was confident of our success, so was I—until I walked into the office library the day before the launch, and stumbled upon a 1942 paper by scientists Able and Noble.

It had a simple point that threatened to defuse our Centaure launch: gunpowder, specifically G20, behaves like sand while the pressure is less than one-fourth of that on ground. It meant that gunpowder just wouldn't fire at an altitude of 100 km. It meant that our igniter would not work. It meant that sodium vapour would not be ignited to discharge its vapour in the atmosphere.

I went to Kalam. He dismissed it initially as some cock-and-bull study. But when I insisted that the study sounded serious, he said we would test it on ground. Again, we had no simulator or a laboratory where upper atmosphere-like conditions can be created. Necessity may be the father of invention; here desperation was the mother of all adventurous innovations. I got a bell jar and kept some gunpowder in touch with a squib. Y S Rajan, an astrophysicist from Physical Research Laboratory who later became the scientific secretary of ISRO and a conscience keeper of Satish Dhawan, offered a vacuum pump. We connected the pump to the sealed bell jar to bring down the pressure to one-fourth. Now we had to see if the gunpowder ignited. It did not. Able and Noble were right.

I repeated the experiment a dozen times, and a dozen times it failed—or succeeded, depending on the way you looked at it. Kalam wanted to see the experiment and I repeated it a few more times, with the same result. Now, Kalam wanted to see up close what was happening to the gunpowder in the jar. The jar was kept on a table in the middle of a room, with the vacuum pump at a distance. Kalam went close and peered into the jar, his nose pressed against the glass, and asked me to fire it.

If the gunpowder fired, it would smash the jar to smithereens; but we knew by now it wouldn't. And Kalam wanted to witness the inertness of gunpowder with naked eyes. The countdown started: 5, 4, 3 ... And then, I noticed that the vacuum pump was not properly connected to the jar. This meant that the pressure would not be low enough for the gunpowder to fire. In other words, it would fire in Kalam's face.

'Stop, don't ignite the squib,' I shouted, and without waiting for the assistant to hear me, leapt over Kalam, bringing him and myself on to the floor. In another second, there was a blast, glass shreds flew all over, I was on top of Kalam.

After the smoke had settled, Kalam sat up and smiled: 'See, it fired.'

This man's enthusiasm for experiments was so much that he was unaware of the potential disaster he had just escaped. I replied, 'See, the vacuum pump is not connected.' I joked that we now not only know that gunpowder does not fire at low pressure, but also that it does fire at normal pressure. The smile on our faces soon vanished when we realised that the sounding rocket with G20 gunpowder could not be a success. Now, who would break the bad news to director Murthy?

There wasn't much choice, and Kalam and I went to the director and explained why the launch could not be a success. Murthy asked me why I did not consider this possibility earlier while designing the igniter. My answer was simple: I did not know about the behaviour of gunpowder at low pressure till the dusty file containing the scientific paper of Able and Noble fell on my lap.

There was no way we could replace the gunpowder with something else at such short notice, and the ground stations across the world were waiting for the launch. Do we call off the launch? That was the big question Murthy had to answer. Calling off the launch would mean that the world would laugh at us saying we can't launch even a sounding rocket. Going ahead with the launch would mean that we could send the rocket up, but couldn't achieve the goal of igniting sodium vapour. There were four rockets waiting to be fired. And all were destined to fail. Murthy decided to go ahead with the launch.

'We can't afford to be laughed at. Let's go ahead,' he said. Later we would have to do a failure analysis to convince the world, though we knew before the failure the reason for it. We launched the four rockets across sixteen hours. They all failed, one after another. While everyone else remained tensed before each of the four launches, Murthy, Kalam and I waited for the inevitable—sad, composed and determined. Much later we successfully launched the Centaure rockets and did sodium vapour experiments by replacing G20 gunpowder with another explosive that did its job irrespective of the atmospheric pressure.

We were learning from every mistake so as not to repeat failures, but there was no dearth of new mistakes. And every time we fell, we made sure that we laughed at ourselves, dusted our backs and walked on to master another lesson.

While the Judi-Dart adventure cost us four rockets, some, like Experiment 45-01 were saved just in time. The year was 1967. The French Centaure sounding rocket had as its payload a transponder developed by O P N Calla and an electron probe by Satyaprakash. For the two things to be released from the rocket, the nose cone had to be separated at a predetermined altitude, and this depended on an ejection mechanism developed by A P J Abdul Kalam and me.

The idea was rudimentary: at the time of lift-off, a timer device would be set off. The timer would be set in such a way that when the rocket reaches an altitude of 63 km, it would activate the nose cone ejection mechanism. A squib would fire and separate the nose cone, letting the electron probe out. The leftovers of the rocket, with the probe and transponder would then plunge into the Arabian Sea. In the less than ten minutes of flight and fall, the probe would study electron density in the atmosphere. The transponder, during the fall and after, would transmit the data to us.

Kalam was the project director and I, the controller. Heads of various systems communicate through the controller who also does the countdown. I was in the block house, a virtual concrete bunker a few metres from the rocket, to have a close view of the launch. About ten minutes before the lift-off, I saw something peculiar: the nose cone, which was to eject at 63 km altitude had already been ejected.

'Controller calling project director,' I announced.

Kalam responded.

'Nose cone got ejected.'

'What?'

'The nose cone has been ejected.'

TERLS director Murthy, who was listening in from the system in his office, asked me to come on the phone. I explained to him what I saw.

'But how can it eject on ground?' he wanted to know. 'It was to happen at 63 km'

It was then that we found that the squib which was to fire at the pre-determined high altitude was activated early, probably because of electromagnetic emission from the surrounding radars on ground. Lesson learned: Squibs should be tested for what we call 'no-fire current', the threshold of the squib to resist triggering through electric current generated by electromagnetic frequency.

The launch was aborted.

Aravamudan, one of the early birds at TERLS, was a man who never lost his cool even during tense moments. His wisecracks, in fact, lightened up such moments.

After the nose cone ejection, I announced: 'Controller calling. Director wants a discussion.'

Kalam replied, 'Which station is this?'

Aravamudan quipped, 'Kazhakkoottam police station.'

At the discussion, P P Kale, head of a group, asked who had developed the ejection mechanism. Someone said Kalam. Kale pulled Kalam's leg, 'Oh Kalam, you just had a premature ejection.' Not getting the pun, Kalam tried to explain the science. Everyone by now knew the reason and laughed. Kalam continued to give lessons on electromagnetic radiation.

In a few days we were back with the no-fire current specified squib, and the rocket was ready for launch. I was back at the block house, this time with Calla, who developed the transponder. Calla, a brilliant scientist who can rightly claim to be the father of indigenous transponders—scores of them now in space letting you talk on your mobile phone and watch television programmes—was also a master of banter. He would talk casually even during the countdown, so much that he could distract others and himself from work.

During the countdown, it was not unusual for systems heads to ask for a 'hold'. It simply meant that there is some correction to be made to a system, and hence the launch had to be held back. Till a few minutes before take-off, the payload is power-fed by an external source. Then, about five minutes before firing, it goes into internal power mode.

This is to save the precious battery that is to feed the payload. Draining the battery would mean killing the transponder and hence nil data.

As the controller, I had to take the call on switching between internal and external power. While Calla kept chatting with me incessantly in the block house, someone asked for a hold just five minutes before the launch, which meant that the rocket was now on internal power.

'How long?' I inquired.

'About 45 minutes.'

'OK, systems to go back to external power,' I said.

'Roger,' said the telemetry guy, confirming that his system went into external power mode.

'Roger,' said the ground station man.

Without blinking, Calla too said 'roger', without switching back to external power.

The moment he said 'roger', I had to take it for granted the transponder had switched off the internal power.

The scientist who asked for the hold got back in thirty minutes to report that he is ready for the launch. And I resumed the countdown. At T-5 (T minus five) minutes, I instructed all heads to go back to internal mode, meaning that the lift-off is imminent. Everyone confirmed with 'roger', but Calla fell silent now. Since he was sitting next to me, I asked why he hasn't said 'roger'.

As if waking up from a dream, Calla asked what my instruction was.

'To go to internal power,' I replied.

'You mean we were supposed to go to external power sometime earlier?'

Now it sank in: Calla's transponder, which had to transmit data, was drawing power from the internal battery, draining it all along. Thirty minutes on internal power means Calla's transponder was dead before the rocket was launched. Time was now running out and technically I could not allow lift-off without a 'roger' from all systems heads which included Calla. I stared hard at him and Calla said 'roger'. Both of us knew the transponder would not work, which meant the probe data will never reach us. Another death foretold. The countdown proceeded and the rocket took off. Everything worked perfectly: The nose cone ejected at 63 km, the probe might have gathered data about electron density in the atmosphere. But there was no signal from the transponder. Everything plunged into the Arabian Sea. Calla kept silent. So did I.

And that remained our secret for many years till I had to tell ISRO chairman U R Rao in a different context. Why I told Rao about it is another tale—that shows not just we the Indian toddlers in space, but even the French masters of rocketry can fail because of callousness.

The French blooper came five years later, in 1972, when they launched the three-stage Diamant-BP4. I was in Paris for the launch, as part of an ISRO-CNES programme. The project director was a man called Roussel. The French, by then precision launchers of rockets, usually have a grand lunch or dinner for every launch, and it is joked that many scientists gather in Paris while the rocket takes off from Hammaguir, Algeria, more for the lavish spread of food than the launch itself.

The Diamant rocket took off and the first three stages burned out beautifully. The fourth stage, which was at the core of this experiment, did not ignite. The launch was a failure. As the grand lunch waited, scientists uneasily stared at each other, thinking if they have to eat a humble pie and move to the dining table. I took Roussel to a corner and asked why the fourth stage did not ignite. It was probably a state secret of the French, but Roussel somehow decided to tell me the truth. 'Promise you won't tell anyone. It didn't ignite because now I realise that I forgot to put the igniter.' I was stunned at Roussel's honesty and a premier space agency's oversight.

Years later, in a casual conversation, U R Rao said space scientists may have several secrets and that they do not share it with the higher-ups despite review committees probing failures. And Rao mentioned the Diamond rocket disaster. He somehow knew about the stupidity of the French failure.

'Do you know why the French rocket failed,' he asked me.

I knew I was breaking my promise to Roussel, when I told Rao yes, I knew.

'You know?' Rao was surprised.

I told him that Roussel had confided in me.

'How can they do such a thing?' Rao continued.

I couldn't contain myself.

'Your boys are also forgetful, Prof Rao,' I said.

'What do you mean?'

I told him the story of Calla's preoccupation in the block house and how he forgot to switch to external power, draining the transponder battery.

MEETING INDIRA GANDHI

Not all countdowns were as casual as that of the Judi rocket that had a 'premature ejection'. To the layman, the controller who was counting 10, 9, 8, 7 … may sound to be the most important person, but in real, it is just another job. But, for some reason, Murthy had put me in that seat often, maybe because he liked the way my voice came through the speakers.

So, on 2 February 1968, the day when Prime Minister Indira Gandhi was to dedicate TERLS to the United Nations, I was asked to do the honours. I was not very amused as this would mean that I may not get to meet Mrs Gandhi who would witness the launch of a sounding rocket and get introduced to the scientists at TERLS, while I will be cocooned in the control room on a campus across the road. But I agreed when Murthy insisted.

Then Murthy said something that made me happy: ten minutes before the lift-off, the prime minister, accompanied by Vikram Sarabhai, will visit the control room to see the countdown. Murthy told me that the controller should look important and should go about his job unmindful of the Prime Minister coming in. On the day, I wore a suit to work and decided to look important.

The countdown progressed smoothly, and at T–minus ten minutes, the door behind me opened and Sarabhai walked in with Mrs Gandhi. I had not forgotten Murthy's instruction, but I involuntarily I rose from my chair. But before I could stand up to greet the important visitors, a hand pressed on my shoulder.

'Sit still,' whispered Sarabhai.

I sat like a school boy and continued with the countdown procedures, my mind racing on whether I would get to shake hands with the Prime Minister. Soon they walked out, and the rest of the countdown went on well.

Soon after the lift-off, once my job was done, I rushed out and asked a driver to take me immediately to the other side of the TERLS campus where scientists were lining up to meet Mrs Gandhi. I was the last to join the line and, by default, the first one to be introduced to the Prime Minister by Sarabhai.

Some of the trials were successes in the first attempt. A payload recovery system, the brainchild of mechanical engineer V Sudhakar, is a classic example of how we, still unsure of making satellite launching rockets, got it right, however, rudimentary the system may sound now.

It was one of those days in 1968 when we—Kalam, Sathya, Majeed and Sudhakar—huddled around our four-table workspace discussing the Judi-Dart rocket. We all wondered when we would make bigger rockets that can launch satellites. Without much scientific analysis, we would do this often. Sometimes we stayed back in the office, sleeping on our desks, sometimes on the beach, stargazing and dreaming aloud. Then Sudhakar had this brain wave. What if we can recover payloads or even rocket parts which fell into the Arabian Sea after our sounding rockets touched a maximum altitude of 70 km. There was nothing much to recover than a few short-life transponders or minor probes launched using hand-out rockets like Centaure from France and Nike Apache from the US, but the idea sounded interesting. The US was then progressing fast on recovery vehicles and probes. We got to the job immediately.

In a few weeks, Sudhakar developed a parachute deployment system to soft-land a decoy payload. I developed the ejection mechanism. But there was no rocket to integrate it with.

'The idea is to see if a hurtling payload would activate the parachute and soft-land on the sea,' said Sudhakar. 'So why do we integrate it into a rocket? Why not drop the stuff from a plane?'

Our enthusiasm was child-like—and infectious within the group. Looking at fishermen's children who flew kites on the Thumba beach, we reminded each other that we are not much different.

We called the Trivandrum Flying Club, which readily agreed to charter a two-seater Pushpak. So, here was the plan—the decoy probe will be integrated with Sudhakar's parachute system, which my ejection mechanism will deploy using a timer activated at the time of release from the aircraft. Pushpak, a flying machine of the 1950s vintage, can attain an altitude not more than 5,000 feet, but for the experiment, that would do. With the parachute deployed, the probe would float, glide and soft-land on the sea surface. On impact, it would release a dye that would turn an area around it a different colour, so that an overflying craft can spot it and we can send boats to recover it.

Pilot Krishnan flew the Pushpak. The probe's descent was filmed. Watching the probe descend for a full fifteen minutes was as strenuous as boring. So we decided to watch the video later to analyse every movement. There was a problem—we did not have a projector room. So off we went, a score of scientists, to Central Theatre, a cinema hall in the heart of Trivandrum that my cousin R Subbiah owned, to watch the recovery experiment. The film, however, turned out to be a damp squib. Mathew, our only photographer who designated himself the chief photographer, did not appear to believe in using the zoom facility of the camera. The result—grainy visuals of a speck floating down the sky. We did not make an issue of it since we were too happy with the grand success of our first recovery system.

A recovery system is imperative for manned missions for the simple reason that we need to get the men and women back to earth after the space flight. Space agencies including ISRO are working on such recovery systems also to reuse some of the rocket parts to save money. When it is not a manned flight, all that has to be considered is if a recovery system is cost-effective. Rocket parts that fall into the sea after each stage separation are no doubt precious, but integrating a recovery system into the rocket means adding to its weight. The thumb rule is that for every 16 kg you add to a stage, the payload weight goes down by 1 kg, which means a lot of money when it comes to satellites with costly transponders and cameras.

Sometime in the 2000s, ISRO did a recovery experiment from the Sriharikota launch facility. I felt sad that not a word was spoken about Sudhakar who conceived the idea and delivered on it almost forty years earlier. Not so surprising, as it comes from an organisation which has done precious little to remember Vikram Sarabhai beyond naming the space centre in Trivandrum after him.

CHAPTER 6

MARIAM'S NAME IS THROWN IN

'I will slap her.'

Anil, the police constable who had first warned me of the bugging device in the room, stood there. 'Tea or coffee, sir?' he said, and I replied just 'yes'. I don't remember what he brought. I sipped the lukewarm drink, unable to taste it. Every bit of my body was paining. The joints were virtually immovable; the ache made me feel each and every muscle in my body.

'They've all left,' said Anil. 'Do you want anything?'

I asked for a newspaper. I asked for an English newspaper since I couldn't read Malayalam. Anil said I would not find anything about the spy case in the English newspapers—it was the forte of the Malayalam papers, this juicy developing story that made every rookie reporter an investigative journalist who unearthed a hidden strategy of espionage or equally important, the favourite positions of the Maldivian women in bed.

Two men came into the room. 'Get dressed.'

I was in the same old brown shirt and trousers that I wore from home to the Vanchiyoor police station on 30 November 1994. It had been five days. I stood up, unsteady. When Anil came to support me, the men abused him. 'You think he is your grandpa?' they shouted. Anil scurried out.

One of the men told me the CBI was coming to interrogate me. Later, I came to know from some of the other accused that the IB men, before handing them over to the CBI, had asked them to repeat the tale they were told. Some of the accused, including the two Maldivian women had given 'confession statements' under duress, and the statements were videographed. I had the suspicion—which later proved true—that parts of my interrogation were also videographed, though without my consent or knowledge. I had refused to parrot their lines, and this man wanted to make a last ditch effort.

'Before the CBI men question you, here is one more chance for you to tell the truth. What was your deal with Mariam Rasheeda?'

By now I was as tired as them of this game. 'Is it a lie you want to record as a statement? Then record whatever you want and claim I've said it,' I said.

One of them tried to be smart. 'Mariam said that she knows you.'

'Can you bring her here and make her say that?' I challenged.

'What will you do if she says that in front of you?'

'I will slap her.'

They said they have in their custody a Pakistani who had corroborated what Sasi had confessed. They wanted a Muslim name from my mouth to be linked to the imaginary spy tale. I looked at the telephone that was, oddly, in the middle of the room. I knew it had a microphone or a recorder. These men were waiting for me to tell the tale the way they wanted. I decided to have some fun.

'I was approached by one Habibullah in 1982,' I started, and had the immediate attention of my interrogators. 'Well, I think it was 1982 ... that's the year you wanted me to say, isn't it?'

They were furious. The recording was being interrupted by the clarification. Every time I built up a tempo, I broke it seeking a clarification about a date. Or I just asked, 'Is that what you wanted me to say?' The officer who I understood to be from R&AW had joined the team midway through the tamasha, and whenever I played the trick he smirked, as if he was getting convinced of my innocence. I am yet to ask him if he knew the truth then.

At this point, someone dashed into the room and said: 'Get ready, we have to move.'

Move where? I wondered. Pathankot? Kashmir? Are they going to finish me off?

The Panama smoker told the man who came with the message that he needed fifteen more minutes. 'We are almost through. Please give us a little more time.'

He then turned to me and said with a sense of great urgency, 'Behave and tell us the plot without breaking in the middle. If you do that, we will release you immediately. Or else you will be taken to hell for further investigation.'

My head was spinning, but I tried my best not to show any emotion. Any hell would be better than this, I told myself. The IB officer was yelling at me to talk. I realised that he was loyal to his masters, whoever that was. He wanted his concocted tale recorded in my voice to be presented to his bosses. I was not going to yield as I knew he did not have much time left to deal with me.

Something told me that the IB's role in this case was getting over, and that I would be handed over to, as one of the interrogators had said, the CBI. In about twenty minutes after his first entry, the messenger came running in again, shouting, 'You know these fellows, they are here. They've already called thrice. If we do not move now, we have to face the consequences.'

'Ok, let us move,' said the IB man. Then, turning to me, he added, 'Mr Nambi, please remember that you should tell your new interrogators more or less the same things we asked you to say. If you don't, you are going to feel really bad about it.'

They took me out of the room, on to the ground floor. Someone handed me a polythene bag, saying it had come from my home. I did not bother to look what was in it. There were four or five constables and a few others taking me to a police jeep. Before I got in, the R&AW officer came up to me, took my hand and said, 'Good luck'. I looked around for the other interrogators, but could not see any.

They asked me to get into a police jeep that was to take me—and the other accused—to the Pallipuram police camp in Trivandrum where the CBI awaited us with handcuffs.

SOLID, LIQUID AND A LOT OF GAS

'The name Sarabhai could move heaven and earth.'

For the common man, space science has been a matter of either wide-eyed wonder or just a waste of money. Almost four decades after Vikram Sarabhai dreamt of making India a space power, we are almost there, but ISRO has not convinced everyone that the toil of so many scientists and the support the organisation got from the government have not gone in vain. India today is among the best satellite launching nations, and is on a promising trajectory towards deep space probes and interplanetary explorations.

What most of the world outside ISRO doesn't know is that this versatile group of scientists and engineers were at loggerheads, more often than not to push for what they thought was better for rocketry and the country. ISRO has been steeped in internal politics, but much of it was battle of ideas, at least in the earlier years.

As early as 1967, I had pushed for liquid propulsion. This was not easy because the Indian space programme then was revolving solely around solid propulsion. Moreover, Sarabhai, an astrophysicist, himself was either not convinced of the capabilities of liquid propulsion or our capabilities to develop it. It was widely accepted that liquid propulsion could send heavier rockets to space, but it was tougher than playing with solid fuels. Now nobody contests that it is the Vikas engine—which I was instrumental in developing—which is at the core of Indian space's work horse PSLV which has had thirty-eight consecutively successful launches till July 2017.

Sarabhai had another pet dream—developing long-range missiles. And he thought missiles have to be built with solid fuel. At the risk of sounding immodest, I would say that I had to educate Sarabhai on this. I plunged into rocket science literature and pored over international project reports involving liquid propulsion. Citing several references, I impressed upon Sarabhai that several missiles were powered by liquid fuel engines. I told him that while India can build its Intemediate-Range Ballistic Missiles (IRBMs) with solid, Inter-Continental Ballistic Missiles (ICBMs) should be powered by liquid fuel. Similarly, I told him, if we are to graduate from sounding rockets to satellite launchers, we have to develop liquid propulsion systems. Sarabhai was convinced.

Kalam, meanwhile, was working on a satellite launch vehicle with solid fuel as the propellant. It later came to be known as SLV-3. While I respected Kalam's dedication to his pet subject—the man literally lived at the workplace, always studying models and putting together solid boosters—I couldn't agree with his eagerness to dismiss liquid propellants as the future. It was a clear solid versus liquid tussle. The US, meanwhile, was planning to land man on moon.

Kalam found a useful friend in M R Kurup who was heading the Rocket Propellant Plant (RPP), which made only solid fuel. Ironically, I, the sole proponent of liquid propulsion, was stuck in the Rocket Engineering Division headed by Kalam.

Parallel to this, another group was pitted against Kalam. It comprised Y Janardhana Rao, V R Gowarikar, Subhash Chandra Gupta, D S Rane, Muthunayagam, Amba Rao, M K Mukherjee and a few others. All of them where PhDs and handpicked by Sarabhai, making it a potent group. But the problem was the eminent doctors did not know how to put a rocket together. The group had scant respect for Kalam and Murthy, who had only a bachelor's degree in engineering. That made me also think how I would survive, leave alone flourish as a scientist, only with a graduation in engineering.

I had wondered why Sarabhai, such a visionary, randomly brought people without assigning a clear job profile. It would become clearer to me soon when Sarabhai himself would open up on his experiment: Grab the best of brains, mostly people who have earned PhDs abroad, and keep them in India. Let them do whatever they want in space science. A structure will emerge sooner or later.

That Sarabhai wasn't too happy with the result became clearer to me a month before his death in December 1971, when he spoke to me before sending me off to a Rolls Royce facility in Scotland. That November he told me things weren't going the way he wanted and that he was planning to revamp the organisations. When I was abroad, Sarabhai was found dead in Halcyon Castle, a seaside resort in Kovalam, Trivandrum on 30 December.

But now, in 1967, Sarabhai was still experimenting. To accommodate the PhD group, Sarabhai founded the Space Science & Technology Centre (SSTC) with himself as the director and Murthy as the associate director. The PhD group would not cooperate with Murthy. On this side, I found it difficult to work with Kalam who was vigorous in developing solid boosters as much as dismissing liquid propulsion. One day, with SSTC in mind, I told him I want to leave. Kalam was upset. Kalam had immersed himself in developing what would later be known as the series of Rohini sounding rockets. Kalam was developing D-75 ('D' stood for Dreamer, according to Kalam, and 75, in mm, was the diameter of the rocket). There I learned from Kalam how sometimes making a small rocket is tougher than making a big one. Around the same time, SSTC also started developing a 75 mm diameter rocket. Ground tests were done in Veli, a sleepy fishing village near Thumba; and often the head or tail part of the rocket would burst in the trial and error run.

I kept insisting that I have to leave Kalam's team. Finally he allowed me to apply to SSTC, which readily took me in. Ironically, at SSTC, I was again assigned work on solid propulsion. As I nursed the liquid dream, Kalam went on to develop larger versions of Rohini, RH300, RH560 and RH1000, which went on to become the booster for the SLV-3 rocket.

In 1969, virtually intimidated by the abundance of scientist scholars around me, I decided to study, lest I might end up an also-ran. A natural choice was a post-graduate course in Trivandrum Engineering College. This was one time I came near regretting my decision not to pursue courses in Caltech University and Princeton University in the US because I had to be near my ailing mother. I got admission for MTech in heat power at the Trivandrum Engineering College. SSTC—and TERLS—then did not have a proper administrative system to even let me know if I could study and work simultaneously. With no guidelines, I registered for MTech, but hardly six months into the course, some administrative officer inquired how I could work and study at the same time. I asked for the rules, but there was none.

Sarabhai had a suggestion: study something on liquid propulsion, my passion, in a foreign university. He could send me on study deputation with a grant if I got admission. I was not sure if Princeton would consider me two years after I did not take up the course, which I was offered, but I applied.

Soon came good news–bad news—I was selected to Princeton, but my course will be on solid propulsion under Prof. Summerfield, a famous solid propulsion specialist. I made my option clear and the university allowed me to choose another professor who would guide me on a masters in chemical rocket propulsion, which was closer to liquid propulsion. Prof. Lugi L Crocco was the man, but he would not take any students now. Clinching that was the first challenge in Princeton. Reaching Princeton itself would have been tough, but for the influence and interest of Vikram Sarabhai.

The letter from Princeton came in mid-August 1969 and I had to join in September. Getting a visa would not be difficult as a student, but those days getting foreign exchange was cumbersome and time consuming. And then, there were government procedures to be followed to send a scientist abroad for study. But when Sarabhai wanted something done, nothing came in the way.

In a matter of few minutes, a committee was constituted to 'evaluate and authorise' my project. The panel comprising E V Chitins and H G S Murthy gave the green signal. I was cleared.

The government of India would pay for my air tickets and I would get a monthly subsistence allowance of $210. My salary would continue to be credited to my bank in India. That was more than a fair deal, but getting foreign exchange to the tune of $1,260 in a few weeks continued to be a tough proposition.

Sarabhai pulled strings. Given that he was among the few in the world who could call Prime Minister Indira Gandhi on the phone whenever he wanted, I was confident of Sarabhai's field of influence across institutions. He asked me to go to the RBI office in Madras as soon as possible and meet Y T Shah. I did not even ask who Shah was; I packed a small bag and headed for the Trivandrum airport.

It was a hopping flight via Madurai; and it turned out to be literally so. The flight was so turbulent that at Madurai airport, all but two passengers alighted and told the airline that since they are not keen on dying they would take the road to Madras. I was one of the two passengers who remained on board to Madras. At the end of the journey, which continued to be turbulent, the pilot asked me if I wasn't scared.

'I was shit scared,' I told him, 'but it wasn't a tough decision to continue on board as getting to Madras late would be as bad as not reaching there.'

The pilot did not ask any further.

At the RBI office, which was as infamous as any government office for their lack of courtesy and abundance of delay, I was treated like a king. When I asked for Y T Shah, an officer said he was waiting for me. Later I realised Shah was a senior official. In an hour, they gave me $1,260.

'The name Sarabhai could move heaven and earth,' I told myself.

But when the moment came for me to board the flight from Trivandrum to Bombay, from where I was to fly to the US, I had a momentary hesitation. I had packed just one ragged suit and a few pairs of trousers and shirts. My wife and our nine-month-old son came to the airport. Looking at them, on my first voyage to the other side of the globe, I thought if it was worth it. Something told me yes.

Sheer delight awaited me on board Air India flight Annapoorna from Bombay to New York. I was in the economy class when Sarabhai, sitting in the business class saw me passing by. He left his seat and took one next to me till end of the journey. As the flight hopped from Bombay to Kuwait, Rome, London and New York, I saw a different Sarabhai— one more introspective and philosophical. He did speak of India's space dreams at great length, but they were punctuated by long spells of silence and then unfinished sentences about his family life. He did not elaborate much on that, but he kept wondering if he was doing the right thing by travelling so much on work and ignoring his family.

I listened without uttering a word. This man had been a tireless traveller. Much like his dreams, his body was often in the sky, I thought, as Sarabhai would be flying almost every day from city to city, inspiring young scientists to do India proud and striking bargains with space-faring countries to help India achieve its aspiration beyond the stratosphere. While in India, he would fly from Ahmedabad to Trivandrum to chair a meeting with us for three hours and rush to the airport to catch a flight to Chennai for a family reunion and be back the next morning to continue the meeting in Trivandrum.

In passion, Sarabhai overtook Homi Bhabha who had handpicked Sarabhai as his successor at the Department of Atomic Energy (DAE), and later for the space mission. Sarabhai simultaneously held the post of the DAE chairman and headed the space programme. From the first job he drew a salary, from the second he took a nominal one rupee before it became fashionable for many politicians to take a token remuneration. And most of his flying was on his own expense. Sarabhai, hailing from an aristocratic family in Gujarat, could afford it handsomely.

At work, Sarabhai exhibited dual nature. At DAE, he was less accessible and sometimes a terror. At the space centres he would throw a hand around anyone and chit-chat. Homi Bhabha was known to be a proud boss who took his dignity too seriously. When Bhabha entered a lift, nobody else would get in. Sarabhai, on the other hand, would squeeze himself to a corner of an Ambassador car after getting five people into the vehicle. When Sarabhai landed at any airport in India, there would be a fleet of family cars awaiting him; but he would hop into a car in which he could discuss rocketry with a colleague on way to one of his umpteen work places.

Sometime during the flight to New York, Sarabhai told me, 'If you come into such a job, then you don't deserve to have a family.' The sight of my wife with our toddler son waving at me at the Trivandrum airport flashed through my mind. I tried to sleep.

At the New York airport, Sarabhai wished me good luck and left. I took a bus to New Jersey where Princeton University awaited me with its invaluable lessons.

CHAPTER 7

CBI TAKES OVER

'Handcuffing is a formality, sir.'

In the jeep was a bearded man. He wore a *kada* on his right wrist. Is this the Pakistani the IB officials claimed to have arrested? For a moment I wondered if some espionage had really taken place. But what was this cock-and-bull story about selling drawings of rockets? That cannot be espionage, I comforted myself.

Later I learnt that the bearded man was S K Sharma, the sixth accused. Sharma, a small-time industrialist, was implicated in the case because he was a friend of Chandrasekhar. Sharma had taken Mariam Rasheeda and Fauziyya Hassan to meet former army brigadier Bhasin who helped Fauziyya's daughter Zila Hamadi get a seat in a Bangalore school. Sharma, like me, had nothing to confess, and the IB men had nothing to show as the balance sheet of our interrogation. The others, however, we came to know later, could not stand the torture and had given statements under duress.

The jeep came to Vazhuthakkad, where DIG Siby Mathews's office was located. I looked around and saw the board 'Babu Raj, IPS'. I was taken in, to a hall. When my escorts moved aside, I realised there was a telephone at my arm's length. I had this urge to pick it, dial home and say I am fine. I stopped myself.

I saw circle inspector Jogesh there. I asked him if I can meet Siby Mathews. The instant reply was in the negative. When I insisted that I have to meet him, Jogesh said the officer did not want to meet me.

I sat on a chair by the verandah and asked the person sitting next to me if he had a cigarette. He looked around, and reluctantly pulled out a cigarette and a matchbox from his pocket for me. I lit the cigarette and inhaled deep. I saw sub-inspector Thambi Durgadutt moving in and out of that police office. He avoided my gaze.

After a few minutes, Jogesh told me that the ISRO spy case has been formally handed over to the Central Bureau of Investigation (CBI). The agency will soon take custody of me and the other accused. I did not know whether to feel happy or sad.

We were asked to get into a van. The destination was Pallipuram camp, another den of criminal interrogation in Trivandrum. The van entered through a wrong gate and had to return and take the right entrance. Everyone, including the policemen in the van, was silent. It was eerie.

We were led to the first floor of a two-storey building on the campus. At the landing on the first floor, someone received us with the simple ceremony of handcuffing us. I tried to resist, but immediately yielded to the coldness of the metal on my wrist.

'Handcuffing is a formality, sir,' he said.

Much like the experience in the magistrate court the day after my arrest, I felt I was watching myself in handcuffs. I felt like a criminal.

Now the CBI had the accused in different rooms at Pallippuram. They were:

Mariam Rasheed (A1)

Fauziyya Hassan (A2)

D Sasikumaran (A3)

K Chandrasekhar (A4)

S Nambi Narayanan (A5)

S K Sharma (A6)

NEW LESSONS, OLD DREAMS

'Mate, you exposed me.'

The Princeton University campus is a knowledge seeker's dream. On the verdant acres, buildings in chiselled grey stones appeared to emerge from the depths of earth, bringing with it buried secrets of yore; their spires seeking greater heights of the azure sky. Towers stood like sentinels of scholarship.

Students and professors—indistinguishable at times—streamed in and out of the imposing buildings that housed libraries, laboratories and dormitories showing virtually no signs of the great ideas they fostered to make the world a better place. During spring and summer, some studied under the trees, on the grass; some others exchanged banter, with salads that came free from the dining room and hamburgers for which they paid.

The campus allowed students who were not just bright, but with a never-ending quest for knowledge. Professors were demanding to the extent that if anyone mediocre happened to turn up there for research, he would live the rest of his life as a frustrated student. Geniuses were tolerated, toilers were appreciated. It was also one of the few universities of the Ivy League that NASA gave sensitive contracts to.

For courses like mine—Master of Engineering Sciences in the Aerospace and Mechanical Sciences—classes happened seven to nine in the morning. Later, one was free to do projects in labs round the clock—you only need to have a technician who would not crib for being forced to put in long hours. The department was spread over 22,000 acres, which included an airstrip and an aircraft.

The first challenge was to register under septuagenarian Professor Lugi Crocco. Considered an outstanding professor, Crocco had stopped taking new students. In fact, he had stopped coming to the campus; the university was happy to have him agree to be on the rolls and guide students from his home.

Those who thought the professor to be prude didn't know the real reason: his wife was bedridden, and he would not move away from her bedside. Prof. Crocco changed my perception of Americans who, I thought till then, lacked the family values we Indians were so proud of.

Prof. Crocco, an Italian who migrated to the US, rejected me outright saying no more students. But I would not give up. I had a trump card up my sleeves: I had studied in great detail Crocco's stability theorem. It was my little secret that I had written to him while at TERLS seeking clarifications on his theorem. My mails never got a reply. When I kept pleading, he asked me what I expected: 'Have you read the Crocco theorem?' I was ready with a 'yes', but he would not be satisfied till I explained the theorem and answered his questions. I passed this exam and Prof. Crocco agreed to take me in with a condition—I had to do projects on campus and go to him at his home only for clarifications. Thrilled, I nodded in agreement.

As for the daily interaction on campus, I had to report to Prof. David T Harrje, who was as genial as he was demanding. There was a NASA project the department was handling and I grabbed the opportunity to work on it. It was on the behaviour of shock waves in a combustion zone, and was crucial for stability analyses of rocket systems. For someone who had attempted trials, errors and fun at the fledgling Indian space labs, this was high grade stuff.

The project involved sending a shock wave—a burst of air through a perforation on a membrane—after firing a liquid engine, and reading the behaviour of the wave. It was tough analysing the wave behaviour. It was pure mathematics, based on the readings. That may sound simple, till we realised that the number of variables here were more than the number of mathematical equations available. So you club the variables and analyse for the bunch. Well, this was complicated stuff.

I kept repeating the experiment well beyond the specified number of times. While this impressed Prof. Harrje, the technician on duty was not amused with the extra work he had to do in assisting me. He was not my concern, so the shock wave lived a hundred lives on the Princeton campus, firing my curiosity, quest and imagination, every time it passed through the perforation before dying its gradual yet quick death. After the initial reluctance, the technicians started spending longer hours with me, and we soon were friends.

What came as a bonus was a NASA fellowship I had applied for while at Princeton. The Government of India's monthly sustenance allowance was $210; the NASA fellowship entitled me for $460. That was big money, which would not come to me directly. NASA would send the money to the Government of India, which had to pass it on to me.

The Government of India promptly received my NASA fellowship money of $460 every month, but gave me only $210, citing some bureaucratic rigmarole. It was only much later after my return to India, and again thanks to Sarabhai's interference, I got those arrears. After my return, I asked Sarabhai's administration head S R Thakur why I was not given the money. He said he tried hard for six months, but could not get it passed. I went on a strike of sorts and stayed away from Sarabhai's meetings, but continued with my work.

After three meetings, Sarabhai sent word. I said I am unhappy that I am not paid my dues. Sarabhai dictated a letter to the first stenographer in sight, saying I be paid the money immediately, whatever it takes, signed it and asked Thakur to process it. Thakur was visibly upset that what he could not do despite six months of efforts Sarabhai could do immediately. But Sarabhai doesn't take such questions. The letter went up to the Prime Minister's office for ratification, and I got my money. I still have a copy of Sarabhai's letter sanctioning the money—and I consider that invaluable.

At Princeton, I was not worried about the extra money since $210 was good enough, and I had a few friends who made life happier. One of them was S N Gupta, a graduate from IIT Kanpur working on a Princeton project on the behaviour of aircraft during turbulence. A trained pilot that he was, Gupta probably had the most adventurous learning on the campus. When the weather is bad and the winds gusty, Gupta would hop into the cockpit of the small aircraft on the campus and fly into the darkest of clouds.

Sometimes Gupta would ask me to accompany him. First hesitantly, later eagerly, I would get into the cockpit with him. He would look out for the toughest patches in the sky to guide his flying machine through. I thought of the bumpy flight from Trivandrum to Madras, from which most of the passengers ran out when it landed in Madurai. It was so insignificant compared to what Gupta was so delightfully going through.

Every time he manoeuvred through turbulence, I sat mesmerised as much by the forces of nature as by man's zeal to tame them more by respecting the elements than disregarding them. At times, science makes you philosophical. Flying a small aircraft through pitfalls in the air should take a lot of science, philosophy and guts. I had never been afraid of flying; and now my adventures with Gupta conditioned me to remain as calm as the pilot when the aircraft is tossed around by atmospheric pressure dips and uneven winds.

So, when TERLS director H G S Murthy, a man of practical jokes, tried to scare aerodynamics engineer Y Janardhana Rao and me on our way from Paris, I smirked. The flight was above the Alps when Murthy, sitting on an aisle seat suddenly craned his neck to look at the engine beyond Rao on the window seat.

'Did you hear that unusual sound?' Murthy said, apparently sensing Rao's fear of flying.

I knew what was coming, and sat still. Rao was a bit rattled and strained his ears.

'Yeah, it must be the pilot adjusting the flaps,' said Rao, more to reassure himself than anyone else.

'I don't think so,' Murthy continued with the prank. 'Sounds like something is wrong with that engine.'

Rao snapped, 'Murthy, now will you please keep silent?'

* * *

Many academic programmes in Princeton worked thus: you enrol as a research scholar, you have to complete seven subjects for credit. This, plus a completed project work will make you eligible for your masters. Many took two—a few three—subjects in a semester of five months, I took four in a semester and three in the next, simultaneously working on the project to complete the requirements for the masters in ten-and-a-half months.

One of the few friends I gained in Princeton was a Russian student. We went on long strolls on the campus. I was surprised as much at his English—he spoke well—as his knowledge of thermodynamics. He had registered for a graduate programme under Professor Summerfield, who is considered a pioneer and a legend in solid propulsion systems.

After a few months of my wondering how he mastered so much on the subject even while doing the graduate programme, the Russian let me in to his little secret: He was a post-doctoral fellow. He was hiding his PhD just to experience Princeton, and work under Professor Summerfield.

I suspected there could be more. Russia, as much as the US, was known for deploying its people at centres of academic excellence to observe developments in strategic sectors. I did not ask him anything to clarify my suspicion; he was a knowledgeable friend I did not want to upset.

It was a usual practice for post-doctoral fellows of Princeton and Caltech, the two great US campuses of scientific research, to present their research/thesis on each other's campuses. This practice was more prevalent between Princeton's Guggenheim Laboratory for Aerospace Propulsion Systems and Caltech's Jet Propulsion Laboratory, both funded by NASA.

One day a Caltech researcher was presenting his research paper in Princeton, and I was there with the Russian friend. In the hall was William A Srignano, a Princeton professor.

The Caltech man went on for an hour explaining his paper, filling the blackboard with mathematical equations that looked like Greek to me. I was feeling lost, when the Russian leaned to me and whispered: 'This guy is bullshitting.'

'What?'

'His equations are fundamentally wrong,' said the Russian.

'Then why don't you question him.'

'No way.'

'Why?'

'I am not here to show off my knowledge.'

'No, you have to speak out. You can't let a wrong pass in such a gathering. It's against the spirit of science.'

I was instigating the Russian.

Finally he sought a couple of clarifications, which the Caltech man explained, again through a maze of equations.

Professor Srignano egged the Russian on.

Now the Russian friend stood up.

'Your theories are against some fundamental equations of thermodynamics,' he told the presenter who now invited him to the podium to prove his point.

The Russian took a piece of chalk and moved to a corner of the podium where the blackboard still had a little space. He started scrawling furiously, reeling out equations all the while. This went on for some twenty minutes. At the end of it, he had demolished the Caltech man's research paper. He walked shyly back to the chair next to me even as Professor Srignano and the rest of the crowd pondered over his scrawls on the blackboard. There was absolute silence. The Russian whispered to me.

'Mate, you exposed me.'

The rest of the audience now grilled the Caltech scholar. The poor man lost it. The incident influenced my perception about two things. One: Russians are sharp. Two: an American university hall full of scientists can easily miss a bloomer in thermodynamics.

Well, if that sounds as a conditioned prejudice, there were others who had more misplaced notions about Indians. It could be out of some one-off experience that a Turkish professor at Princeton had. He believed Indians were poor in mathematics.

The professor was working on a mathematical problem for the class and I kept asking questions. At one point he got irritated and asked me: 'Where are you from?'

'India,' I replied.

'No wonder you can't understand what I am saying.'

This was more an insult for me than shock. It was personal, it was racial; I had never scored anything less than full marks in maths right from school. And to brand Indians weak in maths was a collective affront on a nation that had given birth to such greats as Ramanunjan, C V Raman and Harish Chandra. The professor's remark incited me to work harder on the problem and learn the solution myself.

Time for my sweet revenge came a couple of months later while the Turkish professor was again working on a problem on the blackboard. Midway through an equation he paused, went back a few steps and wondered aloud: 'Where did I go wrong?'

I raised my hand. 'Can I help you?'

'Yes,' he said.

I walked up to the blackboard, and worked out the steps to arrive at the solution. Now I turned to the professor, who was gracefully taking the place of a student.

'Do you understand?' I said.

'Yes,' said the professor.

'I thought you wouldn't, because the solution came from an Indian.'

Later I introspected if I was being childish or cheap. It was my luck that I knew the solution and the class presented an opportunity for me to get back at the professor. I liked it. Later the professor became my well-wisher and came to congratulate me when I completed the master's course.

I thought I was creating a record of sorts when I completed the projects and the course in little more than ten months, given that students usually take at least a year and a half to do the same. Prof. Harrje was sure that Prof. Crocco wouldn't clear my degree so soon, for there was a sense of bewilderment on how I did it so fast. But Prof. Crocco surprised everyone—including me—by giving his nod for clearing my degree. Brocco, an Italian scholar doing a PhD for more than seven years under Prof. Crocco, was happy for me and sad for himself. Brocco was not bad at research, but the highest standards Crocco set for this students made it difficult for anyone trying to pass out of the campus without showing at least some flashes of brilliance. 'The professor,' Brocco told me about Crocco, 'would allow anyone to get a degree, but not an Italian.'

Technically speaking, with Crocco's approval, I was ready to leave the campus with the degree. But Prof. Bill Sirignano, another faculty, wouldn't yield, citing that the ten-and-a-half month within which I completed the programme was too short a period for any student to be awarded a degree. It was another matter that there was no time frame for degrees—only that you had to meet the academic criteria, which I had by putting in longer hours.

'Why don't you do the project a few more times and make it terribly attractive?' he said.

I said 'yes'.

According to Prof Srignano's calculations, that should keep me on the campus—and the project—for a good one-and-a-half months, so that there is a 'respectable' year into my graduation. I disappointed him by doing the extra repeats in ten days. Without the assistance of technicians Lawrence and Ken, who were now active participants in my project and passion, this would have been impossible.

Now I had completed the extra work, well within eleven months. Prof. Harrje now had another plan to keep me in the degree project for a few more months: I should visit a few reputed space science institutions in the US. I would get an inclination of what Prof. Harrje, as a willing patriot of the American system of grabbing Indian scientists, only later, but I readily agreed. After all, an Indian space scientist getting access to Goddard Space Flight Centre, Aerojet General Corporation, Bell Aerospace, Hercules Powder Company, Thiokol Chemical Corporation, Boeing and half-a-dozen more companies was rare. I decided to play along—and win.

The benefits of the fleeting yet unrestricted visits I considered big. At the end of it all—which was another month—I had a fair idea about developing both solid and liquid propulsion systems. I had also made acquaintances who would later prove useful for ISRO. One of them was a gentleman called Delwell, who was then with Boeing. Later, after he joined Airbus Industries as a technical director, he approached me with a barter: I should influence the India government to buy Air Bus aircraft; in return he would give me the total stage engineering of the Viking engine.

My faint suspicions about some people trying to delay my stay in the US took the shape of clarity soon when I got a call from a person called Eugene Scott of NASA.

'We will be happy if you stay back in the US,' she said.

These guys were poaching. All those conducted tours to the US installations were to impress me about the facilities the US has against a country like India struggling to understand the basics of space science. There was no doubt that they had impressed me, but I could not wait to get back to India where Sarabhai waited with his dreams—and my wife and son with theirs.

I called Sarabhai.

'Leave the nasty guys and take the next flight,' he said.

I remember Sarabhai adding that he would speak to Arnold Frutkin. The name didn't ring a bell till I realised later that Frutkin, the man who Sarabhai wanted to give a piece of his mind to, was the deputy director of NASA's International Programs Office during the US's space race with the USSR. Later he was designated the associate administrator for external relations. With Sarabhai gone, only Frutkin, still alive at 98 at the time of writing this, would know what Sarabhai told him about the American poaching attempt.

I returned to India in September 1970.

CHAPTER 8

OFFICERS WITH REAL NAMES

'If you have done no crime, you have nothing to worry.'

At the Pallipuram camp, I was taken to a room where a CBI officer introduced himself as superintendent R S Dhankar, the CBI's chief investigating officer in the ISRO spy case. He showed me his identity card. It was a refreshing change from the IB's shady ways. I instantly thought that he was a good person.

Dhankar asked me to sit on a cot before leaving the room. I was left with an ageing police constable who introduced himself as Darshan Singh. A genial man in his late fifties, Singh remained with me throughout my stay here, attending to every need of mine. This god-fearing man gave me strength to face the rest of the interrogation. He would console me, never getting tired of repeating that the truth will eventually come out.

On 5 December, around 2 pm, I had my first lunch in three days (I had stopped taking food on 2 December, while being tortured by the IB officials at Latex Guest House). By now I realised that all the accused in the case were here. In fact, it was a big hall, partitioned with curtains.

In the adjacent portion were Chandrasekhar and Sasikumaran. The two Maldivian women would be somewhere in the building, I knew.

Finishing my lunch, I sat on the cot, my left hand cuffed to the leg of the furniture. Could they have arrested more people in the fictitious case, I wondered. Who could have been behind this sordid drama? My thoughts were interrupted by a man who briskly walked into the room.

He was tall, slim and fair. His eyes were almost blue, and his nose sharp. Later I was told his name was M L Sharma IPS, an inspector general of CBI from Delhi. He radiated authority and intelligence in equal measure. He came to me as if to ask me something, but stopped himself. Abruptly he turned back and left in the same pace he had come in. He entered the adjacent 'room' where Sasi and Chandrasekhar were lodged. I could not see what was happening there, but could hear every sound.

Suddenly the CBI officer was shouting. 'You bastard, you sold the nation to the enemies. You call yourself a scientist ... how do you call yourself an Indian first?'

Sasi was saying something, but his voice was so feeble that I could not make out what it was.

There came Sharma's voice again. 'You speak about law? If I am convinced that you have done this crime, I will make sure that you will spend the rest of your life behind bars.'

Then he turned his ire towards Chandrasekhar. For a few minutes, the CBI officer's voice reverberated through the building.

Something told me that Sasi had met the Maldivian women earlier, and that he had done something—though definitely not espionage—that gave the police a reason to link ISRO with the Maldivians and the cooked up case. I was angry with Sasi for having landed me in this cesspool, and even felt a tinge of glee when Sharma shouted at Sasi. I was also scared of this officer though I had nothing to hide.

Sharma marched out of Sasi's 'enclosure', his boots making the tap-tap sound that added to his authority. Sensing my fear, Darshan Singh came and sat by my side.

'Saab, if you have done no crime, you have nothing to worry. Sharmaji is such a great person that he will find out the truth, and he would hurt no innocent,' Singh said.

The old man, now wearing a white kurta-pyjama, was such a contrast from the Kerala police constables that I doubted whether Singh is really working for an investigating agency. During the rest of my stay there, Singh made sense of his demeanour: He had seen it all—people who were wrongly framed and criminals who were rightly exposed—and that wisdom was radiating from his speech and action. Singh, he told me, was to retire in three months.

Now I saw Sasi and Chandrasekhar leaving their room, must be for interrogation. They returned after a couple of hours. I knew it was my turn next.

AN EXPLOSION AND AN OUTBURST

'But why the resignation?'

No sooner than I returned to India, I found myself again in the vortex of the liquid-solid turmoil. Kalam was keen on me working with him on the SLV project, which at that time appeared the most promising project. Though I was not very happy at SSTC, which again worked more on solid propellants than liquid fuel, I found here a better opportunity to push for my pet project, which I was sure would one day take heavier satellites to space.

Kalam's SLV was on stream because it was approved as a project, while my liquid engine was still a concept, and hence categorized under research and development. Projects always got—and continue to get—more funds and human resources, while concepts remain just that till they are approved as workable projects. Sarabhai, my biggest moral support was by now no more—he was found dead in a hotel in Kovalam on 30 December 1971.

But I had faith in Satish Dhawan who had taken the place of Sarabhai, but Dhawan couldn't ask for more money—he could get it if he did—since I had nothing much to show on the ground for a liquid engine as a bright promise.

In mid-1968, the propulsion division was working at a feverish pace to launch the first multistage solid-fuelled sounding rocket named Rohini. During this period a small team consisting of T Sriram and A Chandran developed and tested the country's first indigenous liquid propellant engine named LPM-0. This was quickly followed by 30 kg and 200 kg thrust engines. Another team comprising A Chandran, Sivaramakrishnan and E V S Namboodiri had put together a 600 kg thrust liquid engine.

The Americans, Russians and the French were using 240-tonne cluster engines using four 60 tonners. In comparison, our 600 kg engine was but a tad better than a Diwali rocket. Nevertheless, I made an attempt to put together a rocket using the engine. Since a 600 kg thrust was too meagre for a launch, we used a solid booster, and soon a two-stage rocket called LP-006 was ready for testing.

The solid propulsion groups working within SSTC and TERLS were still unconvinced about the possibilities of a liquid engine, and this fired my ambition more. After successful ground tests, we had the rocket at the Sriharikota launch pad.

It was a sunny morning at Sriharikota on 15 May 1973 when LP-006 lifted off with the first stage solid booster and the liquid engine as the second stage. All eyes, literally, were on the liquid stage. A few seconds after the rocket rose to the sky, it disappeared from our sight. And the radar didn't pick up any signals from the rocket thereafter. Since the rocket had no payload which could have communicated to the ground station, there was no way to confirm if the second stage performed as planned.

A majority of the scientists who had gathered at Sriharikota, including quality control head M C Mathur, said the launch was a failure. I argued it was a success. My logic was simple: the radar might have been at fault. And, with the sun bright on the eastern sky, we could not see the second stage ignition and performance, which could have been possible on a clear night sky.

Throwing a challenge at the majority who called the launch a failure, I said we are ready with a second LP-006 engine and my team could launch it within a month. This time we would do it on a night, when the sky is clear, so that we can see with our naked eye, the entire burnout of the rocket, irrespective of the performance of the radar. My detractors, possibly convinced that I would bite the dust, agreed.

Eighteen days later, on 2 June 1973, we were back at Sriharikota on a starry night. As the countdown progressed, my heart thumped against my chest, but on the outside, I wore a confident look. My reputation and dream were at stake. LP-006 lifted off majestically, and both the stages performed—in front of our eyes—perfectly. Unlike the previous flight, this one was instrumented and tracked well by the radar which confirmed normal performance of the engine. There was applause.

Modesty escapes me at times of both triumph and tribulation.

'See, now you all agree that the previous launch was also a success; only that we couldn't watch it against the day sky,' I said.

The dispute continues to date, and it is time for me to confess: While my argument about the backlight that blinded us from seeing the second stage burnout still stands, I believe my trained eye could not have missed the brilliant flare from the liquid engine. Yes, privately I had told myself that the first attempt was probably a failure. In the absence of a scientific validation either way—whether it was a success or a failure—I stood my ground then. And for good reason: conceding would have meant a deathblow for the liquid concept, and I was keen on a second attempt.

Now that we had proved the might of our 'Diwali rocket', it was time to dream bigger. While the Russians were using 110-tonne liquid engines, I thought it was not out of place to think of a three-tonne liquid engine. But, with the project yet to be officially recognized as one, we were working with the meagre allocations for R&D. Our first necessity for a three-tonne engine was a ground-test facility. The 600 kg stuff could be tested on the Thumba beach with some rudimentary stand, but a bigger version needed a better facility which would cost some money.

The group that still refused to see merit in the liquid engine tried to put up barricades. Many came up with a variety of reasons to stymie the liquid engine test facility. Some of their points were arguable, many were absurd. Some said it was dangerous to have the facility at Thumba, some others found the very idea of storing liquid propellants an invitation to disaster. Proponents of this risk theory got a shot in the arm when U Subbaiah Pillai, a curious and sincere technician did something foolish: to see if we had enough red-fuming nitric acid, which was then used as the liquid propellant, he bent over the storage tank. As the name suggests, the acid when exposed to air, gives out noxious red fumes. Pillai fainted and had to be taken to a hospital for first-aid. All hell broke loose. The see-we-told-you chorus became unbearable.

What they probably knew was that such propellants as red fuming nitric acid are kept in large barrels even on college campuses. In fact, testing a liquid engine is safer than a solid test: a propellant flow can be stopped at will, if something goes wrong in a liquid engine. This is not possible with a solid engine, which is like igniting compressed gunpowder. I would not give up, and decided to test the engine.

They suggested that I take the engine to Sriharikota for further tests. It was not a bad idea, since Sriharikota had much more uninhabited space. I agreed, though I realised that their idea was to drive the liquid engine out of Thumba, than to offer a better alternative. The island with Bay of Bengal on a side and a lagoon on the other three sides, was indeed a safer place, but Sriharikota had no facilities for our stay: There were a couple of rooms for our team of more than twenty people.

The first test was a resounding failure, literally. An explosion ripped through the engine, smashing the test stand that holds the engine to smithereens. I was devastated.

A failure analysis later showed that the reason was the water we used to calibrate the system before filling fuel. To save fuel, water is passed from a tank to the engine, with several filters on the way, to gauge the flow of the liquid. Through mathematical calculations, we would make corrections based on the difference in the viscosity and other parameters of water, before cleaning and filling the system with the liquid fuel in place of water. Our calculations were based on the presumption that the water is pure. It was not. Fine suspended particles in water settled as sediments on the filters and the readings we got were erroneous. When we filled the fuel and fired the engine, we were unaware that the anomalies in the calculations would result in a heavier flow of the liquid fuel. The result was the disaster.

The team went into mourning. By now I thought that I would not get another chance to push for the liquid engine. Not only that the test was a failure, the explosion had destroyed the test stand which then cost around Rs 2 lakh. The team asked what we should do. I asked them to pack up and get back to Trivandrum. I did not want to get back to Trivandrum, where my detractors waited gleefully. I went to the SHAR (Sriharitoka Range) guest house in Poes Garden, Chennai. The guest house, always open for us space scientists, had a few rooms. The manager asked me how many of us were there. I said I was alone. He said a room was available for me, but the other two rooms where occupied by Satish Dhawan and Brahm Prakash, then director of Vikram Sarabhai Space Centre.

Now I knew what to do. I grabbed the first piece of paper I could lay my hands on, wrote my resignation letter and walked into the room where Dhawan and Brahm Prakash were in a discussion. My face was roasted red from the long hours in the sun. I handed over the letter to Dhawan. He studied me for a moment, then asked what had happened. I explained that the test was a failure, and that I think I am incompetent to continue in the organisation.

'And, yes,' I added. 'I have caused a loss of about Rs 2 lakh by blasting the test stand.'

'But why the resignation?' Dhawan demanded.

By now I was fuming. I had great respect for Dhawan, but at this moment, I blew my fuse.

'These guys,' I said, referring to the large majority of scientists, engineers and administrators at VSSC who were trying to quell the liquid engine concept, 'are kicking me around like a football. And you people do nothing to support me. Enough is enough. I want to leave this organisation and do something else for a livelihood.'

Dhawan and Brahm Prakash remained silent through my twenty-minute outburst. Then Dhawan spoke something to the effect that I had misunderstood him. I realised that I had been harsh, but even now I was too hurt to mellow down.

'I am not saying you are inefficient,' I continued. 'But I have to say that you are not doing your job by keeping silent when others are trying to ride roughshod over me and destroy my dream of making a liquid engine, which would be much superior to the solid ones.'

'I think you need rest,' said a calm Dhawan. 'Why don't you retire for the night and let's talk about this over breakfast tomorrow?'

Back in my room, I repeatedly washed my face and found that my eyes were red-shot. May be it was the sun, may be it was my anger. Through the restless night, I had hazy dreams of red-fuming nitric acid.

The next morning, I met Dhawan and Brahm Prakash in the guest house dining room for breakfast. Dhawan, as calm as ever, was seated at the head of the table, flanked by us. I was feeling slightly better than the previous night. Dhawan did not get back to my allegations of some people trying to scuttle the liquid engine concept and my accusation that he was being a silent spectator. But he appeared to have considered seriously whatever I had told him.

'Failures are part of the game,' Dhawan started. 'You have been trying something that you strongly believe in, and I appreciate that. Now, why don't you try for some collaboration with a country willing to help us develop this engine?'

There was not any country then, keen to join hands with us, I knew, but Dhawan's words sounded encouraging. I also realised that even if I strike a deal with another country for the liquid propulsion system, it would not make me happy till some seniors continued to disregard the promise of the liquid engine. By now I was convinced that they either did not understand the future or chose to ignore it to further their own interests.

'Collaborations I can look for,' I said. 'But only if I can report to you …'

I sensed an unease in Dhawan, and quickly added '… formally or informally.'

Dhawan patiently explained to me how as an organisation I couldn't overstep my seniors and report to the chairman directly.

'I will monitor your project, and you can interact with me anytime you want to,' he said, 'but the administrative hierarchy should remain in place.'

I got the message.

Dhawan and Brahm Prakash appeared to be satisfied that they could drive some sense into me, and stop me from quitting. They obviously wanted me to believe that by postponing this discussion from the previous night, they had given me time to cool down and think. That was true. But it was equally true that they wanted time for themselves to placate me with a new idea and retain me.

I was finishing my bread and fried eggs when Dhawan cleared his throat. 'Now, with your permission,' he said, taking out the resignation letter I had given him the previous night, 'May I do the honours?'

He tore the letter and threw it into the bin.

★ ★ ★

We soon did three more ground tests—two short duration and one long duration—which were successful. The first test flight, however, was a failure. An analysis showed that it was because of 'combined beating and sloshing', a phenomenon little-known to us then. In simple terms, 'combined beating and sloshing' is similar to the movement of water in a tanker on the move. Liquid fuel, while flying, would beat and slosh, resulting in variations in flow, thereby upsetting our calculations. Later we developed methods to minimise, if not prevent, these anomalies.

A year later, after I left for Vernon to head a team of sixty-odd Indian scientists to work in collaboration with the French to develop the Viking-Vikas engine, the three-tonner was successfully flown twice by a team comprising my colleagues A Chandran, D Subramanyam, M K Narendranath, D Anandan, Mohammed Muslim and O P Varshney.

In the absence of a project, the three-tonne engine was abandoned. It was anyway a technology demonstration project.

CHAPTER 9

A PLEASANT INTERROGATION

'Sleep as much as you want.'

5 December 1994. My interrogation call came at 6.30 pm at the Pallipuram police camp.

Someone removed my handcuffs and escorted me to the room at the farthest end of the first floor of the Pallipuram camp.

The room had a large table and several chairs around it. M L Sharma sat at the head of the table on which were several files and papers. On his left was seated P M Nair, DIG of police. This was the man who had come to the Vanchiyoor police station on 30 November, soon after my arrest, masquerading as a journalist from outside the state.

Nair was on another official assignment, and was about to return to Delhi when he was asked to stay back and nose around before the CBI officially took over the ISRO spy case. At the Vanchiyoor police station, he was eavesdropping at the policemen and journalists who, he later told me, had bought the spy story before even questioning anyone.

Nair spoke fluently in Tamil, Malayalam, Hindi and English (what other languages this polyglot was proficient in, I knew not). He was trying to be tough, but failed miserably. He just could not hide his ingenuous cordiality, even while trying to sound tough.

Sharma again introduced himself and Nair, and the two showed me their identity cards. It was the CBI style: no intrigue about them, only a no-nonsense approach to unravelling the truth.

Nair spoke, 'The first time I saw you, this morning, I got the feeling that you will speak the truth. That's why I kept this session with you the last. Now, Mr Nambi Narayanan, tell us all about you and the charges you face.'

He was firm and clear in his words, but very different from the threatening ways of the Kerala Police and the IB. I felt reassured.

I sat still for a minute or two, gathering my thoughts. I decided to be as articulate and lucid as possible. I divided my story, mentally, into three parts. First, my family background, my financial situation and my commitments to my sisters and some other relatives; second my professional background and achievements; and the third about whatever little I tried to understand about what they called the ISRO spy case.

I tried hard not to show my emotions as I spoke about my father, mother, my commitment to my sisters, their marriage, my struggle through the engineering college and the lost opportunity to study abroad because of my mother's ill-health.

Sharma and Nair listened intently, in silence.

The second part of my story was more of a presentation of pride; how I joined ISRO, my meeting and association with Vikram Sarabhai and A P J Abdul Kalam; how I led a team of more than fifteen Indian scientists to collaborate with the French and develop the Viking/Vikas engine which helped launch India's first two PSLV rockets only months earlier. I also told them something I had not told anyone else: my plan to quit ISRO sooner than later, purely to make more money so that I can take care of some dependents in my extended family.

The two officers sat poker-faced.

The third part, I told them, about the so called espionage case, was just a figment of imagination. All that I knew about the case was through the questions the IB men had thrown at me. I told Sharma and Nair that this case is a complete frame-up since rocket secrets cannot be transferred through paper, it needed intense hands-on collaboration and training for years—the way we developed the Vikas engine. I raised the suspicion that I could have been falsely implicated in the case, but I did not know the reason beyond the fact that several people in ISRO were not my fans since I was known for bulldozing through official barricades to achieve my goals, which included the making of India's first big liquid propulsion systems. I also told them that I found the IB interrogation fishy as they came with a story and kept amending the plot as and when I demolished some parts.

The two officers kept taking copious notes. I spoke for hours and it must have been past midnight when I finished. Sharma, for the first time, stood up and offered me a cigarette. I took it. I was at ease with these officers, though exhausted.

Sharma and Nair asked a few questions about my belongings—some home appliances, which I understood they had listed out after a search at my place when I was in custody (later one of them told me that the search yielded nothing suspicious). I gave them a list of things I owned, some of which I had brought back from France.

They asked about my association with the other accused. I told them I knew only Sasi and Chandrasekhar.

'Are you sure?' Sharma asked.

I replied in the affirmative, and he did not ask any more questions that day.

'You may go and take rest,' he said. 'And you need not bother about waking up early, sleep as much as you want. We want you fresh tomorrow.'

I went back to the room and my left hand was again handcuffed to the leg of the cot. Lying there with my hand thus extended gave me a shoulder pain, but the exhaustion took over and I fell asleep.

THE FRENCH CONNECTION

Kanwal Grover stunned everyone at Le Lido, sponsoring half a bottle of champagne to each of the 2,000 guests that night.

Much before Dhawan asked me to look for foreign collaborations, I had initiated it when Sarabhai was alive. Sarabhai, with his global network of contacts, had initiated talks with SEP, a private French company working on propulsion systems for Centre national d'études spatiale (CNES), the French space agency, which was a member of the European Space Agency (ESA). In the early 1970s, Sarabhai wanted me to go to Paris and explore the possibilities of a tie-up from which we could learn more on solid propulsion.

SEP had its solid propulsion centre in Istres and a liquid propulsion system centre in Vernon. Its Boardeaux facility dealt with control rockets and some defence-related development; SEP also had a cryogenic lab in Villaroche. Understandably, I was eyeing a joint venture with the Vernon centre.

P Souffle, a retired French army officer, was the chairman and managing director of SEP, and Rene Morin was the commercial director. The two gentlemen were cordial to me and Nandakumar, my deputy on the electronics side. SEP wasn't convinced about the capabilities of Indian space engineers in developing high-end rocket engines, but was keen on doing business with India. We did not want to buy rockets from them, and hence there was no deal in sight. There had to be a way out. And that is when I bumped into Kanwal Grover.

Nandakumar and I were at Le Lido, the most famous address of entertainment on Champs-Elysees, Paris. Champagne flowed at the night club where the high and mighty rubbed shoulders amidst cabaret and burlesque. Suddenly, the music stopped and the manager of the club came on the microphone.

'We have a distinguished guest from India. Ladies and gentlemen, let's welcome Mr Kanwal Grover,' came the announcement.

A smiling, balding gentleman stepped on to the stage, took the microphone and thanked everyone. And then he announced that he was ordering half a bottle of champagne for every guest that night. The crowd went into a rapturous applause; I remained dumbstruck thinking who this wealthy Indian was. The guests, like us, had paid 250 Francs for an entry into the club, and got half a bottle of champagne on the house.

Grover was soon to impress me more as a businessman of rare acumen and a sense of selflessness that only patriotism can infuse in a man. He was the main catalyst for ISRO striking a deal with SEP in 1974 to develop the Vikas engine. Viking, Vikas's French counterpart, continues to fire the famous Ariane rockets. Grover would also go on to be famous in India as the man behind Grover Vineyards that brought quality wine to India at an affordable price.

On that night at Le Lido, Grover happened to sit near me. We started talking about the French weather, and were soon engrossed in a conversation about rocketry and India's struggle to develop rocket engines that could be used for satellite launches. I learned that Grover was an agent for HMT milling machines. France wanted many such machines; HMT in India was making them, but was not adept at selling them abroad. Grover, with his impeccable communication and networking skills, made a roaring business out of the opportunity. He was also trying to be an SEP agent, which he became before striking the Indo-French deal.

With Souffle and Morin being friendly, and a good push at the right time by Grover, the French allowed me to visit many of their propulsion facilities, including a missile-making centre. Later I had wondered why they let me in there—to impress me with their technology that they were keen on selling or the belief that an Indian scientist wouldn't be able to take away anything from a cursory visit of a missile-making facility? The missile facility, however, remained out of bounds for foreign scientists soon after my visit, and I was probably the only one from ISRO to have had a ringside view of the early French missiles. The French were not foolish by letting me in, though. One cannot develop a rocket by seeing how it is made, not even if given detailed drawings of all the systems. If that was the case, a small-scale industrialist doing a metal plating for a rocket part should be able to replicate the rocket since he, like any other contractor, is given the blueprint. Lack of this basic understanding was to make many believe in the ISRO spy case of the mid-1990s, as the Indian Intelligence Bureau concocted the story of us selling the Vikas engine and cryogenic engine secrets to Pakistan through two ill-educated Maldivian women.

A rocket cannot be made with just the know-how. You need the 'know-why'. And, for that, you need to work with the masters for years, be part of the design, development, tests and reviews. That's what more than sixty ISRO scientists did for five years alongside the French at the Vernon facility to develop the Vikas engine.

Some simpler systems, however, can be replicated once you have a close, long look, provided you know not just the design and theories, but also the material used. One such was the six-component static solid motor test facility we had access to in Istres. The concept of a solid motor test facility is simple: the motor or the rocket itself sans payload is kept in a horizontal position against a reinforced concrete wall. At the point of contact between the motor and the wall would be strain gauges. You fire the rocket motor which pushes against the concrete wall and the strain gauges pick up and measure the force exerted by the motor. Calculations give you the thrust to see if it is good enough to take the desired mass to the altitude of your choice.

At Thumba, we had a test facility which served our purpose of testing small solid boosters, but in comparison to the French, ours was at best primordial. A six-component test facility, the kind SEP had at its Istres centre could not just measure thrust, but also give accurate readings of variations when the rocket motor was tilted. In other words, it gave details of quantum and direction of the force. While allowed to roam around the Istres centre—we were in France, visiting several such facilities across two months—we were picking up these details.

Nandakumar, an electronics engineer from IIT who later set up the ISRO satellite tracking centres across India, took notes of measurements and instrumentation. I studied the location and functional details. On our return, we replicated the six-component facility at Sriharikota, which came to be known as STEX (Static Test and Evaluation Complex). This was later upgraded as the Vehicle Assembly, Static Test and Evaluation Complex (VAST).

But all these were just useful sideshows in my search for the right liquid engine. I kept pestering Morin. He showed me an engine called L-17, trying to sell it to ISRO. An outright technology transfer was not my idea; I wanted an ISRO group to work along French scientists to develop an engine. By doing this, we would not only gain hands-on knowledge and skills, we could also tweak the engine to suit our future needs. L-17 did not appeal to me for another reason: it was a pressure-fed engine, which was not ideal to work upon for futuristic missions. I wanted a turbo pump-fed engine with higher thrust level.

The next candidate was a liquid engine called M-40, which had a thrust of 40 tonnes. It used nitrogen tetroxide (N_2O_4) and unsymmetrical dimethyl hydrogen (UDMH) as fuel. Morin said they were planning a 55-tonne thrust rocket and wanted to upgrade M-40 for that. Grover, a constant companion in our dealings with SEP, realised the potential for a France-India tie-up on this. When he proposed this to SEP chairman Souffle, he dismissed it saying Indians wouldn't have the expertise to work with them. That was a notion that the ISRO team of scientists would soon demolish to show how Indian engineers can be as good, if not better, than anyone if given an opportunity. Grover went to great lengths to convince Souffle that though ISRO had not developed big rocket engines, its scientists were much more than a bunch of greenhorns. There were young scientists who had passed out of IITs, our premier engineering institutes, Grover reasoned. He asked Souffle if he considered me, a graduate of Princeton University, as any less capable than their scientists. Souffle appeared convinced.

I shuttled between Trivandrum and Paris for the next three years, trying to firm up the collaboration. Parallel to this, Sarabhai had been trying for a German joint venture, which did not take off. And Sarabhai did not live to see the results of our French connection: the Vikas engine.

Even as I was working on the French option, Sarabhai was talking to some German scientists, especially a professor called Prof. Armin Dadieu. The Germans were masters of metallurgy and fabrication. Germany's has been an unfortunate degeneration in the field of space and missile technology after its defeat in World War II. As early as the early 1940s, Germany under Hitler had developed a liquid rocket called V-2. Hitler wanted to use V-2 with a warhead. In other words, as a missile. But there was a hitch: V2 did not have a guidance system to hit targets. The Germans still gave England the scare, randomly firing V-2 with warhead across the English Channel. It was using some of the unexploded V-2 rockets, called Operation Backfire, that the British started their missile and rocket programmes, which continue to be heavily dependent on the Americans.

I knew Dadieu as a close associate of Wernher von Braun who developed the V-2 engine. Dadieu was also a friend of Sarabhai—both compelling reasons for me to get close to him. Whenever Dadieu came to India, I would try to strike a conversation with him about V-2, thinking that he, as a liquid propulsion scientist would know much about the wonderful rocket of the times. The man was taciturn. Whenever I asked about the rocket, Dadieu, who was fluent in English, would feign that he could not follow me, and would switch to German. Only much later I realised the reason for Dadieu's reticence: he had worked closely with von Braun to make V-2 rocket that sent shivers down the spine of England and her allies during the war. He simply did not want to talk about his brainchild whose versatility prompted the US and its allies to impose sanctions on Germany to stall its rocketry.

When it came to economy of words, no different was Dadieu's companion Muller who kept visiting India, too, frequently to make me wonder about his intentions. I still don't know what brought him to ISRO so often, though we did not strike a deal with him.

After Sarabhai's death, Dhawan, the new ISRO chairman, took forward the French collaboration attempt. Following my outburst and the resignation episode at the ISRO guest house in Chennai, after the failure of the three-tonne liquid engine test, I worked harder on the possible tie-up with SEP, France. After more than a year of correspondence, when Souffle and Morin mentioned their plans to upgrade M40 to 55 tonnes, we found an opportunity to collaborate and learn.

Besides trying to get some money from us, the French were also driven by a sense of competition with the US and the USSR, who were making great strides in rocketry. And they were competent to put themselves on a par with the Americans because of their sheer capabilities in developing flying machines. Concorde was a classic example of French expertise in aviation. The Americans had made supersonic fighter planes, but making a big civilian aircraft that could break the sound barrier remained a pipedream for the US. Aerospatiale-BAC flew the first Concorde as early as 1969, and entered service seven years later. The US tried hard to develop and fly its equivalent, but in vain. The French success with Concorde was so difficult for the US to digest that it banned Concorde from its airspace after many years of trans-Atlantic flights by Air France and British Airways. The US gave some safety concerns as the reason, but within, its spin doctors knew what the consequence would be. Without flying across the Atlantic, a supersonic civilian plane cannot be viable. Concorde, which had twenty planes and one crash (in 2000) in its twenty-seven years of flying, had its last ceremonial flight in 2003.

It was this confidence that drove France to plan a geosynchronous satellite launch vehicle in the early 1970s. And it presented us with an opportunity to further our agenda. It was an ambitious project at that time. The three-stage vehicle called LIIIS would be an all-liquid fuel vehicle, including a cryogenic upper stage.

Configuring a satellite-launching rocket is a top-down process, literally, starting from the payload under the nose cone and planning down to the first stage engine and boosters. The first thing to decide is the orbit—you have to be clear on where in space you want to place the satellite. That depends on what you want the satellite to do, which again decides what kind of a payload you need. If it is for communication, you need transponders; earth-watching satellites need cameras.

The weight of the payload decides the configuration of the rocket as there should be optimal balance of the payload and propellants. The stages of the rocket—solid, liquid or cryogenic—are dictated by this balance.

While India continued its romance with solid propellants ignoring the merits of liquid fuels, the French were among the earliest to plan a geosynchronous satellite launch vehicle powered entirely by liquid fuel, given that cryogenic engine, too, deals with liquefied gases. For a primer, here is a quick list of advantages of liquid over solid: a liquid engine can be tested repeatedly before being flown using the same hardware after cleaning and reassembly, enhancing reliability; a solid engine burns itself out, which means every engine you fly is a new engine as what you have tested is but a similar engine, not the same. Liquid engines can control the flight of the rocket through gimbaling; a solid engine needs external control systems which incur more cost and additional weight. If India realised these benefits, perhaps, its PSLV would have been an all-liquid and more versatile rocket. One need not look farther than our GSLVs, which have all its engines propelled by liquid fuel—but for the solid strap-on for initial thrust—to understand this.

Solid gives good initial thrust for lift-off, but it burns out much earlier than a liquid engine. A crucial engine was far superior to both, in terms of burning duration and energy quotient. A liquid engine can be stopped and restarted during tests and flights, ensuring better fuel efficiency; a solid engine once ignited, cannot be stopped.

Liquid propellant engines can be tweaked and upgraded for different uses; a solid is virtually as rigid as the fuel.

Propellants are not just to take a satellite to space; they are needed to keep it in orbit. Once in a designated orbit, the satellite moves around the earth by forces governed by gravitational pulls of the earth and other celestial objects, but it tends to stray from this path. Liquid propellants come in handy here, as they can be fired for very short durations and stopped at will. Position sensors and onboard computers work in tandem to fire small control rockets fitted to the satellite to push it back to the orbit whenever it tends to deviate. Geosynchronous satellites that orbit the earth at an altitude of 36,000 km, often swing wildly on different planes. To keep such swings below 3 km from the orbital plane, several control rockets fitted on different planes of the satellite are fired.

The French considered all these—and more—while configuring LIIIS. It was decided that the rocket would have a one-tonne payload. In those days, calculations of the rest of the rocket were made on scientific gut feeling; today you have mechanisms for precise calculations of every stage and component. So, it was presumed that a cluster of four M-40 engines could form the first stage booster. The second stage was to be a single M-40 engine, and the third stage a cryogenic engine called HM-7, above which the 1-tonne payload would be integrated.

All these went for a toss when the scientists realised that the payload would weigh 1.5 tonnes, and not 1 tonne as originally planned. Now this meant enhancing the boosters, reconfiguring the vehicle. Many high-end rocket engines are upgraded versions of smaller engines, but beyond a point upgrading becomes a misnomer as the new product would virtually be a new engine, though with the basic concepts of its predecessors. In fact, M-40 is such an upgraded—or redeveloped, depending on the way one looks at it—version of several of its earlier versions. Our own little 3-tonne liquid engine was a 'grown-up' version of our 600 kg engine.

Now SEP conceptualized an upgraded version of M-40, with a 50-tonne thrust, but they did not call it M-50. Instead, they named it Viking-1. This, still, wasn't good enough. Then came Viking-2 as a

55-tonne engine, and Viking-3, a 60 tonner. It was a cluster of four such engines which went on to power the first stage of the first Ariane flight in 1977. Ariane used a Viking-4 engine, a slightly modified version of Viking-3 with an extended nozzle that would yield 73-tonne thrust in upper atmosphere, as the second stage, and the original HM-7 cryogenic engine as the upper stage.

Jointly developed by SEP and ISRO, Viking-3—Vikas for Indian rockets—continues to be the second stage of PSLV, India's most consistently successful launch vehicle. But how the joint venture came about is another tale of intense lobbying by friends like Grover, some smart deal-making by me and a crafty contract writing by T N Seshan, who was the administrative director of ISRO.

CHAPTER 10

CONVINCING THE CBI DIRECTOR

'We are terribly sorry.'

7 December 1994. When I woke up, my hand was paining. Early morning, an officer came and introduced himself as Surendra Pal, deputy superintendent in the CBI. This appeared to be their custom: every CBI officer introduced himself, complete with designation, to all the accused. This helped me to a large extent, to believe that they, unlike the IB officers, had no hidden agenda. As I told my well-wishers later, the IB was framing a story, the CBI was finding the truth.

Surendra Pal was of fair complexion and medium build. He was unassuming, but spoke with the air of a man who had done his homework. I learned that he had met a lot of people in ISRO and outside to gather much information about me and the functioning of the organisation. In the course of his interactions, Pal had got friendly with some of my ISRO colleagues perhaps to glean more than what was told. During his short stay there, he said he had fallen in love with Kerala's greenery. But he missed the 'north Indian' food. Once when he told this to Mohammed Muslim, an ISRO scientist, Muslim supplied him a steady stream of rotis from his house.

This became news to a desperate journalist of a Malayalam newspaper who wrote that some of my colleagues were bribing a CBI officer with food. The source, obviously, was within ISRO; and this spoke of the internal petty rivalry that existed in our organisation.

Now, soon after introducing himself, Pal sat opposite my bed and asked: 'Who is Madhu?'

I could not remember the name instantly. And then it came to me.

'Madhu, is an attendant at the Liquid Propulsion Systems Centre where I worked.'

A casual staff, Madhu was a young and energetic man with ten years in ISRO. He was mostly attached to my office. I asked Pal why he asked about Madhu.

'No, nothing … I just wanted your opinion on him.'

I said he was an honest and hardworking employee. Later that night Pal would explain to me the reason behind his query: the IB had stated in its report that Madhu carried the 'documents' to my car, and my driver Sukumaran took them somewhere.

Now I remembered one of those IB men telling me that my office assistant and driver had 'confessed' to the crime of carting away state secrets from ISRO. Those monsters would have tortured my poor guys to 'confess', I thought. I was furious.

I was partly wrong. Pal told me that the IB men tried their best, but both Madhu and Sukumar maintained there was no wrong doing.

'Hats off to Madhu,' Pal said. 'He stuck to his statement till the end that Nambi Narayanan never used to take any documents home. At one point, the lad told the investigators that if they wanted him to say that Nambi did take documents, he would do that, but he would also add that what he said just now was a lie. The IB officials were stunned by the man's conviction that you can do no wrong. Driver Sukumaran also stuck to the statement.'

Pal had evidently questioned Madhu and Sukumaran—and many others—and was by now convinced of the IB fabrication.

There was an hour's break when I returned to my room. When called back, I found Surendra Pal and P C Sharma, with them Ahmed, the managing director of Hotel Fort Manor, Trivandrum. Ahmed was known to me as he played host to ISRO guests, especially Russian scientists who visited our centre in Trivandrum as part of the cryogenics project.

Also, I used to visit Hotel Fort Manor with a few friends for an occasional drink. We would take our drink to the hotel and buy only water and snacks. Ahmed would refuse to take money from me, but I always insisted on paying my bill. Since Ahmed had instructed the waiters not to give me a bill, I used to get the bill directly from the counter and pay. The interrogators, having collected these bills, wondered why we bought only water and snacks.

Some of these bills the CBI found during their search of my home. And that explained why the CBI officers had called Ahmed. They asked us to identify each other and we did even exchange pleasantries. I told the officers about my visits, and that Ahmed used to take good care of the Russian scientists who stayed in his hotel. The officers bid Ahmed bye.

The day passed with intermittent inquiries by M L Sharma, P M Nair and P C Sharma. These were more of clarifications, and I was joining the dots myself: the CBI, even while carrying out its independent investigation, was sending out its people to interview and interrogate a large number of people mentioned in the IB report. I realised that by now the CBI had seen through the IB plot to fabricate a spicy international spy case. It was getting increasingly clear—to the CBI and me—that the IB's was not a slip, but a concerted effort to make up a conspiracy that never was. Was it for the high some lowly IB officers might have got from it? Or is there a bigger conspiracy? Clarity would soon emerge.

✳ ✳ ✳

8 December 1994. By 3pm, the Pallipuram camp became active. Officers were moving around with files, making clarifications and exchanging notes. One of the officers soon told me that CBI director K Vijaya Rama Rao was coming. An hour passed and an officer came to tell me that Rao wants to meet me.

I was taken to a room where sat a man in a white shirt, a blue suit and a matching tie. He stood up – quite tall, I thought—walked towards me with his hand in a pocket from where he fished out his ID card. 'I am K Vijayarama Rao, the CBI director,' he said. He shook hands with me before making all of his colleagues introduce themselves to me.

Many of them had introduced themselves to me earlier, now they did it again, coming forward one by one, inspector general M L Sharma, deputy inspector general P M Nair, who later became a consultant for TIFR; Ashok Kumar, then an SP who later became the Tamil Nadu DGP; R S Dhankar, who was later examined as a witness in my compensation case against the Kerala government; Saxena, P C Sharma, who later became NHRC member ... Having endured IB's nameless agents of torture for four days, these investigators with real names came as a refreshing change, even a ray of hope that I would finally be heard.

'We will be happy if you tell us the truth,' Vijayarama Rao said.

I felt relieved with his manners, but his next sentence wasn't so soothing.

'Do you think your colleague Sasikumaran might have sold some drawings to foreigners?'

It was an old question, to which I had explained repeatedly to different people there is no way rocket technology can be transferred through drawings. But this time the question indicated a couple of things: one, Rao had scant respect for Sasi who he was convinced had met the Maldivian women; two, he realised that I had never met those Maldivian women.

Now I too had reasons to hate Sasi who must have met the women and hence landed ISRO in trouble.

My answer to the question, however, was a quick 'no'.

I made a request. 'Instead of this session beginning with your questions, shall I first explain how the Indian Space Research Organisation works?' I said.

'Please do,' said Rao.

I was ready to repeat what I did with the first set of CBI investigators.

I asked for a pen and sheets of paper. When they came, I assumed the air of a professor and started drawing the organisational chart of ISRO. Running the CBI officials through the hierarchy of Indian space programme, I showed them where I stood—not so high on the seniority list, but holding some crucial posts including those of the project director of liquid propulsion and cryogenics. By explaining how the organisation and its people worked, I hoped, I could drive some sense into these gentlemen and show that such a spy case can only happen in the fertile imagination of some vested interests.

'How much of it is classified information?' one of the officers asked, about the drawings of rocket engines and other parts.

'Nothing,' I replied. 'Nothing in ISRO is classified or de-classified. Drawings and documents are there for any scientist to refer. Though there was no ban on taking out drawings, rarely did a scientist take them home.'

The CBI men asked sensible questions, and appeared to be—in stark contrast to my previous interrogators from IB—unprejudiced and receptive, even while keeping their trained scepticism intact. The interrogation went on from 7:30 pm on 5 December to 2:30 am the next day. I didn't have to think for half a minute before answering any of the questions—they were direct; and since I had nothing to hide, I elaborated on every point that I knew of.

At the end of it all, Vijayarama Rao took both my hands in his and said, 'We now have a clear picture. I don't know how this whole case has come to this stage. We are terribly sorry.'

I looked into his eyes for a moment, then broke down. I wept like a child for a couple of minutes. There was pin-drop silence in the room. When I regained my composure, Rao asked me to calm down, that justice would be delivered. He left the room saying, 'Ask our men whatever you want.' From that day, my handcuffs were gone.

After a few hours, in the morning, I asked for breakfast. Constable Subhash brought bread and omelette. He said now I was allowed to take visitors. The first one to visit me was my son. I inquired about my wife. My son was silent for a moment, then he spoke: 'She doesn't know what's happening.'

I didn't understand the gravity of that statement then; only later would I know that she, after witnessing my arrest, had gone silent and was sinking deeper into depression that would soon leave her deranged.

'Console her,' I said. And he left, sobbing.

That night Subhash asked me if I wanted a drink. I felt like having one, but wasn't sure. When I returned from the rest room, I found a pint of rum under my pillow. I returned the bottle unopened to Subhash the next morning. I have not been a heavy drinker, but have enjoyed an occasional whiskey.

HOW WE CANNIBALISED A ROLLS ROYCE LAB

'You eye liquid stuff anywhere you go,' Sarabhai said, 'and now you have got something too.'

When SEP decided to upgrade the M-40 liquid engine to a 60-tonner, I knew it was our best opportunity to strike a deal with France to be part of the project and learn in the process. I kept pestering Grover to push for it and he continued to impress Souffle and Rene Morin. It was late 1971, months before Sarabhai's death. I kept telling Sarabhai that we should not let go of the opportunity.

The process was set in motion by my visit to Paris, and P Souffle and Morin coming down to India. While this was on, Sarabhai got news that the UK, which then had a fledgling yet promising space programme was winding it up after the US impressed upon it that it was duplicating efforts and, as a natural ally, the US could launch British satellites.

The UK had begun its space programme in 1957, and its Ariel series of satellites, starting with Ariel 1 in 1962, were launched by the US. The British embarked on an ambitious project to develop a satellite launch vehicle in 1957, but the project called Black Prince had to be shelved three years later for want of funds. They, however, put together a rocket called Black Arrow, which launched the Prospero satellite from Woomera, Australia in 1971. Black Arrow had three failures since 1969, before putting Prespero in a low earth orbit. Prospero, which studied the effects of the space environment on satellites, remains the only British satellite to be launched by a British rocket. The UK continues to be dependent on NASA for its satellite launches.

It was around this time that Sarabhai, ostensibly knowing my fixation with liquid systems, asked me to visit a Rolls Royce space science facility, which would soon be dismantled as part of the UK's decision to shelve its active space programme. The facility at Spadeadam in Cumbria, had a new hydraulics laboratory the company had put up at 400 million pounds. A F Cleaver, the director of the Rolls Royce lab was a former British army officer who had served in Mumbai. Cleaver said he never agreed with the way his country looted mine, and wanted to give back whatever little he could.

'What can I give you?' he asked.

I felt like a child in a toy supermarket. I wanted everything I saw around.

'Why don't you give me this hydraulics lab?' I said.

The lab, which offered simulation test for fluids with a complex system of gauges, was any fluid dynamics engineer's dream place.

Cleaver remained pensive for a moment, then said, 'You mean your scientists want to come here and do experiments? But the problem is we are going to break this down soon.'

'What if I ship this out?'

No sooner had I blurted out my request, I wondered if I was being too audacious.

'Do you mean what you said,' Cleaver's face lit up. 'It would be fantastic if you could do that. It is better that India put this to good use than us dumping it.'

Cleaver said he was feeling guilty that Britain did not allow India to partake in the industrial revolution, and found this an opportunity to pay back, however minor this contribution would be. He said he would give the entire hardware free of cost, only that India had to pay for dismantling the set-up and shipping it out. Here was a 400 million-pound lab, all ours, if we could disassemble, ship and reassemble it. I had no idea where I would find space in India to set this up, but I nodded vigorously.

I called Sarabhai who sounded impressed. 'You eye liquid stuff anywhere you go,' he said, 'and now you have got something too.'

I hated the British rulers of India, especially Robert Clive who was instrumental in the East India Company's systemic exploitation of India. I asked Cleaver if he could tell me where Clive's resting place was. Cleaver asked around his colleagues, but none of them knew. Later, we discovered Clive's tomb at Moreton Say, near his birthplace of Shropshire. It was a non-descript resting place for a man who established the British crown's military and political supremacy over India. Call it puerile or profound, I felt a strange sense of satisfaction standing there.

In less than twenty-four hours, I would stand frozen in disbelief and uncertainty, as the BBC flashed the news of Vikram Sarabhai's death.

ISRO deputed Ratnaraj Jayamani, who later became the first project director of GSLV, to bring home the Rolls Royce hydraulics lab from Spadeadam. He did a meticulous job getting people to disassemble the hardware and pack them. However, when one of the packs reached the airport, it was found to be too big to get through the mouth of the cargo hold. After a few weeks, a cargo aircraft carrying what was once a hydraulics lab flew to Trivandrum. It was only then we realised that we don't have a place to set up the lab. We emptied two of the three ISRO apartments in Veli Hills in Trivandrum, and converted them into a godown for the precious consignment. As the two apartments could not take them in full, some of the gadgets and parts were kept in a basement of the security building. Cleaver would turn in his grave if he knew what happened to them.

The heap of tubes and gadgets, which once formed an enviable laboratory in Spadeadam, was systematically plundered by our scientists who took them away for experiments. As the custodian of the consignment, I made some attempts to get a piece of land to set up the laboratory, but wasn't successful. So, here came scientists, one asking for a recorder, another taking away a pressure sensor, a third one snatching a flow meter. After giving up on setting up the facility on a new campus, I silently let these go, in a heartrending way, that it was probably better at least some of the hardware were put to use than let it gather rust. There were times when it also occurred to me that some people who did not want ISRO giving thrust to liquid propulsion systems would have derived great pleasure in seeing what was happening. Before my eyes, the Rolls Royce hydraulic laboratory was cannibalized.

Today, ISRO has a good test facility at Mahendragiri in Tamil Nadu. Had we found a place like that in 1971, the lab would have continued to be an envy of the world. Still, the Rolls Royce lab, forty-two years vintage, could have been incomparable for its simplicity and functional efficiency. After the development of Vikas engine, all we have been doing is improvising on it, the cryogenic engine being an exception. Now, if India wants to develop a totally new concept rocket engine, we would have to set up a lab like the one Cleaver so generously gave us away, only to be wasted.

This could have never happened if Sarabhai was alive. For he was the man who sent me to Spadeadam to take a look at the facility, though he wouldn't have dreamed of Cleaver gifting us the lab. Had Sarabhai lived a couple of more years longer, the Rolls Royce lab would have found a second life on a new campus in India. If a new campus was hard to come by, I was sure, Sarabhai would have set it up at one of the educational institutions, probably IISc, Bangalore, in which he had an abiding interest.

He had close ties with the then IISc director Satish Dhawan, who succeeded Sarabhai as the ISRO chairman, after M G K Menon held the post of interim chairman for less than six months. Probably Sarabhai saw a crucial role for Dhawan in India's space programme. When Dhawan visited TERLS sometime in the late 1960s, Sarabhai asked Dhawan to visit the high altitude rocket test facility at Tennessee, US. Dhawan did as directed and submitted a report to Sarabhai.

CHAPTER 11

BACK IN COURT

'Do you have any complaints?'

9 December 1994. Around 10.30 am I was asked to get ready to be taken to the court of the additional Chief Judicial Magistrate in Trivandrum. While getting into the police van at Pallipuram camp I saw Kurein E Kalathil, a friend of mine.

I waved at him. Kurien looked tense, hesitated for a moment, and waved back. He obviously did not want anyone to see him wave at me. Later, I came to know that Kurien was called to be questioned about his connection with me.

Kurien was introduced to me by Vijayan, a common friend. Later my son found a job in Kurien's office as a computer programmer.

After Sasi's arrest, Kurien used to call me, asking what it was all about. I would tell him that it appeared to be a case of mistaken facts, that the idea of selling rocket technology through papers was laughable. When I was arrested, Kurien might have been shocked. And when the CBI officers landed at his office, he must have been paranoid. This explained why he was hesitant to wave back at me as I was leaving for the additional Chief Judicial Magistrate that morning.

In the police van I found the two Maldivian women, Mariam Rasheeda and Fauziyya Hassan. It was the first time I was seeing them. I felt overwhelmed by anger and hatred towards these women, for the IB men had told me that they had confessed to having taken the rocket drawings from me. It was only much later that I realised that the women, innocents themselves, were tortured to name me. But now I just could not stand the proximity of these creatures with whom I was forced to travel to a court.

I had told M L Sharma that I had never met these women, I remembered, but why did he not crosscheck this with the women in my presence? I had an urge to ask Sharma to do it then and there, but I stopped myself. Later when I realised the professionalism of Sharma and his CBI colleagues, I had only praise for the way they dealt with the case.

In the court room, the magistrate pointed to the CBI officials and asked me, 'Do you have any complaint against them?'

I said 'no.'

Since there was no representative of either the Kerala Police or the Intelligence Bureau in the court, I took the question as whether I had any complaint against the CBI officials who had produced me in front of the magistrate. This was later misinterpreted by the Kerala police to be presented as if I have no complaints about the state police, IB or the CBI.

The CBI told the magistrate that they wanted to take us, all the accused, to Ernakulam, as it was getting difficult to question us in Trivandrum were the media was on an overdrive. For this we had to be produced before the Chief Judicial Magistrate court in Ernakulam. The court readily agreed.

SARABHAI: AN ERA ENDS

'We came together from Bombay and he returned alone, in a body bag.'

Having got Sarabhai's green signal to sign the contract to dismantle and take home the Rolls Royce hydraulics lab, I was at the YMCA in London on 30 December 1971 when BBC flashed the news: 'Eminent Indian astrophysicist Vikram Sarabhai was this morning found dead in a hotel in Kovalam in south India.' I reread the scroll to make sure that I had got it right. It was at first unbelievable, then unacceptable to me. I dialed the BBC, which confirmed the news.

Besides the personal loss I was yet to come to terms with, I wondered what would become of India's space programme and my experiments with liquid propulsion. I took the next flight to India. Landing in Bombay, I hesitated for a while what to do. Sarabhai's body, I knew, would be taken to Bombay on way to his hometown in Ahmedabad. I asked an airport staff if he knew about the body arriving, but he had no clue. Then I thought the body would still be in Trivandrum for an autopsy. So I took the next flight to Trivandrum. Only on reaching Trivandrum did I realise that the body was taken to Bombay soon after I left. No autopsy was conducted, apparently on the wishes of his wife Mrinalini Sarabhai. His wife, somebody said, had spoken to the Prime Minister, and the Kerala Governor P Shiv Shankar was said to have received a call from Delhi instructing him to ensure that Sarabhai's body would be handed over to the family without a scratch.

At Trivandrum airport I saw S R Thakur, Sarabhai's chief administrative officer, running towards me. He was weeping like a child. Thakur, who was Sarabhai's shadow, had accompanied him from Bombay to Trivandrum only the previous day. Thakur couldn't find place on board the plane that carried Sarabhai's body to Bombay, so here he was to take another flight for the funeral. Hugging me, Thakur sobbed. I could feel his tears wetting my shoulder.

'We came together from Bombay,' he said, 'and see, he has left alone in a body bag.'

I couldn't rush back to Bombay, and hence missed Sarabhai's funeral. About a month later, I waited at the Trivandrum airport where Sarabhai's son Kartikeya and a few others brought the ashes in an urn to be immersed at Cape Comorin, where three seas merged at the tip of the Indian peninsula. When Kartikeya, with the urn in his hand, emerged from the arrival lounge, I ran towards him. With several seniors of ISRO having lined up to receive the ash, some found this to be a disregard to protocol. I cared a damn! Sarabhai never followed the protocol when it came to getting work done—or when appreciating a work well done. In 1970, when Union Minister K C Pant visited TERLS in Trivandrum, some fifty scientists had gathered at the canteen where, on a mezzanine floor the minister sat with Sarabhai. There were scientists much senior than me in the group, but Sarabhai singled me out, and called me on to the mezzanine where the two sat having food. He then introduced me to Pant as 'my Princetonian'. Sarabhai was obviously not bothered about the seniors watching the three of us chit chat in the exclusive zone, since he sincerely felt I deserved appreciation. He must have done the same to several other deserving scientists.

Hierarchy meant little to Sarabhai who would casually drop by at my—and many others'—desk for a chat or take me for a stroll along the Thumba beach to discuss something. Still struggling to let the tragic news sink in, I remembered the day the handsome man in white kurta-pajama stood before me, a rookie engineer working on an explosive bolt at TERLS in 1967. His first words to me rang in my ears, 'They call me Vikram.'

Having reconciled with Sarabhai's death, now I wanted to know about his last hours. Sarabhai, staying at Halcyon Castle, a British era bungalow tucked away on the campus of a luxurious hotel overlooking the Arabian Sea, had met a few scientists the previous night, the last one being B Ramakrishna Rao, a contemporary of Kalam. I met Rao, but instead of a hint of the cause of Sarabhai's death, I was let into the sad tale of Rao who lost in Sarabhai, his last resort to prove his innocence over charges of misappropriation in ISRO.

Rao told me Sarabhai had been meeting several people, as usual, giving instructions and listening to their concerns. Rao had a grievance: he was accused of taking away from VSSC an air-conditioner and a few equipment to his house without permission. This amounted to stealing. Rao told me that he had indeed taken some gadgets home, but not the air-conditioner, with oral permission from Sarabhai who understood that Rao, a senior scientist, could at time work from home.

I believe in Rao's tale, for I know he was a conscientious scientist. I also knew Sarabhai's style of functioning, often giving permission to do things and getting the paperwork done later so as not to delay work. Sarabhai didn't disregard the bureaucratic system, but he bent it as he willed to enhance efficiency. I remembered how he had constituted a committee and made it approve my Princeton education within a few hours, and how he pulled strings at RBI to arrange for foreign exchange within a day. Not too different was the way Sarabhai ensured that I got the NASA fellowship money, which the Government of India refused to pay me even after my return from Princeton University.

Rao said he was discussing with Sarabhai how he was being crucified for nothing. Sarabhai had assured him that he would make it official that Rao had taken the equipment home officially. 'I will take care of it,' Rao quoted Sarabhai as saying. 'It's eleven, and I have to catch up on sleep before my early morning walk.' And Rao left the place a relieved man. The next morning, he was to wake up with the double shock of having lost his boss and the prospects of facing charges of theft.

'Sarabhai was the only man who knew I was innocent,' Rao told me, crying. 'And now he is no more, I will die a thief.'

Rao wasn't wrong. He was suspended, transferred and persecuted. He died an unhappy man.

Theories abounded about Sarabhai's death, and I found it only natural for people to talk of such an unnatural death. A 52-year-old man of many virtues and virtually no vice, dropping dead on his bed after a perfectly happy night in a hotel room. I knew Sarabhai never smoked or drank. Many who had seen him at parties, which he used to network rather than shake a leg, moving around with a glass in his hand, probably didn't know that it was a diplomatic show. I had watched closely several times to catch Sarabhai take a sip at least at the end of the party, but that was never to be. He was health conscious and went on regular morning walks. And without a postmortem done on his body, the cause of his death would remain disputable, if not unknown.

THE REAL MISSILE MAN

Vikram Sarabhai is rightly known as the father of Indian space science. And by virtue of India's early attempts to project itself as an aspiring space power for peaceful purposes—TERLS being dedicated to the UN in February 1968 was seen by some as a step in this direction, though Sarabhai was clear about the benefits of exposure and learning opportunities India would get by keeping TERLS accessible to other space agencies—Sarabhai was also seen as the mascot of this propounded Indian space philosophy. But probably more Americans, than Indians, knew that Sarabhai's dreams extended to making India a missile power.

A thin, not-so-hazy, line separates satellite launch vehicles from missiles, as both are essentially rockets. One has a satellite as the payload, the other has a warhead. One is designed to go into space and never come back, the other may go into space or to a lower altitude before landing back on earth, at a predetermined target. One develops, the other destroys.

I sensed Sarabhai's interest in missiles as early as my first interactions with him. If pursuing liquid propulsion system was my passion, persuading our people, including Sarabhai, to believe in it wasn't easy. There were times when I wondered why Sarabhai, such a visionary, glossed over my arguments for developing a liquid engine, while he encouraged solid propulsion projects. Sarabhai had bought the PVC propellant making technology from France and set up the Rocket Propellant Plant (RPP) in Trivandrum. M R Kurup, who headed RPP, became a natural 'ally' of Kalam who was working on the solid-propelled SLV, in the solid-liquid tug-of-war. I was alone.

I found reason in the argument that we cannot ignore solid, since the technology was available and rockets were indeed fired using the propellant, but what troubled me was the indifference to liquid propulsion systems, which were far superior though more difficult to develop. It took a while for me to realise that Sarabhai's support for the solid group had another core reason: solid propellants, he believed, were inevitable for developing missiles.

I heard this from the horse's mouth once when I was arguing my case in private with Sarabhai.

'But missiles are made with solid propellants,' he remarked.

I got the message. I spent longer hours in the library to find a convincing reason to push for my pet project. I went back to Sarabhai and impressed upon him that liquid not only did work for missiles, it was imperative if India was to develop intercontinental ballistic missiles that would go to space before returning to earth to strike targets anywhere on the globe.

The US wasn't ignorant of Sarabhai's network of friends. Even before trying for an ISRO-CENS France tie-up, Sarabhai had forged an ISRO-DFVLR programme with Germany. This brought German scientists like Dadieu and Muller often to ISRO facilities, and Indian scientists had several exchange programmes with the Germans. Sarabhai saw that Germany's space programme was on a downslide because of the post-war sanctions, and in it he saw a dying opportunity to collaborate with the Germans and learn from them the art and science of rocketry. Sarabhai may not have told many people why he held Dadieu too close, but I knew later that the engineer who worked on V-2 rocket that had stunned the Allies more for its audacity than accuracy could be an invaluable friend for anyone planning to make missiles.

For Sarabhai, such powerful people as Arnold Frutkin, deputy director of NASA's International Programs Office, was just a telephone call away, but the US was obviously not among those keen to see India make strides in space. Sarabhai realised this, and it might not have been incidental that Japan, another spacefarer that he reached out to was, like Germany, on 'the other side' in World War II.

Sarabhai struck a cordial relationship with Hideo Itokawa, the father of Japanese space programme. Working on Japan's Pencil rocket in the mid-1950s, Itokawa had earned the nickname Dr Rocket. Sarabhai also knew Itokawa's central role in designing the Nakajima Ki-43 Hayabus Oscar fighter during World War II. Sarabhai initiated a programme with Japan, with scientists exchanging ideas, albeit in a general way. The US had imposed sanctions on Japan, limiting its technology experiments to low thrust rockets after the war. As a restrictive inducement, the US supplied high thrust rockets to Japan, stopping it from developing its own. But Sarabhai knew the Japanese still possessed the know-how. With faith in the Japanese wisdom on onboard-control systems and the German mastery over fabrication both not allowed by the US to be put to use by those countries Sarabhai was trying to forge a deadly brotherhood.

The US was ostensibly unhappy with India cozying up to its enemies, but Sarabhai was too big for the Americans to show their displeasure in the open, especially when India maintained its posture of being an aspiring space power for peaceful purposes. Sarabhai was taking on the Americans in the American style—assertion through diplomatic deception.

It was never lost on the US though it was often glossed over in India that Sarabhai held the dual posts of the chief of the country's space programme and the atomic energy department. Add to that, his proximity to none less than the Prime Minister of the country, and it made Sarabhai a man not just with a purpose, but the means to achieve it. It could have been more than disconcerting for the US.

I have never been an insider of the country's atomic energy programme, but my proximity to Sarabhai allowed glimpses of his long-term plans as much as his immediate priorities. One such plan came to fruition on 18 May 1974, two-and-a-half years after Sarabhai's death, when Buddha smiled and India became the first nation outside the five permanent members of the United Nations Security Council to trigger a nuclear explosion. There may be nothing on record, definitely not in public domain, to show Sarabhai's involvement in India's show of nuclear might in the Rajasthan desert, but it will be foolish on anyone's part to think that a nation could explode a nuclear device in less than three years. Sarabhai, no doubt, was at the core of the Pokhran exploit.

Homi Bhabha handpicked Sarabhai to succeed him as the head of the space programme evidently because of his eagerness to make India a nuclear power too. Bhabha, in a way, was the World War's gift to India. Bhabha, then a nuclear physicist in Britain, was on a vacation in India in September 1939 when the war broke out, prompting him to stay on in India. Bhabha took up a teaching job at the Indian Institute of Science (IISc), Bangalore, then headed by C V Raman. How he persuaded then Prime Minister Jawaharlal Nehru to initiate India's nuclear programme and launch the Atomic Energy Commission barely a year into independence is history. The bomb was Bhabha's goal. In Sarabhai, Bhabha found a scorer.

When Air India flight Kanchenjunga 'accidentally flew' into Mont Blanc in the morning of 24 January 1966, as Wikipedia puts it, Bhabha, 56, was among the 106 passengers who died. Five years later, Sarabhai, 52, was found dead in a hotel room in Trivandrum.

CHAPTER 12

JOURNEY WITH MARIAM AND FAUZIYYA

'Wait, you will soon know.'

For the first time, all the accused in the ISRO spy case were together, in the police van to Ernakulam. Each of the accused was guarded by a constable; the Maldivian women had with them a woman constable each.

While the presence of the Maldivian women in the vehicle angered me, I wasn't any less irritated about the others including my colleague Sasikumaran. It appeared to me that Sasi had indeed met the women though there was no espionage possible, I knew. But it was all because of his acquaintance with the women that ISRO and I were in this soup. Above all, he had apparently confessed to the crime, dragging me too into the cesspool of a fabricated spy case.

I kept to myself throughout the journey though Sasi and Chandrasekhar tried to strike a conversation by apologising for their fake confession. They tried to smile at me once in a while as the journey progressed, but I refused to look at them.

About four hours into the journey, we reached Alleppey. On to an unused road parallel to the highway, the van pulled over, and we were given lunch—a few chapattis packed from the Pallipuram police camp, and a few bananas the policemen had bought from a shop. The van had all its windows shielded by shutters pulled down, but one of them had a gap. Through this some passersby were trying to peep in. The constables shouted at them, and asked us to finish the lunch quickly so that we could resume the journey.

We reached Ernakulam around 5 pm. The van meandered through narrow roads to the CBI office on the outskirts. By now somehow word had spread about the ISRO spies being taken to Ernakulam, and a crowd had gathered at the CBI office there. Alighting there, we were made to sit on the foyer. Policemen were struggling to stop the surge of onlookers keen on getting a glance of Nambi Narayanan, 'the traitor'.

About fifteen minutes later, we were taken to the court of Chief Judicial Magistrate Ganeswaran Nair. The magistrate asked the same question: Was I ill-treated by the CBI? I replied 'no'.

The magistrate made a note and looked at me with disdain. He remanded us in police custody for fifteen days. The rituals were not over yet; we were taken to a CBI special court in connection with another case that charged Sasikumaran with amassing wealth disproportionate to his known sources of his income. The rest of us, the charge read, had abetted him amass that wealth. CBI special judge Diwakaran remanded us in CBI custody for fifteen days. This second case, I understood later, was to ensure that the ISRO spy case accused remained in jail longer so that the CBI got enough time to question us and complete the investigation.

When we came out of the court, the crowd had swollen and the police had to use mild force to take us to the police van. Soon we were back at the CBI office foyer. We were given tea. I was in a daze, unsure where I would be taken next, when Sasi said to nobody in particular that one of the guards had told him that we would be taken to Delhi.

I asked CBI officer Dhankar what next.

'Wait,' he said. 'You will soon know.'

Around 8.30 pm, dinner was served—chapatti, again. I did not touch it. Around 10.30 pm, a CBI officer told me that the same night we would be taken to Madras as nowhere in Kerala we could be interrogated because the media and the public refused to go away. Soon we were in cars that drove straight to the railway platform, entering the station through a special gate.

At 11 pm, the Trivandrum-Madras Rajdhani Express pulled into the Ernakulam station. We were made to board a first class compartment in which other passengers were not allowed. Accompanying us were M L Sharma, P M Nair and a few others, including Thiagarajan, a superintendent of CBI who was also in charge of the bureau's Cochin office. A pleasant man in his early 50s, Thiagarajan spoke in Tamil. Deposing in the Rajiv Gandhi assassination case, years later, he would later admit that he omitted a detail from the statement of one of the accused, Perarivalan.

I could not sleep through the journey. I asked Dhankar why we were taken to Madras, and whether more investigation was needed. I was under the impression that I had proved my innocence to the CBI. Dhankar did not reply to any of my questions.

'Be calm, sleep well,' he said.

STRIKING THE FRENCH DEAL

'We have much more than fifty fine engineers.'

Uncertainty stared in the face of ISRO after Vikram Sarabhai's death. The government appointed the then electronics commission chairman M G K Menon to the post of ISRO chairman, as an ad hoc measure. Menon was a gentleman, but Sarabhai's shoes were too big for him. A few months later, however, ISRO got another visionary and a natural leader, Satish Dhawan at the helm. Dhawan was to take forward Sarabhai's agenda, and become one of the three great chairmen India's space programme had. The third was to be U R Rao, who succeeded Dhawan. ISRO, thereafter, never had a chairman of such calibre.

The French deal was the first major project Dhawan inherited from Sarabhai, and brought to fruition. As the person who initiated the talks with SEP, I remained ISRO's prime representative for the project. With SEP keen on only selling an engine, and I keen on a collaboration, there appeared to be no common path till SEP realised that the M-40 engine cannot be upgraded beyond a specific limit for LIIIS, the proposed geosynchronous satellite launch vehicle. This meant developing a new engine, and here came our opportunity to strike a deal.

But it wasn't easy as SEP wanted money, and ISRO didn't have much to offer. Kanwal Grover, who became an SEP agent, worked on the deal more for his love for India than anything else. Such was Grover's commitment to the national interest that he forwent his commission to make the deal work. When he saw a possible negotiation over joint development of the new engine, Grover asked me bluntly how much money India could spend on the deal.

'Not a paisa,' I said.

'Then how? The French want money.'

'We will do a barter.'

I didn't realise what I had just said. A barter? What do we have to give in return? We are still a bunch of scientists firing sounding rockets and struggling with a three-ton liquid rocket engine, which appeared to be a toy against the 60-tonner the French were about to develop. But that triggered a chain of thoughts in me, eventually leading to a contract so ingenious that we partnered to develop the Viking-Vikas engine along with the French with no money going out of India. What's more, India got a transducer-making facility, which is still churning out the tiny pressure sensors used in rockets, with machines and know-how from France.

Here is how we made it.

I told Grover that India will not be able to spend even a rupee in cash, but our manpower could be bartered for the technology. About fifty of our engineers would come and work in France along with SEP men to develop the engine. Grover laughed.

'As if you have so many engineers good enough for the job,' he said.

Again, without thinking I said, 'We have much more than fifty fine engineers.'

I was trying to convince myself than Grover, who soon agreed to take up the proposal with Souffle and Morin. The SEP heads found merit in the barter proposal, and here I made the offer irresistible for them and, at the same time, gave India the opportunity to learn a technology that was a closed secret among space-faring nations. I was told an average SEP engineer earned 25,000 Francs a month.

'Fifty Indian engineers will do the same work for 3,000 Francs a month,' I told Souffle and Morin. 'You save 22,000 Francs per person per month. That is 1.1 million Francs for fifty people. Which means you save 13.2 million Francs at the end of the year. If the project is to go on for five years, it converts to 66 million Francs at the end of the project.' That was some impressive mental arithmetic!

Before Souffle could reply, I dangled another carrot. France was making transducers for 14,000 Francs a piece. India will make it for half the price, provided the French transferred the technology and gave us machines and raw materials. Left unsaid was that the transducer deal, which I offered as a bonus, would add to ISRO's kitty an auxiliary asset.

But the contract threatened to fall apart just when it was to be signed. Souffle and Morin had been visiting India as much as I visited France to work on the contract. At one point, there was some serious disagreement over the transducer project. Besides some haggling over the transducer price, the French felt that India was getting the technology too cheap. The credit for ironing out these differences should go to Grover. When the French expressed their reservations over signing the contract, Grover came to me.

'Nambi, all your efforts have gone to the dogs,' he said.

When he explained the problem, I realised it was tough to renegotiate the deal; only some glib talk might salvage it.

'Now,' I challenged Grover. 'Show your salesmanship and get it done for India.'

Grover did just that. Souffle and Morin were in Bangalore, and Grover invited me for breakfast along with them at Windsor Manor. Grover had this compelling argument in favour of the contract. He told Souffle and Morin that it was much more than a joint-development of a rocket engine; that it was the beginning of a business deal and friendship the French would find rewarding in future.

'SEP would gain much more than what you think,' Grover told them. 'And, have you seen the business opportunity here? If the deal goes through, the European Space Agency (ESA) can sell geosynchronous satellite launch vehicles to India, and make a lot of money. India would otherwise go to the US for these rockets.'

It was a double-edged argument the French couldn't ignore. Grover displayed his selflessness in pushing for the contract by telling SEP that he would not take the commission the company was to give him. Morin agreed to consult the European Space Agency (ESA) and get back. I knew Morin had a soft corner for me. Our friendship had blossomed by the side of the negotiation that went on for three years. I had also impressed him by casually slipping in this bit of information that I was a student of Professor Crocco. Morin's wife, like Crocco, hailed from Italy, and he was a fan of the professor.

Four days after the breakfast, Grover called with the good news. SEP, with permission from the French Government and the European Space Agency, was ready to sign the agreement. India would draw up the contract, the French would suggest changes. The barter deal sounded simple, but we had to be careful while drafting the contract.

That part of the job was left to Seshan, the man of impeccable communication skills. The history of contract writing is punctuated by examples of treaties going kaput or getting misinterpreted to one party's unfair advantage because of a misplaced comma or an incorrect preposition. But perfection was Seshan's forte. He dictated the entire contract draft—about fifty pages—in one go, pausing only for breath and, rarely, for what appeared to be a momentary mental juggling for the right term in a crucial sentence. When stenographer Datta Guru gave him the typed text, Seshan ran a pen through the document, the tip of it touching the paper only a few times to inject a comma or to replace a word. The contract was sent to SEP for its approval, and on 24 August 1974 Seshan signed it on behalf of ISRO.

A couple of weeks before that, I was in a meeting with Dhawan when Seshan walked in with the news that the French had accepted the contract. It was expected, and we shook hands with each other. An excited Seshan, then had this to say: the French were also willing to give India a cryogenic rocket engine. Seshan, an IAS officer, was not a scientist, but he often understood—sometimes better than my scientist colleagues—the importance of being futuristic when it came to rocket science.

'They say they will give us the cryo engine for just Rs 1 crore,' Seshan told Dhawan.

I knew about this offer, for SEP had indicated this to me a few times. I kept out of it since I wanted Dhawan's focus on the liquid rocket engine deal. Seshan probably chose the wrong occasion to say this, for I thought Dhawan was either in one of those rare moments of foul mood, or he was too relieved that the French deal has come through, and was not in a great hurry to think of another round of negotiations till this one was done.

'Seshan, this is technology,' said Dhawan. 'You please focus on administration.'

Seshan, a man of considerable and justified ego, was too proud to even argue.

'Yes sir,' he said, and sat through the meeting in silence.

Dhawan was soon his jovial self, and had evidently forgotten the snub he had given Seshan. About half-an-hour into the meeting, discussing a concept, Dhawan turned to Seshan.

'What do you think of it, Seshan?' he asked.

'It's technology sir,' Seshan retorted. 'I will focus on administration.'

He delivered that sentence poker-faced, no emotion in his voice. Dhawan and I exchanged a quick glance and got on with the discussion. I believe Seshan must have felt satisfied, if not happy, that the meeting in which his suggestion was dismissed also presented him with an opportunity to get even with the chairman of ISRO.

History proved that Dhawan was making a big mistake by not taking forward the cryogenic deal of Rs 1 crore that Seshan had suggested. When India signed a cryogenic deal with the Russians in the early 1990s for Rs 235 crore, the French were again negotiating for a deal worth Rs 900 crore. The enormity of the historical blunder of turning down the French offer of 1974 dawned on me while chatting with a French official in the 1990s. When he spoke of the Rs 900 crore they were expecting, I casually asked him if he remembered an offer they had made fifteen years earlier to sell a cryogenic engine for Rs 1 crore.

'Yes, I know,' said the French official. 'And I also know that it would have been the most foolish deal we would have made.'

Another negotiator chipped in, 'Back then, we didn't know the value of a cryo engine. You realise the worth of anything only when there are takers. We had the engine and wanted to sell, but there were no takers.'

It became abundantly clear to everyone that India had let go of a golden opportunity, but Seshan never harped on the message he took to Dhawan, the snub he got and the revenge he relished. True to the spirit of the Indian civil services, Seshan never displayed insubordination, but never shied away from putting forth his opinion. His bosses may have had their way, but Seshan had his say. And, when he was vested with the powers, he showed how to wield it—and show results.

Seshan, who wore many hats, is today known to many Indians as the former Chief Election Commissioner of India. Holding this post from 1990 to 1996, Seshan showed what the real powers of the CEC were. How many of his successors learned how to put their foot down is history that the political class is yet to digest. Feeling helpless when Seshan tightened his grip on overspending candidates during general elections, one politician called him an Alsatian. Seshan enjoyed the sobriquet, and even popularised it. At public meetings, when he is introduced to the audience, he would say: 'For some I am T N Seshan, for a few others, I am AL-Seshan.'

Seshan remains a friend and well-wisher of mine. Years later, in 1997 when the Supreme Court was sitting in judgment of the ISRO spy case, Seshan was among the signatories of an open letter that asked to end the harassment meted out to me.

The open letter said: 'We are choosing this route to express our concern because of our inability to intervene meaningfully in the complicated chess board of moves and counter moves that seem to make inevitable the continued persecution and traumatisation of a valued colleague.'

In a gist, the letter said the ISRO espionage case had done immense damage to my morale, and revealed that India's space programme was no longer immune to outside interference; it could derail India's space programmes and adversely affect national interest.

The others who signed the statement were two former ISRO Chairman—Satish Dhawan and U R Rao, UGC Chairman Yash Pal, National Institute of Advanced Studies Director Roddam Narasimha and then IIM Professor S Chandrashekar, the father of Indian remote sensing. A year later, the Supreme Court acquitted all the accused in the ISRO spy case. The men who conspired to shatter my life and India's space dreams still await punishment.

If Seshan was so disciplined not to argue with his superiors like Dhawan, he was also a ruthless task master for his subordinates. And this he did with no agenda than conscientiousness, for he felt if someone was not doing his job, he doesn't deserve the job. For the accounts and administrative staff who faltered at work, Seshan was a terror. Once when I was in his office, Seshan summoned an accounts officer who had been sleeping on a file for long. The officer tentatively walked in and stood across Seshan's desk.

'Have you drawn your last month's salary, Hariharan?' Seshan said in a deceptively polite tone.

'Yes sir,' came the answer.

'Then go and deposit the money back in the ISRO account. You don't deserve that money.'

As the officer stood hanging his head, Seshan thundered: 'Go jump into the first agglomeration of water that you see.'

I had to look up the dictionary for 'agglomeration'. This man was as bombastic as he was original.

CHAPTER 13

IDENTIFICATION OF RAMAN SRIVASTAVA

'No, I don't know him.'

10 December 1994. Around 8.30 am, the Rajdhani Express rolled into Madras Central. It was a familiar station for me. I had been here several times, one of the memorable occasions being in 1967 when I was on my way to the Ammunition Factory in Kirkee, Maharashtra.

Stepping out of the train, it was a pleasant experience to be not mobbed by people and media. It must have been the same feeling for the CBI officers. We got into a Tempo Traveller that drove to Greenways Road, a leafy neighbourhood in Madras. When the vehicle turned into an old bungalow, I had little idea that this would be my home for another ten days.

The colonial-age building stood on a huge wooded campus. The ground was carpeted by dry leaves and fallen flowers from yellow pods. Adding to the coolness of the Tamil month of *Margazhi* was the shade thrown by the canopy of hundred-year-old trees. Not a bad place, considering that the Latex Guest House and Pallipuram camps were my shelters for the past ten days.

The comfort was short-lived. I made a few inquiries and was told that the bungalow was the famous 'Malligai', used by the Special Investigation Team that probed the Rajiv Gandhi assassination case to interrogate the accused three years earlier. Third degree measures used to extract information from the Rajiv case accused were popular. A shiver ran down my spine.

Each of us was given a room with an attached bathroom. There was a cot, a bed sheet and a pillow. Was there a blood stain on the bed sheet? I was not sure then, but soon I would see many such patches on curtains and linen on the furniture. Malligai had a history of being a torture house. Were these telltale marks of third–degree measures that accused in many cases were subjected to? Or were they just props to scare you so the interrogators could get the accused talking without having to try too hard? I was not sure.

Probably because it was a Saturday that we arrived, for two days there was not much of questioning. The next round of action was to begin on Monday.

12 December 1994. It was night by the time a constable asked me to go meet M L Sharma in a room upstairs. Seated opposite to Sharma was a man in a grey safari suit. He wore a black 'tilak' that devotees got from Ganapathi temples in Kerala. He looked perturbed.

Sharma offered me a seat.

'Do you know him?' he asked me.

'No.'

'Take a close look at him, you may be able to identify him.'

I looked at this man again.

'No, I don't know him,' I said.

Now Sharma turned to the man and asked him if he knew me.

'Yes,' said the man in the suit. 'He is Nambi Narayanan.'

I was surprised—and worried if this was another ploy to implicate me in the case by producing a false witness.

Sharma asked, 'For how long had you known him?'

'Oh, I've never met him,' said the man in the suit. 'I've seen his photograph in the newspapers in connection with the ISRO spy case.'

I was relieved.

Sharma introduced this man to me as Raman Srivastava, the inspector general of police, Kerala. We shook hands.

The CBI officer turned to me.

'But then, during the IB interrogation you gave a statement that you knew Raman Srivastava.'

'Never,' I said. 'I never said so. In fact, they beat me up for not saying that I knew Raman Srivastava.'

At this juncture, P M Nair and Ashok Kumar showed some files to Sharma to correct him that it was not Nambi Narayanan, but Sasikumaran who had given a statement that he knew Raman Srivastava.

A while later Sasi was brought in. Sharma repeated the same question to him. Sasi said he could not identify the man.

'Then why did you tell the IB that you know him?' Sharma said.

'I did not initially,' said Sasi, 'but when I was tortured and threatened there was no option but to give a statement the way they wanted.'

Then came Mariam Rasheeda, and the same question was repeated to her. I was surprised when Mariam named him as Raman Srivastava.

'How do you know him?' Sharma asked.

'Inspector Vijayan had shown me this sir's photographs.'

'One look at those photographs and you remembered Raman Srivastava?'

'I was given training by inspector Vijayan,' Mariyam was stuttering with fear. 'He showed me several photographs and told me to memorise his face and name. I have never met this gentleman.'

'What about this man?' Sharma told her, pointing at me.

'I have never met him till my arrest. I first saw him in the police van. But the inspector showed a few photographs of his, too, and trained me to remember the name Nambi Narayanan.'

Fauziyya's identification exercise too went off on the same lines. Chandrasekar and S K Sharma were brought to identify Srivastava, and both of them failed to do so. In fact, all the six accused told the interrogators that they have never seen this man in their life, earlier.

I felt sad for the senior IPS officer. A man respected in service and outside has been dragged into this cesspool. How? Why? I was to learn how bitter politics between two factions in the Congress in Kerala— one led by then Chief Minister K Karunakaran, and the other by A K Antony and his Man Friday Oommen Chandy—made this officer a scapegoat.

It was no secret that Srivastava was one of Karunakaran's favourite police officers.

GETTING READY FOR FRANCE

'I am sure you can handle this.'

According to the French deal, scientists and engineers of ISRO and SEP would jointly develop the rocket engine, and India would provide a little more than fifty people at any time for the hundred-man year project. SEP would assign our men for 75 man years and I would lead the rest of the team which would put in 25 man years. The project later got extended to 135 man years.

Getting the deal signed was quite an achievement for me, given the inherent opposition to the development of liquid propulsion systems, which the 'solid guys' thought was way outside our sphere of capabilities. It was gratifying that Sarabhai and Dhawan saw merit in my argument for developing liquid systems. Some said they agreed to try for the French deal just to get rid of 'Nambi the nag', thinking that the deal would never come through. Whatever the bosses' intention were, I had won a small battle here.

But the challenge had just begun. The first task was the selection of the team of more than fifty scientists and engineers who would go to Vernon. Given the aspirations, competition and a fair amount of internal politics made it a tough job.

Pessimism about the liquid engine project pervaded top down in the organisation, which was so used to focusing only on solid propulsion systems. But, at least at the lower and middle rungs, getting into the joint venture team was a big dream. A few were genuinely interested in the challenge to learn a new technology; fewer understood its future applications; many just wanted to go to France.

It was understandable, for so far only a few individuals and small groups had travelled abroad, that too on short assignments. Here was an opportunity to live and work for at least a year, may be more than three years in Vernon, just 75 km away from Paris.

Adding to the attraction, those selected for long duration— we would send back people and bring in new members to suit the requirement to meet the planned man hours—could bring their families along. The only ban was on pregnant or ailing wives, as the medical cover for the scientists and families was limited, even non-existent in a sense. This was to prove a big challenge for me in the immediate years to come.

As soon as applications for the Project Vikas team were invited, there was a rush. Some 1,500 people applied within a week. We needed, at a time, a little more than fifty people and, on the whole, some hundred people. Dhawan constituted a selection committee with him as the chairman, all group directors as members, besides me as the member secretary. It comprised V R Gowarikar (solid propellant director), A E Muthunayagam (propulsions director), S C Gupta (control, guidance and instrumentation), Amba Rao (structures), A P J Abdul Kalam (SLV-3 project director), Y Janardhana Rao (aerodynamics), M K Mukherjee (materials and quality care), Brahm Prakash (VSSC director), T N Seshan (administration director) and U R Rao (satellite division head).

The first task of the selection committee was to shortlist 500 from the 1,500-odd applicants, and then handpick fifty-five for the first team.

A caveat: since the team was to report to me through the long assignment abroad, I wanted scientists and engineers who were not just brilliant, but also those who shared with me the fire in the belly. And yes, they all had to do what I wanted them to—and that was nothing personal, since all I wanted was to master this technology, though you could accuse me of doing it my way. In short, I did not want men, even if qualified, with the wrong attitude. While I went about ensuring that the team was to my liking, I expected allegations of favouritism. As long as my conscience was clear, even with the little tricks I played to handpick one man over another because I thought he shared my passion and the goal, I cared a damn when I overheard whispers that 'Nambi is playing a game.'

A confession: I did play more than a game to ensure that virtually every team member was to my liking. But this in no way compromised on the skill sets of the candidates. I will put it this way: I never selected someone just because I liked him, but I helped a few of my favourites to beat their peers in the final round of selection. Here's how.

To ensure that no mediocre scientist or engineer got selected, we made the primary criterion that the candidate should have got a 'very good' rating for three consecutive years in their annual confidential report. This weeded out a large number of applicants. Having already dubbed it a 'Nambi show', the selection process did not get enough participation from some seniors like Gowarikar and Kalam.

While Gowarikar was less adept at masking his disinterest, Kalam played the 'trust' card.

'I am sure you can handle this, you go ahead with the decision,' Kalam once said when I sought his signature on one of the selection files.

I knew I would go ahead with the decision, but to preempt any hitch, I sat on Kalam's desk till I got his attestation. This I diligently followed at every juncture of the selection process. I could deal with nasty whispers, but I did not want any hole in the paperwork that would give my detractors a chance to derail the project. I got Gowarikar, too, to sign on the dotted line.

After the initial screening, I played my trump card: let's have group discussions of the shortlisted candidates. Those watching me closely with suspicion knew what I had in mind, but there was simply nothing in the process that anyone could protest. A group discussion brings out the best in the candidates in a transparent manner, giving no scope for allegations of foul play. At the same time, it gave me an opportunity to stump my detractors.

I did favour a couple of people who I was keen on having in the team since I was convinced of their skill sets and was a bit worried if they would underperform in the group discussion, and hence get rejected. I alerted these men a couple of days in advance to prepare for the discussion. You can argue this as an unfair practice—and it is, viewing it from the point of view of the other candidates—but here was a situation that made it imperative for me to get the candidate who would do as I directed. This was crucial for the mission, since anyone doubting the need for a liquid propulsion engine would be an impediment to the mission. And even while tipping off 'my men' to come prepared for discussions, I ensured the final selection was on merit. Their performance as part of the project later proved me right. My conscience remains clear.

I maintained this approach throughout the project, till 1980 when the last batch of our scientists returned and we eventually put together the Vikas engine (which till date is at the core of our Polar Satellite Launch Vehicles). Then I did not know I had adopted the philosophy of USA Today founder-editor Al Neuharth: be as nice as possible; only as nasty as necessary. It helped in dealing with some shortsighted Indian scientists; it triumphed over some shrewd French friends. That's another series of mind-and-matter episodes that would soon unfold in the beautiful countryside of Vernon, France.

When the final team was announced, complaints poured in that the team comprises only Nambi's men. I had expected this, and there was ample reason: no person from solid propulsion systems was selected for Operation Vernon. When a few rejected candidates complained this to Gowarikar, I asked a simple question, 'How could a solid propulsion man be in a liquid propulsion project?' That silenced the dissidents.

And then there were complaints that were absurd. One such was that I handpicked H S Panda because he was the son-in-law of Banamali Babu, a Congress MP from Orissa. Truth be told, I did not know about his background till the allegation surfaced. Panda was an IITian, and an excellent engineer. Those were reasons enough for me to have him in the team.

In four months, the team was ready. It had a few veterans of varied expertise, but many members were as young as in their twenties. The average age of the team was thirty. I, the team leader, was thirty-three.

We were ready to rub shoulders with French scientists and engineers, and now we realised a problem: the French spoke little or no English, and none of our men knew French. It was time for school. The VSSC conference hall in Trivandrum turned into a French tutorial for two months. But, at the end of it, our men still couldn't make out a croissant from a cake. The tutorial was a disaster. We decided to get French lessons in the best place—France. The French, too, realised the futility of working together without sharing a language. SEP was magnanimous to spend 25,000 Francs to educate our men. Berlitz School of Language did in twenty-one days what our *desi* French tutor could not for two months. At the end of the three-week course, our men could hold a civil conversation with our French brothers.

Talking of civility, it also took a session by Seshan and Brahm Prakash to sensitise the team on French manners. Many of our scientists were travelling out of the country for the first time. Seshan spoke about how to behave in a foreign land.

Next came the question of medical cover for the team. ISRO was not yet a government department—it was an autonomous institution reporting directly to the prime minister. It had its positives and negatives. While the autonomy and the direct access to the PMO helped the organisation surpass red tape to ensure speedy clearance of projects, the employees did not enjoy benefits including medical cover that government employees were entitled to.

Seshan, the administrative head, worked out a basic medical cover, but that was too insufficient to deal with any serious situation as healthcare was prohibitively expensive in France. To minimise damage, we advised the team members to get basic medical checks done in India before flying. Dental problems need to be fixed, they were told, and do not take pregnant wives to France.

The rest of the formalities were a breeze, with the government fast-tracking our visas and other documents. I was given the powers equivalent to that of the head of the department of the government. I was so confident of the team that I readily agreed to SEP's condition that if anyone is not up to their mark, they could send him back to India, albeit in consultation with me.

All set, the weight of the moment started pressing on my shoulders. Having worked through the labyrinth of the French negotiation and the back-and-forth trips to finalise the intricacies of the deal, I was brimming with confidence, but I realised that it was the first time I would be leading such a big team on an endeavour abroad. Dhawan was solidly behind me, and Seshan was always there to help with administrative matters, but I needed much more, some courage of the mind and soul. And who else to turn to than Vikram Sarabhai, who continued to live in me during times of soul searching.

I had learned a lot on man management and delegation from Sarabhai, and this included some lessons on how not to do certain things.

Sarabhai's disarming charm was enough to keep his flock together, with no murmur, but bereft of such a gift, lesser mortals like me could not afford to be as lenient with people as the great man was.

Sarabhai's style of letting anyone do anything had baffled me to a level of silent disagreement. There was no iota of doubt that Sarabhai was a man of great vision, but there were times when I felt he, having brought bright Indian scientists from the best of international universities, did not know what to do with them.

This was not lost on Jacques Blamont, a French astrophysicist whom Sarabhai brought as a consultant at the time of setting the Space Science and Technology Centre. Blamont, who was in awe of Sarabhai's energy and optimism, however, had a word of advice to him, 'You need to put your guys in their squares.'

Once I mustered enough courage to ask Sarabhai, 'Do we have a plan of action here?'

Sarabhai had smiled and said: 'The plan will emerge once we let people do what they want and realise what they are good at. I am not sure if it is the right thing to do, but I feel it's the right thing to do now. It's an experiment.'

Never again did I broach the topic.

If he allowed me to go to Princeton University to study liquid propulsion, and gave the nod for the French connection, it was partly because of his theory of letting people do what they want to do. So, in a way, I was a beneficiary of some of Sarabhai's ways of which I was critical about.

I remember a conversation with Sarabhai where he showed great interest in liquid propulsion; it was about the V2 engine developed by the Germans. His eyes lit up when he was told about how the Germans used the rocket engine to fire ammunition across the English Channel during World War II. He probably saw liquid also as a fuel for missiles, but for now, solid was ruling the roost, and Sarabhai did not want to disturb the course.

Given Sarabhai's deep sense of patriotism and interest in matters of the nation's defence, though he remained India's face of peaceful application of space science, a missile-powered India could have been well within his agenda.

While many Indians may still disagree with this, the US and some other developed nations realised this early, and they were not happy with it. Do I have proof for this? Not everything can be proved, like the cause of death of Sarabhai.

CHAPTER 14

MEETING KARTHIKEYAN

'Pray to God, he will come.'

17 December 1994. The last few days had passed uneventfully. There was virtually no interrogation; I presumed the CBI officers were documenting the identification parade of IG Raman Srivastava on 12 December, besides crosschecking the information the accused gave. This was the diligent practice of the investigating agency. Soon after getting a statement from the accused, an officer or a constable would visit the place or the person, or summon the person, to verify the accuracy of the information provided. In case of any inconsistency or discrepancy, the accused was questioned further. Clarity, it appeared, was at the core of a CBI investigation.

Now was the time for some more seniors of the agency to take stock of the investigation. On 17 December, such an officer came. He introduced himself as Arun Bhagat, an additional director of CBI. This man, in his fifties, was a symbol of maturity. His questions were sharp, his listening intense and his inferences considered. Bhagat appeared to have studied in detail every available paper in connection with the case, including the IB investigation report.

He was shocked to learn that the IB had adopted third-degree methods during my interrogation. He kept asking other colleagues for details and corroboration, apparently taking pains to understand what had gone wrong with this case, and where. After an hour of questioning,

Bhagat left saying 'the truth will be out soon'. Bhagat later became the IB director and presided over the ouster of one of its joint directors, Ratan Sehgal, who was caught having secret meetings with US intelligence officials in Delhi in 1996.

18 December 1994. The next to meet me was CBI Additional Director D R Karthikeyan. P M Nair took me to Karthikeyan who headed the special investigation team that was probing the Rajiv Gandhi assassination case. It was only three years since the former Indian Prime Minister was killed by a human bomb of the Liberation Tigers of Tamil Eelam (LTTE).

Karthikeyan was visibly worked up, probably because of some tangles in another assignment.

His first question was blunt: 'What is your relationship with the two Maldivian women?'

I replied I had never met the women till my arrest and the investigators brought me face to face with the co-accused.

Now he was asking questions which I had answered several other officers many times. I presumed that Karthikeyan, unlike Bhagat, had not gone through the case files, but his questions were equally sharp. Having dealt with hardcore militants of the LTTE, grilling me would have been a child's play for the officer. Firing a question, he would expect an immediate answer; he disliked silence. I tried my best to keep up with his pace, giving answers immediately. Whenever I had to think over something like a date, I told him I need to think. He questioned me for four hours.

Later I understood that both Bhagat and Karthikeyan were reviewing the draft of the CBI investigation report to ensure that the conclusions were watertight. At the beginning of the questioning, Karthikeyan had appeared to be an irritable man, but at the end of four hours he looked content, and said, 'truth will prevail'. It appeared to me that CBI officers were instructed to say this like gospel at the end of each interrogation.

While leaving Karthikeyan's room, I read a poster on his wall that said 'Pray to God, he will come. He will not come quick, but be assured He will come.'

VERNON, HERE WE COME

'Bring back lessons every day from work.'

Excitement was palpable as our first team of about fifty people were ready to leave for Vernon. A commune of hardly 10,000 people then, Vernon in the Upper Normandy region was known outside France only because of the rocket engine-making facility. About 75 km north-east of Paris, it had the quaint charm of an expansive village than a small town. River Seine flowed not-so-quietly; on its serene banks, children played, farmers grew mustard.

In early August, 1974, our engineers K Lakshminarayanan and M K G Nair made a pilot visit to Vernon to arrange accommodation for the team. Once they identified an apartment complex at the St Marcel community, about 10 km from the SEP campus, I went to sign the housing contract. The apartments were of varying sizes, from single-bedroom to four-bedroom facilities. This posed a practical difficulty as most of the scientists opted for smaller houses to save on rent and heating.

I charted out a plan: all the apartments will be in a pool from which each would be allotted on lot. Irrespective of the size of the apartment, the rent would be the same, which was the average. None protested. One of the four-bedroom apartments was converted into our office. As the team leader, I had the privilege of having a room. In another, I got some fifty chairs for the team to meet. I took along two draftsmen, Muthuswamy and T K Lakshmanan, and a personal assistant Unni Paramangalath, who also went through a screening. Adding a photocopier machine, ISRO's first foreign office had just started functioning. H R S Mani, who was in charge of quality control, helped with administration.

Since we were dealing with blueprints of rockets, buying a photocopier in our name would invite a lot of questions. I got it in the name of the Indian embassy. My personal assistant, I was clear, should be most trustworthy, since we would be dealing with sensitive stuff. According to the Government of India rules, any foreign assignment has to recruit exclusively through the ministry of external affairs. But I did not want an 'outsider'.

Seshan worked around this problem and ensured that I got the man I wanted, Unni, a trusted stenographer from Vikram Sarabhai Space Centre. Unni, proved to be much more than that. He meticulously documented our meetings, filed and tucked away drawings and documents, and ensured that our dispatches went back to India without being opened even by the Ministry of External Affairs (MEA) officials.

Our team members came in batches, most of them with their young wives. I brought along my wife, five-year-old son and three-year-old daughter. By September, the team of sixty was in place. We decided to meet at the office conference hall after the first day at SEP. The first meeting wasn't a happy one. Every one found out of place at SEP, and we realised that without learning French, our mission will be useless. Our men could not even exchange pleasantries with the French. After a crash course by Berlitz School of Language, however, our scientists were bubbling with confidence.

The first challenge to the joint venture came in early 1975, a few months after we had set up base in SEP, as the European Space Agency (ESA) was founded with the merger of the European Space Research Organisation (ESRO) and the European Launcher Development Organisation (ELDO). ESRO was formed in 1964 with ten European countries to do scientific research in space. It stemmed from the previously existing CERN, the European Organisation for Nuclear Research.

ELDO had come into existence after the British Blue Streak Missile Programme was called off, and as a joint venture to develop the Europa satellite launcher. When the satellite programme failed to show results, the two organisations merged to form the ESA.

Soon after taking over as the first director general of ESA, Roy Gibson, a British technocrat who was ESRO director till then, wanted an amendment to the ISRO-SEP contract on Viking. He wanted the part of a clause that said ISRO should use the technology 'for its own use' be changed to 'for its own peaceful use'.

ISRO had the contract with SEP, and was not answerable to ESA, but SEP, as an agency that eventually came under ESA, had to consider the amendment. T N Seshan, India's master craftsman of contracts, was called in to negotiate. I accompanied Seshan to meet the SEP heads. Seshan was firm that the word 'peaceful' cannot be added to the contract.

'You will have to insist that the contract with India will remain intact, with no changes,' Seshan told SEP honchos.

When the SEP men insisted, Seshan said he would consult 'the highest office in India' and get back. The next day he was back at the negotiation table. 'The Government of India does not want any change to the contract. If this contract is annulled for this reason, we may have to review scores of other contracts we have with France,' Seshan said.

Now the ball was in SEP's court. They had to convince ESA that they could not afford to lose the many lucrative pacts France had with India. I don't know if Seshan ever spoke to 'the highest office in India', but SEP allowed the contract to remain the way it is. We were back at work in the SEP labs.

There were, however, more surprises. For one, the engineers in the seventy-five man year group were not put in the Viking technology section. There was no arguing with the French, so I decided to turn this into an advantage by getting five of our scientists as part of another crucial project SEP was working on—the HM7 cryogenic engine. Getting a glimpse of cryogenic development was a godsend, but we had some lessons to learn.

The members who worked with the French on HM7 brought documents and sketches associated with their work, and Unni religiously photocopied and stashed them away. How wrong were we, thinking that these papers would help us make a cryogenic engine. These files still gather dust in a safe in ISRO, and we got nothing out of it. This was the point I would tell my interrogators twenty years later: know-how does not help you make rockets, you need know-why. And this comes only with working with the masters for long years. My point: the case that I handed over drawings of rockets to Maldivian spies is a figment of imagination, a useless lie. If rockets could be made with drawings, India would have by now sent men to Mars.

Our routine at Vernon was something like this: a bus would take us to the SEP campus every morning at seven. On Mondays we worked till 5.30 pm, on Tuesdays and Thursdays till 5 pm, and on Wednesdays and

Fridays till 4.30 pm. Sunday was a holiday. Every day after work, it was imperative for everyone to gather at the office apartment.

'Bring back lessons every day from work,' I told the team.

And they brought to the table every evening, their experiences and, specifically, details of the Viking subsystems they came across.

This is when it dawned on us that several subsystems of the Viking project were out of bounds for us, since the contract did not include them. This exposed our rudimentary knowledge in attempting to put together a rocket engine as much as the French's shrewdness in keeping intricacies out of the contract. For instance, we made sure that the contract gave us access to development of turbines, pumps and gas generators. Design and development of the combustion chamber, engine and nozzle were also part of it. Little did we know how to store gas. We had no idea, and according to the contract, we will have no access to closed-loop control system, the network of valves, thrust frame, pre-pressurisation and fill-and-drain system for gas and fuel. Without these, our rocket would be slightly better than a Diwali firecracker.

Desperation drove me to virtually everyone who mattered at SEP. With some I reasoned that the joint venture would be futile, at least for the Indian side, unless our scientists were included in the design and development of all the subsystems. With some who knew this, but still stuck to the written word of the contract, I pleaded. When there was still reluctance from some quarters, I used threat dipped in sadness, 'If the contract has to be implemented in the present form, we would have no choice but to go back without even attempting anything.'

The combination of tactics worked. The French wouldn't rewrite the contract, but unofficially allowed us to be part of everything that went into the Viking project. Some people like Morin were considerate, and hence allowed this; but for a majority of the SEP heads, the 'compromise' stemmed from their belief, which sooner than later turned out to be false, that the Indian scientists and engineers cannot build a rocket even if they are allowed to work here for five years. In other words, we were taken for granted as a bunch of inefficient men masquerading as scientists to have a long, paid vacation in France. We were just too eager to prove the French wrong, and we did it in a few months, after which the Indian scientists were acknowledged as some of the best SEP had seen and worked with.

This we achieved through hard and systematic toil. To begin with, I drew up a ten-phase programme, which would take us from scratch to rocket engine.

The ten phases were roughly as follows:

Phase 1: Identification of subsystems and sub-subsystems, breaking them down to the last, nut, bolt, pin and clip

Phase 2: Specifications, with tolerance levels of each subsystem

Phase 3: Detailed drawings

Phase 4: Materials, nomenclature and specifications

Phase 5. Fabrication technology

Phase 6: Non-conformances and acceptance criteria

Phase 7: Detailed design report

Phase 8: Fabrication and assembly

Phase 9: Cold tests and hot runs

Phase 10: Integration of the rocket engine into the stage

I insisted on deploying Indian scientists in such a way that they would mix with their French counterparts and not remain segregated. Some were not very happy with us not sitting together. I explained to them that integrating ourselves with the French would help us learn the language quicker. What I would tell them only a little later was that this would enable us to learn not just French, but the French way of making rocket engines.

Once we broke down the project, I put one man in charge of each subsystem. This took us three months. Every evening at six we assembled to discuss what was learned that day. Once a week, we also met to listen to team leaders talk about what they tried but could not learn, and why. I was clear in my mind that we should not only be able to make the rocket engine ourselves, we should also be able to upgrade it to launch heavier satellites into the geosynchronous transfer orbit. The Viking engine we were working on (Viking-4) had a thrust of sixty tonnes, and I was dreaming of a 100-plus tonne engine to launch heavy satellites. For many, this was a joke, as India had nothing in hand. We were just tottering around the idea of developing a liquid engine with the French, and here I was dreaming things that made several friends burst into laughter.

Some who pulled my leg did it often to defuse my tension than bring me down. Some others back in India, who either did not yet realise the potential of liquid propulsion or just refused to think beyond solid, tried more silent games. But, having come to Vernon and set up the team on the most ambitious of projects, I could not care less for my detractors. As for those who made my plans the butt of many banter, I laughed along.

Truth be told, ISRO still did not have approval for a liquid engine rocket. Then why was I sent to France with a team to work on liquid propulsion? Dhawan himself laughingly answered this in a meeting, taking some by surprise. 'Nambi was chewing my ears and eating my brain, talking about this liquid thing. I thought I can be at peace by sending him away for a few years.' I joined the others in the laughter, but I knew that Dhawan had realised the potential of liquid propulsion, though ISRO had not put in place a system to pursue the technology.

And this meant that even if my team went back to India with the know-how and the 'know-why', we wouldn't be allowed to put together a rocket. And that is what happened once we returned after mastering the engine in 1979. I was not allowed to fabricate the engine.

But I did not need permission to make a model of the engine, which I had named Vikas. With the enthusiasm of a nursery kid using matchboxes to make a train that he can never have in real, I put together a model, of the same size as the original, with all the moving parts. Only the materials were different and, of course, the engine did not work. But it looked as good as the real one. This was not just an act in self-gratification. I had a plan.

I set up the model by the foyer of Vikram Sarabhai Space Centre, a place nobody visiting the centre, including the chairman, could avoid. I got a platform built around the upper part of the engine, and a stair case leading up to it, so that one can touch, feel and see the parts of the gas generator, the turbo pump and the feed lines. At the foot of engine sat a board that read: 'I am Vikas engine. I have a thrust of sixty tonnes and my specific impulse is 295 seconds. By the way, I am an orphan.'

I was in great pain when I wrote the word 'orphan'. Not just because I was displaying the result of my toil as a fatherless child, but to call Vikas an orphan was like turning a dagger inside me. And here is letting you into one of my best kept secrets—something which even some ISRO chairmen would find new. While the French had already named their engine Viking, I decided, at the time of drafting the contract itself, to give it an Indian name.

Vikas means development in Sanskrit, and this was easy to sell within ISRO as a nomenclature, but I had seen another adapted anagram in the name. For me, Vikas stood for Vikram A Sarabhai. I shared this only with Seshan, who readily agreed, but he advised me to keep it to myself. Not because anyone would challenge the genius of Sarabhai—just that I did not want to go through the bureaucratic process of approvals ISRO was infamous for, especially when it came to naming projects and centres after a person.

So, as Vikas stood at the foyer, VSSC employees stopped to take a close look, then read the board. Some frowned, some smirked. All I cared for was Dhawan's reaction. And that came soon. On his way to the conference room, Dhawan paused at Vikas, admired the model and then read the board before walking away. I was disappointed. But not for long. At lunch break, Dhawan took me aside. I knew what was coming.

'So, why is Vikas an orphan?' he asked.

'Because it is one,' I replied. "Because even after developing the engine, we don't have a project to fabricate and test Vikas."

Dhawan did not pause to say: 'How much money would you need to make a real, working engine?'

'Rs 60 lakh.'

'I'll get you Rs 1 crore,' Dhawan continued. 'Go make the engine.'

I was not too excited yet, for this ad hoc measure meant little more than delaying Vikas's funeral.

'But what will you do it with the engine if there is no project to fire and fly it?'

'You just make the engine.' Dhawan was curt.

I started the process of procuring material, and this proved to be tough since virtually every piece had to be imported. I had foreseen this day when we were in Vernon, and had been sending our scientists to visit the facilities of component makers for SEP. This was as much for their education as for establishing a rapport with the component manufacturers who would be of use to us later. The UK-based *Avica* made metallic bellows, which are joints with great strength and flexibility; *Le Joint Francais* made 'O' rings, which went into virtually every joint; *Casa* in Spain was the supplier of tibia, a valve feed-line joint. We had made enough acquaintances in these companies, but when we finally needed the components, they cited a practical problem: it would not be viable for them to supply in small numbers.

After much pleading and pulling strings, we managed to get most of the components, but a particular variant of aluminium was hard to get. We needed 20 kg of it, but the supplier would not give anything less than a tonne. There was only one man to go to. Rene Morin not only arranged for the aluminium, he did not even charge for it. When I asked for the bill, the good old friend said, 'No bill, only goodwill.'

But when the consignment landed in India without a bill, our Customs department was not amused.

'Why are the French sending gifts to ISRO?' a Customs officer asked.

I lost patience. There was no point in educating the officer on the Indo-French friendship.

'Release the consignment or face consequences.' I blew my fuse.

No department had the courage to hold back for long the property of ISRO, which was by now under the department of space that reported directly to the Prime Minister. Customs obliged.

By the end of 1982, we completed fabrication of one-and-a-half Vikas engines. That is, one fully functional engine, and another with little more than the turbo pump, but without combustion chamber and nozzle. To get the engine tested and integrated to a stage which would later be the core of India's most successful rocket PSLV was another long struggle. And that's another tale.

CHAPTER 15

FOUR LIES AND A TRUTH: TESTING THE LIE DETECTOR

'Can I test the machine?'

19 December 1994. This was an exciting day, I was to take the lie detector test. I had heard about this contraption that forensic experts wire to accused and ask questions. Despite being a scientist, I had no idea how it worked—till Dr Lahari, who came to test, explained it to me.

The doctor from the Central Forensic Laboratory was in his sixties. His wrinkles spoke of his experience, mostly results of frowns, I thought. He explained that it is not mandatory to take a lie detector test in India; it can be done only with the concurrence of the suspect. In the US, it was admissible evidence in a court of law; in India it was not a primary evidence.

He gave me a thorough briefing of the working of the polygraph machine. Electrodes would be connected to my index finger and to the fourth finger of both my hands, besides instruments keeping a tab on my blood pressure, pulse and other vitals.

If I tell a lie, there will be a minor change in my biochemical signals, which result in microscopic sweating of my fingers. Moisture will change the capacitance between the electrode and my finger, which will be captured by a computer and shown on a screen. This would be corroborated with variations in readings of other vital parameters. Dr Lahari said he had 'absolute faith' in the machine that has never betrayed him.

'Can I test the machine?' I asked Dr Lahari.

He was taken aback.

'Test the machine, eh?'

Soon he regained his posture. 'Why not, tell me how do you want to test this machine?'

'You said the machine would catch a lie, but it wouldn't catch a truth, right?

'Right.'

'OK, I am going to write five names on different pieces of paper. I will tell you the five names and keep one of the pieces with me.'

Lahari was amused now; I continued. 'You have to call the names, one by one, and ask me if the piece of paper in my hand has the name. For all the five names I would say 'no', which means I have said four truths and a lie. I hope your machine will catch that one lie, and only that one lie.'

I was fighting tears as I wrote the names Meena (my wife), Sankar (son), Geetha (daughter), Ayyappa (the lord) and Nambi. But as Dr Lahari started the trial, I was enjoying it.

'Mr Nambi Narayanan, does the name on the paper in your hand read Meena?'

'No.'

'Is it Sankar?'

'No.'

A pause.

'Geetha?'

'No.'

A longer pause.

'Ayyappa?'

'No.'

'Nambi?'

'No.'

Dr Lahari showed no change in his expression through the exercise. Now he told me which one of my 'no' was a lie. To remove any doubt in my mind about it not being a guessing game, he showed me how the amplitude of the line graph on the screen had jumped when I said 'no' when asked if the name on the paper I held was 'Geetha'. I looked once again at the paper on which my daughter's name was written.

I asked for a repeat trial, still holding the same name in my hand. Dr Lahari asked the same set of questions in a different order. This time, too, the graph corresponding to 'Geetha' showed marked variation. I agreed to take the test.

The questions were a mix of different things in no particular order. It was clear that the intention was not to test one's values, but to detect the lie from a bunch of truths.

Samples:

Is your name Nambi Narayanan?

Do you work with the ISRO?

Have you met Mariam Rasheeda?

Have you received money from Fauziyya Hassan?

Do you know Raman Srivastava?

Have you ever stolen anything from your house when you were a child?

Have you done any crime?

Have you stolen anything from your office?

Do you think Sasikumaran would have done some espionage?

Have you met Zuheira?

Have you received any cash from a Pakistani?

The questions went on, some sets repeating in different combinations. At the end of it, Dr Lahari sat glued to the monitor. His eyes were moist. There was not a single lie.

Dr Lahari got my signature on all the graphs and reports. I went back to my room.

A LIFE LOST, TWO SAVED

'Can you help us save a baby?'

Our arrival in France transferred the sleepy St Marcel community into a bubbling mini-India. Vendors came with bread, milk and meat, and became friendly with the Indian community. Our scientists' wives, especially the Malayalees, boasted that they would learn French faster than the men, since they got to interact with hawkers who spoke no other language. We wished them all the best. And, at the end of a few months, our women could barely pronounce 'bonjour'. On their part, the hawkers went back speaking Malayalam.

Having come to know about the large number of Indians who had moved into St Marcel, a French social security volunteer named Mary came to meet me. Mademoisille Mary was to soon endear herself to our community by becoming a champion of our causes—monetary, medical and social. She was a godsend in many ways, as the Government of India had not only failed to offer social security measures to the scientists on assignment, it even denied the team a basic medical cover. One of the first things I did was to create a medical corpus fund with every scientist pooling in an equal amount, but this was grossly insufficient if any one of us had a serious ailment. And, as fate would have it, there were three medical emergencies within the first two years.

The first such crisis was because of a scientist breaking the Vernon recruitment rule that nobody should bring pregnant wives along. The scientist, who was married only for a few months before he was selected for the Vernon team, did not disclose the fact that his wife was in the early stages of pregnancy. In April 1975, she delivered a girl with a congenital problem of one of the lungs.

The newborn was put on ventilator, and the daily bill came to 800 Francs. There was uncertainty on how long she could be kept on the ventilator. Doctors said her condition was deteriorating, and the normal practice in such cases is to keep the baby in the ventilator for not more than three days. The baby's parents were probably not informed now about the gravity of the situation.

'What does that mean?' I asked a doctor.

'Well, that means the end of the treatment.'

'That's murder,' I said.

'Medical protocol, sir,' the doctor said.

I pleaded that the baby to be kept on the ventilator for some more days.

'How many more days?'

'Five more days,' I said.

There was no basis to my saying five more days. The number just came to my mind as one that the doctors may agree to. And they did.

The infant's condition rapidly deteriorated after three days on the ventilator. And, on the second day of my borrowed time, her second lung, too, was affected. How many more days can we keep her on the machine? Where do we go for the mounting hospital bill? There was only one person to go to. I called Mademoissile Mary.

'Can you help us save a baby?

Mary readily agreed. But, again, the question of how many days cropped up. I repeated, 'five more'.

Mary asked me what after that. I said I don't know. Just that I didn't want to be a party to the decision to pull the plug. My wife kept telling me that I should never allow that. 'Maybe break the rules, confront people, beg or borrow,' she said. That's exactly what I have been doing.

Mary kept footing the bill and, on the second day, the baby's health started improving. They soon healed. In a couple of days, she was off the ventilator. Today, she is a successful professional in Bangalore. Thirty-seven years later, in 2012, at an apparel showroom in Thiruvananthapuram (earlier Trivandrum), a mother and daughter walked up to me.

'Do you remember me?' asked the older woman.

'Sorry, I can't recollect.'

'What about my daughter? Do you remember her?'

'No,' I said.

The woman identified herself as the wife of a scientist who worked in my team in Vernon. "And this is my daughter born in Paris.'

I was not sure if she knew that her daughter had come back from the jaws of death soon after her birth.

The next year, our collegue Panda was diagnosed with a tumour outside his food pipe, pressing against the heart. If left untreated, he wouldn't live too long, said doctors at Hospital Beaujon, an institution that Christiaan Barnard, the first surgeon to transplant a human heart, was associated with. Panda could not swallow anything, and the tumour was found to be life-threatening. A long journey could endanger his life, the doctors had said, and an immediate surgery, more complicated than an open-heart procedure, had to be done. The cost: 800,000 Francs (Rs 16 lakhs then).

I asked the Government of India for money, and my point of contact was a joint secretary, department of space. The bureaucrat said the scientist was not entitled to treatment abroad, and that none of the government rules provided for any allowance.

'Pack him to India,' he said.

'You mean pack his dead body?' I yelled back.

When he continued to be intransigent, I manipulated the French hospital to issue a formal letter saying the patient cannot be moved without the risk of fatality. The IAS officer was a veteran of such situations. Much later, on another occasion, he had the temerity to remind me that we had taken a loan (to furnish the St Marcel apartments) without the government's permission. I gave the official a taste of his own medicine. When we took the loan, ISRO was an autonomous body. It came under the newly-formed department of space only less than a year earlier. The department, hence, had no power to reclaim a loan disbursed by the government before it came into being.

Now, Panda's life was at stake.

I remembered now that his father-in-law was Banamali Babu, a powerful Congress MP from Orissa. During the team selection for Vernon, it was this bit of information that some people in ISRO had lapped up to campaign that I had included Panda in my team because of his political connections. Conspiracy theorists always find admissible evidences to build their case, but time eventually demolishes it.

Panda's wife said she would talk to her father Banamali Babu and pull strings in the Government of India to fund his surgery. Panda, an idealist, would have none of it. I do not know if there was any other reason for his refusal to take help from his father-in-law, but Panda put pride and principle before his life. And that should tell the conspiracy theorists something about the IITian getting into ISRO's Vernon team using his father-in-law's Congress connections.

When we all gave up hope of keeping Panda alive, Mademoisille Mary came like an angel. She said she would arrange the money through social security donations and from well-wishers. Many people in the team felt bad that we are forced to take money from a foreign land to save one of our scientist's life; I shared their sentiments, but told everyone that we have no time to waste debating over dignity.

Having said that, I was not yet ready to give up. As a last resort, I wrote a letter again to the joint secretary, this time marking a copy each to the Prime Minister's Office, the Ministry of External Affairs, and the ISRO chairman. We are going ahead with Panda's surgery, I said. I feel sad that we are taking money from our hosts, and this clearly shows how much India cared for its citizens, leave alone its scientists. But I have no choice, I said.

Till now I do not know what happened, there was an immediate response from the department of space, saying that the Government of India would fully fund Panda's treatment. Doctors again warned that the surgery was complicated. The best they could promise was a 50% chance of Panda coming out of the operation theatre alive. Panda came out alive after a successful surgery. On his return to India, he continued with ISRO for a while before moving to the Balasore missile launching facility. He went on to contribute a great deal to India's space programme. He had another child. His wife became close to my wife, and they almost became part of the family.

Thinking of bureaucrats like this joint secretary, I wonder how Indian Civil Service produced two distinctly different sets of people— one blinded by the rule book, and the other who devised ways around rules to see the larger good and national interest, without breaking rules. Seshan belonged to this latter category, so did M A Vellodi, who was additional secretary in the department of space.

Vellodi was to the point and did not like unnecessary formalities. Once he accompanied Dhawan to the US, and on their return stopped over at France to visit us. It was our monthly custom to have a pot lunch, where every scientist's family would bring a dish and we would meet at one of the houses. That day it was Mohana Prasad's turn to host lunch. Mohana Prasad kept asking Vellodi if he can serve him a second helping of rice. Vellodi said 'no'. When, after a few minutes, Mohana Prasad asked him the same question, Vellodi snapped: I told you no. If I want something, I will help myself.'

Vellodi was also a stickler for time. At any meeting, he would be there a minute in advance. But what surprised me more was that he would also fold his files and leave the meeting at the scheduled time even if the meeting was going on. This was more so during lunch time.

He kept his composure at all times—even after a bad car crash that left Vellodi and A E Muthunayagam, my immediate boss and head of Auxiliary Propulsion Systems Unit, injured in 1972. After a visit to Sriharikota, I had returned to the guest house in Madras by evening. When Vellodi and Muthunayagam, who were also at Sriharikota, did not return to Chennai till late night, I made some calls. I was told their car had met with an accident on the highway, and the two were admitted to the Government General Hospital, Chennai.

I rushed to the hospital. Muthunayagam was to soon fly to the US to present a paper in Louisiana. Muthunayagam, in a state of sedation, was speaking incoherent things; doctors said it was trauma-induced. Vellodi appeared composed.

It wasn't medical miracles all the way in France. Scientist S C Ghosh's wife delivered a stillborn, a few more fell ill, but we managed the situations with the corpus fund. Finally the government provided the medical cover, which still wouldn't have been adequate to cover the expenses in a case like that of Panda.

I lobbied harder for a medical cover for the team and, by the second year, we got one. The clearance, however, was cumbersome in parts and arbitrary on the whole. A medical practitioner was appointed in the community to certify prescriptions and treatments. For routine purchases of medicines, however, this was helpful, though not all medicines were reimbursed.

On one of my visits to the Indian Embassy in Paris, I saw Sondhi, an administrative officer. He was sitting with a list of medical claims, with two pens in hand. The officer ticked some names on the prescription red and some others green. Green meant approved, red rejected. I asked Sondhi if there was a criterion followed for denying some claims.

'Yes,' replied Sondhi matter-of-factly. 'The government has clearly listed out medicines and services which can be reimbursed.'

He did not have a medical background, and hence I was impressed by the pace at which he marked the prescriptions with red and green. I was wrong. Soon I found that Sondhi had rejected and approved the same medication on different occasions. I confronted him.

'Why do you make an issue out of this, Mr Nambi,' he said. 'This is something all offices do. When the auditor goes through the claims he would look for a few rejections. He will be happy with the meticulous work I had done.'

There was no point arguing with this man. I left.

While the two major medical needs tested my patience with the bureaucracy, what turned out to be a litmus test for my nerves was guarding the secret of the death of a scientist's son. S Balakrishnan, a brilliant mechanical engineer was among the short-term recruits we brought from ISRO to work in SEP to generally give them a little exposure. At any point there would be not more than three such scientists, and they would return to India after three months at Vernon. We had an apartment for them, or some of them shared the place with bachelor colleagues.

Balakrishnan was to work in the programme coordination group headed by A Sampath. It was March 1975. Within a week of his arrival, I got a call from his father D P Subbaiah. Balakrishnan's one-and-a-half-year-old son was dead. The boy had fever and, before the doctors could diagnose, he died. Do we tell Balakrishnan? By the time he reaches home, the funeral would be over. And he would not be allowed to come back to Vernon. Subbaiah was sobbing uncontrollably over the phone.

I told him to just listen as I talked. At the end of it, he should take a decision. I presented the pros and cons of Balakrishnan returning to India, mostly cons. I felt his return would deny him a good exposure that would help the young scientist a great deal. Back in India, he would join the rest of the family in mourning, and can do little else. I told Subbaiah that I may sound even heartless, but I am just being clinical, dispassionate, though the news was extremely saddening to me. Having said this, I wouldn't insist on Balakrishnan staying back. His short stay at SEP was not crucial for the project, I could spare him, but he had much to gain.

I told Subbaiah, 'My advice would be to not break the news to him till he completes the assignment. At the end of it, we will tell him. He would be extremely shocked, even furious at me, but I can handle that. Now, it's your decision.'

Subbaiah agreed. 'You are the best judge of my son,' he said. I hung up.

I didn't speak about it even to my wife. It was tough keeping such a sad secret. Balakrishnan would accompany me sometimes for shopping in Paris, and pick up toys for his son. I would discourage him from buying them, saying you get better things in India. I lied through my teeth. I sobbed within.

Balakrishnan did very well at SEP and it was time for his return. I helped him deposit his bags in the car. M Parasu Pillai, another scientist was travelling with Balakrishnan back to India. Once Balakrishnan had got into the car, I took Pillai aside. A Sampath, who was heading the programme coordination group, was with me.

'Pillai, I am giving you the toughest assignment ever.'

Pillai and Sampath looked curious with this introduction.

I said, 'Minutes before the aircraft touches down in Trivandrum, you have to tell Balakrishnan that his only son is no more. That the boy died a few days after Balakrishnan reached here. That his father spoke to me and I suggested that we keep it a secret till you complete your assignment. That your father agreed to it.'

Pillai put his hand to his forehead, and walked into the car. I waved them goodbye. Turning around, I saw Sampath frozen. I shook him.

'What happened?' I said.

Sampath puffed his cheeks, he wasn't blinking.

'Sir, now I am really scared of you. Now on I can't see you the way I had so far.'

I didn't analyse the meaning of what Sampath said, and just replied, 'Now, let's get back to work.'

Later I learnt that Balakrishnan was, as I expected, furious at what I had done. His father explained for many days the conversation he had with me. Two weeks later, I got a letter from Balakrishnan. It was a detailed letter, written by a man who had gone through untold sorrow, helplessness and fury to emerge strong-willed and mature. It said that he felt I did the wrong thing by not telling him because his immediate return could have been some solace to his wife. He also felt that I was right, since the three months in Vernon added immensely to his understanding of space programmes and that he felt more confident of contributing for India.

On my return to India, Balakrishnan actively participated in the development of the Vikas engine, without once talking about the episode. Even today, I am unsure if what I did was right. I have no right to sit in judgment of this decision, which I forced on Subbaiah. After reading the letter twice, I plunged back into work at SEP.

Life or death made no difference to the bean counters in the government departments. As such the division of our scientists into two groups—one called the '75 man years group' (75MYG) headed by SEP officials, and the other the '25 man years group' (25MYG) reporting to me—was causing me problems. The 75MYG scientists enjoyed privileges of SEP, including vacations.

'Soon expect a rebellion if you don't remove these discriminations,' my wife warned.

SEP would transfer a lump sum towards an account I operated, towards salaries of the 75MYG scientists. The Government of India paid for the 25MYG men. Initially, all were paid the same salary of 2,500 Francs, but in the second year, SEP effected a pay hike that ironically added to my problems. Now there was a 5-Franc difference between the salaries of the two groups, and this was a disparity that could create some bad blood. I decided to hold back the difference amount till the Government of India too matched the salary. This was only a matter of a few months, but it had the potential to trigger the rebellion my wife had forewarned.

Now, the specially-created salary account of the team had some restrictions. I can draw money from the bank to disburse the salaries, but I cannot deposit. The only two accounts from which the bank accepted deposits were those of the Government of India and SEP. So I withdrew the difference amount of 5 Francs every month that added up to 2000 Francs after a while. I kept the money in the office apartment, with Unni as the custodian.

Then came a nuisance in the form of an auditor from the London office of the ministry of external affairs. The auditor called up to say he would be in Vernon the week next. I said he was welcome. Later, I realised that he had expected me to pick him up from the Vernon railway station and bring him to our office. I had some important work to do at the office, and didn't care for bureaucratic subservience, which anyway an auditor didn't deserve from a team head of ISRO.

When the auditor landed at our doorstep, I gave him a quick introduction of the team and left him with Unni, our office assistant who was up-to-date with the accounts. 'You may talk to me after Unni explains everything,' I told him and took his leave. Unni later told me that he was bitter throughout the stock-taking. First, he questioned Unni about the purchase of the photocopier machine. Why in the name of the Indian Embassy, and as a purchase of the department of space. Unni noted down such 'big' questions, which he promised that I would later answer. The auditor was apparently finding nothing he could question, when he chanced upon the 2,000 Francs kept in the office safe. He went bonkers.

'What's this?' he asked Unni.

Unni explained, but the auditor insisted it was outside the rule book. Unni asked him what he should do with the money now.

'Deposit it back into the bank,' the auditor barked.

Unni explained the rule that didn't allow us to deposit money, only withdraw.

'Then send it to India,' the auditor said.

Unni said it was not possible unless there is a written instruction to do so.

By now the auditor was fuming: I had denied him the pleasure of being chauffeured from the railway station, and left him with an office assistant who had the temerity to speak back to the officer from the Indian Embassy. The auditor left in a huff.

I don't know what report he submitted to the government, but I did report to Seshan the overbearing attitude of the auditor. Seshan asked me why I made an issue with the auditor. I replied that it was him, not me who made an issue. Later, Seshan told me that I did the right thing. 'You don't know much about bureaucracy, but your way of dealing with him worked. Or else these guys would road-roll you,' he said.

CHAPTER 16

RETURNING TO KERALA

'Can you get me a drink?'

On 20 December 1994, the return journey from Chennai to Ernakulam began. I was relieved, thinking that the ordeal is over and we would be released on reaching Kerala.

Inspectors Narpath Singh and Dhariyal took us to the train. P M Nair and R S Dhankar were in a coupe. The CBI team soon got information that the news of our return has been leaked and the media was thronging the Ernakulam railway station. The team decided to take us to Alwaye, and from there to Ernakulam by road.

The next morning we got down at Alwaye. Though it was an unscheduled break, a large crowd had gathered to see the spies. Mariyam Rasheeda and I were the prime attention.

As I was escorted out of the station, a young man shouted, 'Nambinarayana …'

I turned around and stood there, staring at the crowd. Some shouted *charan* (spy) and *rajyadrohi* (traitor). I stood composed. Once the shouts subsided I looked at the young man who had shouted my name and said aloud, 'Aniya (brother), you will soon know I am not a spy, just a victim of a conspiracy.'

Before he could react, the policemen took me inside a van.

We reached the Chief Judicial Magistrate court by noon and were soon remanded in judicial custody for fifteen days. The next stop was the CBI court, which too remanded us in judicial custody for fifteen days.

The van took us to the Ernakulam sub jail in Kacheripady. It was the first time I was getting into a jail.

The sub jail was a small facility, with five or six cells on two sides of a corridor. The jailor, a man called Joseph, was perturbed that such 'high-value accused' were brought here and he would be held responsible if something happened. The 'something,' he said later, was the probability of us escaping.

'I live a modest life out of my meagre salary,' Joseph told Sasi. 'You are big shots.' Joseph pleaded with his seniors to get us shifted to the Viyyur Central Jail, some 85 km away in Thrissur, but this night we were to stay here.

We were soon in the jail.

'We have some guests,' said Chandrasekhar, soon after we men were locked inside a cell.

'Who? Where?' Sasi asked expectantly.

'There,' Chandrasekhar said, pointing to a couple of rats scurrying across the floor.

The rats appeared to be unmindful of our presence, as if they have lived all their life in the company of human beings, which was the case.

Chandrasekhar now had a request to Sasi, 'Can you get me a drink?'

'Are you mad?' said Sasi. 'We don't have money, and even if we have, they will break our neck if we ask for a drink.'

Now Chandrasekhar and Sasi were whispering something, all I could hear that they were taking my name. I had not spoken to them or with any of the other accused ever since the arrest.

After a couple of minutes, Chandrasekhar and Sasi slowly moved towards me with a smile.

'Chandra has managed to hide Rs 500 he had got from a visitor,' said Sasi.

I kept silent.

'If we ask the policeman he would shout,' he continued. 'But you may be able to convince the warden.'

I knew it would not work, but got this vicarious pleasure of making Chandrasekhar lose his Rs 500.

'I will try,' I said.

Chandrasekhar and Sasi were elated.

Next time when a policeman came near our cell I called him and gave him the Rs 500. My co-accused had no idea that I had not asked him to get anything. The policeman, happy with the Rs 500 bonus for nothing, told me that we would be shifted to the Viyyur Central Jail in Thrissur the next morning, and sauntered off.

The two men waited through the night waiting for a tipple. I feigned sleep. Amidst the most harrowing experience of my life, here in a jail for the first time, in the company of menacing mice, I had a hearty laugh.

LESSONS IN VERNON

'I can weld like a dream, sir.'

In Vernon, my priority was to acquire the liquid propulsion technology as early as possible and get back to India. I had a mandate to head the team for five years. Members of the team had tenures varying from a year to three, and the plan was to send back a few who had finished their part of the job and bring in a few others, depending on the emerging needs and our men's specific area of expertise. On the whole, more than a hundred scientists and engineers worked on the project that lasted till 1980, and at any given point of time there were about fifty of them working at SEP.

While the primary job was to acquire the 'know-why', I realised this could be done only by winning the confidence of the French without being too intrusive. Joint development contracts have been drawn with mutual benefit, but there was always competition. Partners, in a way, practice cautious camaraderie.

It was tough to win the confidence of the French who initially looked down upon our men. There were even a few who found fault with Rene Morin, the commercial head, for having got a bunch of greenhorns into SEP just because the French wanted to do business with India. It is another matter that Morin, who stood by us during difficult times, had a technical qualification and confidence in Indian scientists. The coming years proved that Morin stood by us, from the turbulent days of signing the Viking contract to its execution and PSLV launch. Morin had been a friend of India worthy of at least a Padma Shri.

Dedication was the hallmark of our engineers in Vernon. Ramachandra Rao, who worked on a mathematical modelling of the Viking engine, continued to work despite a fracture he suffered. Rao had left his wife back in India as her father was ailing. Months later, when she joined Rao, her father had died. The couple kept this a private tragedy, and did not share it with us, lest Rao's work in Vernon be affected.

Besides sweat, our men had plenty of skills. Particularly two incidents proved our worth to the French, one demonstrated our skills, the other our knowledge. The former came from welder Samuel Raj. The uninitiated may consider a welder's job a lowly one, but engineers are indebted to a good welder. A good understanding of the behavior of metals and alloys gives him the foundation on which he can employ his skills that get better by the day. In other words, his job demands knowledge, dexterity and experience.

'I can weld like a dream, sir,' Raj said. And he was not boasting. He possessed all the qualities I mentioned, in abundance, and was a star at ISRO. And that's why I took him to Vernon. The welder's job here was quite challenging. For one, he had to work on AZ5, a tricky aluminium alloy. While a machine does inert gas welding at places like the injector through which the fuel and oxidiser go into the combustion chamber, a dome has to be manually welded onto the injector rim. Such is the caution employed that it takes four months to put the injector dome in place, if people worked in sixteen-hour-a-day shifts.

It was tough, but I was confident that Raj could pull it off. But there was a hitch. SEP and many aerospace industrial units in France allowed only those certified by the Institut de Soudure (French Welding Institute) to work on the welding floor. I vouched for our man's skills, but the French would have none of it. A rule, after all, was a rule. So, our star welder was given strips of aluminium to play with, while the certified welders worked on the dome and other critical structures of the rocket engine.

How does one get a certificate from Institut de Soudure, I inquired with some SEP heads. They just smiled. It was indeed very tough to pass the test. Many of the master welders at SEP had cleared the test after a minimum of three attempts. SEP officials said it would be a waste of time and money—yes, taking the test cost a bomb—for Raj to attempt it.

Having seen the SEP welders at work, I knew Raj could match them, if not outclass them. When I insisted, SEP was kind enough to give me a loan to apply for Raj's certification. Raj took the welding test and passed it in the first attempt. SEP engineers were so much in awe that they got the administration to waive off the loan they gave for Raj's test fees. A star was reborn in Vernon.

Raj was inducted into the core team of welders working on the injector dome. The professionals that they were, the French welders and their supervisors held back no praise that our man deserved. A few weeks later, as I was noting how the experience he would gain here in Vernon would be significant for us when we got back home to put together the Vikas engine, Raj came to me with some 'confidential' news. SEP had offered him a job with ten times the salary he was drawing at ISRO.

Raj had told his prospective poachers that he would do nothing without my permission. I told him to the offer, and he did it without any questions. Later, visiting his house on the outskirts of Nagercoil after his death, I felt guilty for not allowing him to go. He had left behind his family in a modest house he had built with a loan, which was yet to be repaid. Raj could have built ten palatial houses by now, I thought, had I allowed him to take up the French offer.

He welded some of the crucial parts of the first few Vikas engines and PSLV rockets. He was also instrumental in training welders of Godrej and MTAR Technologies, which now mass produce Vikas engines for ISRO. Samuel Raj—like many others in ISRO who never bothered to blow their own trumpets among the cacophony of self-promotion—died as an unsung hero soon after the first PSLV took to the skies in 1993.

After the welder impressed SEP with his skills, it was time for us to prove our utility when it comes to reviews and analysis. SEP had two technical bodies to review projects—Review Critique Definition and Review Critique Design. I was a member of the former. It defined and discussed specifications of an engine like operating pressure, stress levels and temperature. Looking at the results, it analysed if the specifications were achievable and, if they were not, it set new ones that were again dynamic. In short, it gave a direction to the development of a rocket engine.

Review Critique Design (RCD), on the other hand, was more critical when it came to understanding the 'know-why'. It went into why some specifications were not met. In other words, it analysed test failures. Earlier, blasts were not uncommon at rocket engine testing sites, but by now computers had taken the controls, aborting tests before they cross the danger mark. So, tests would leave us with many unanswered questions like when a test was aborted due to fluctuating pressure, was it because of pressure variation or the misbehavior of a pressure sensor (India was providing pressure-gauging transducers as part of the contract that got us to Vernon). The outcome of Review Critique Design analyses became inputs for the next test.

I decided to approach the men who mattered. And they were not very encouraging to the idea of an Indian trying to gain access to an exclusive club of analysts who designed future technologies of space. SEP honchos laughed when I expressed my wish to be part of Review Critique Design. Technology head Bachelot ruled it out upfront. Viking project director Dorville explained that SEP never allowed foreigners to be part of Review Critique Design; the few exceptions have been Europeans, given that SEP was part of the bigger European Space Agency.

I realised that request would not help. It was time to change tact. I had to impress upon the SEP top brass that I can bring to the RCD table something significant. I already had a little ammo. With help from my colleague Ayyappan Pillai, an IITian specialising in combustion, I had ascertained that the Viking engine had a low upper stability margin. The engine is designed to have an operating pressure of 52.6 bars (approximately 750 lbs per square inch). The operating pressure of a rocket engine is determined by several factors, primarily by the quantity of fuel and oxidiser entering the combustion chamber. We found out that the engine would become unstable due to vibration when the pressure goes up by about two bars. If, for various reasons the pressure goes up beyond the margin, the engine would blast. A system like this one should have ideally had a minimum upper stability margin of five bars.

How did we find this out? Normally during development, specifications given by a team are taken for granted. Here, we, as part of our learning rigour, never accepted weights and measurements given on paper—we did our own assessment. So, looking at the given operating pressure of 52.6 bars, I was curious what the stability margin was. This, because I wanted to upgrade the engine we were co-producing, once back in India to carry heavier payloads than those planned by Viking. The man to go to was Ayyappan Pillai, our instability expert. Pillai ran a computer programme to tell me that the upper stability margin was low. That is, the engine would start vibrating a couple of bars above the operating pressure, indicating instability. An unstable engine would send the rocket away from the desired trajectory and, worse, trigger an explosion.

I knew Pillai had just handed me a trump card, and I played it. During a casual conversation with Dorville, I let it slip that I felt the stability margin was low. Dorville didn't take it seriously, but he was curious.

'Why do you say that?' he said.

'I get a feeling it is low. And yes, I have my reasons to feel so,' I said.

Dorville neither agreed nor disagreed, but the game did work. Dorville must have reported the information to his senior colleagues. And soon there was a discussion. When asked if I could substantiate my suspicion over Viking's stability, I suggested we run a test to ascertain it. They agreed.

Pillai had done a computer analysis and had employed Professor Crocco's theorem of instability to confirm Pillai's findings.

So, here I was, confident yet anxious of the static test results. They ran the test by firing the engine and slowly increasing the operating pressure. At around 56 bars, Viking was showing a tendency of instability. Dorville was shocked. Ayyappan Pillai and I were right. The French were impressed. Soon, I would be invited to the high table of Review Critique Design.

It is another matter that the French went ahead and produced more than thirty Viking engines with the low margin of stability since they had mass fabricated combustion chambers, before our theory was validated. The Arianne vehicle, which used the first set of Viking engines, were designed with four first stage engines and one second stage engine, which meant the rocket used five Viking engines for a launch. The first launch (L-01) was a success, the second was a failure because of the low stability margin in one of the four engines of the first stage. We were getting validated, again.

The French held a review committee that discussed the low stability margin. After long discussions, the committee decided to discard the more than twenty engines with the old specifications, and improve upon the safety margin to make the Arianne flight more reliable. It was now, in 1981 that ISRO had developed a 350 kg satellite, and Ariane offered to launch it free of cost. It was a win-win for both. The French wanted a payload to test the efficacy of the improved Viking engine, India needed a rocket to take its communication satellite to space. Since it was an experiment, technically speaking, the French offered a free ride. The satellite came to be known as APPLE (Ariane Passenger Payload Experiment). It was a success.

I am not sure if the French would acknowledge that we had contributed to the improvement in the safety margin of the Viking combustion chamber, but I was happy that it got me into the Review Critique Design of SEP. Here everything was on a need-to-know basis. You just could not shoot questions to enrich your knowledge. You could make observations and, if vital to the point being discussed, air your views. It was not a place to clarify your doubts. But that wasn't a problem. Mere observation of the RCD proceedings gave me invaluable insights. And this changed the way I perceived certain things, from as simple a process as recording minutes of a meeting, to quality control.

At ISRO, documentation of meetings was considered a clerical job, and it got done in a haphazard manner. Notes are taken randomly, and someone would put it together with deviations from what was originally spoken at the meeting, and the official signed minutes would be ready weeks later, only to be stashed away in cupboards to gather dust. At RCD, minutes were meticulously recorded, as and when people speak. At the end of a meeting, the minutes are read, signed, distributed to the participants, and stored for reference.

Probably the biggest takeaway for me from RCD was the way the quality control team coordinated with the development team. At ISRO, the two teams are often at loggerheads. I hated the quality control guys, I saw them as people always eager to throw a spanner in the wheel. Now, I realised that I should respect them. But back in India, when I was in a hurry to bring liquid technology, there were enough instances when I thought quality control head M C Mathur was unnecessarily creating hurdles for me. There were already seniors, including solid propulsion proponents Kurup and Gowarikar, refusing to see reason in liquid, and Mathur's quality control team made it worse.

My struggle to test and fly the three-tonne engine, which we developed on the lines of SAM7, a surface-to-air missile Russia had given India, added to my hatred for the quality control team. First they didn't allow me to test the engine in Trivandrum, saying it was unsafe. Then, after the first ground test failed, leading to my resignation that Dhawan never allowed, the first flight of the three-tonne engine failed in 1973. An analysis showed that it was due to combined beating and vortex, some complex fluid behavior. But more than analysing the failure and speeding up correction, Mathur kept harping on 'I told you so'.

I remember standing by a blackboard, with a chalk in hand, explaining things to a senior-level meeting when Mathur said this again. I flung the chalk in no specific direction and shouted, 'Mathur if you know how to do it, do the damn thing.'

Mathur was composed. 'Why are you getting agitated, Nambi,' he said. 'It's my job to question and clarify.'

I was still fuming. 'Yes, it is your job to stall development of a liquid propulsion engine. And your job is much easier than mine.' I stormed out of the meeting.

I was reminded of this spat while seated at RCD where the French disagreed with each other with extreme civility and professionalism. But then, SEP was not ISRO. At ISRO, often people with no hands-on knowledge in propulsion systems and development are put on quality control. Often, like the planning and programme group, it was considered a dump yard for the bosses to send underperformers. Here at SEP, quality control has always been headed by a person who had got his hands dirty on the work floor. Our structural engineer H R S Mani, an IITian from Bangalore, imbibed these lessons in quality control from SEP and helped ISRO adopt it in a professional way.

Earlier, my scant respect for the ISRO quality control teams coupled with my impatience to deliver made me take several impromptu decisions based on my hunch feeling. Let me confess that sometimes this was in contravention to protocol. One such decision came with sufficient risk. And here is one of the best kept secrets.

After the untimely and shocking death of Vikram Sarabhai on 30 December 1971, Satish Dhawan was to take over as ISRO chairman. But at the time of Sarabhai's death, Dhawan was midway through a programme in the US, and the government appointed M G K Menon as a short-term chairman. Menon, a physicist mentored by Homi J Bhabha at the Tata Institute of Fundamental Research, was then the electronics commission chairman.

ISRO had developed the Rohini-560 rocket, and Sarabhai had appointed me the chief of Rocket Assembly and Test Facility (RATF), which was part of the Space Science & Technology Centre (SSTC) in Trivandrum. Soon after taking over as the chairman, Menon wanted to witness a static test firing of the Rohini rocket. Arrangements for the test were on at a great pace and I, as the RATF chief, was overseeing them. It was the new chairman's first visit to the centre and we were eager to demonstrate our readiness.

I was on the test stand when pressure pick-ups (transducers) were being mounted on the head-end of the rocket. Thankaiyan, one of our best fitters, was at work. Consistent good work and laurels can make one overconfident, and Thankaiyan was no exception to this rule. He used a normal spanner to tighten the screw, against the norm that specifies use of a torque wrench that allows to preset and limit the extent of tightening. I had told him on earlier occasions not to rely always on spanners, but Thankaiyan felt his experience was superior to the precision of the torque wrench.

As Thankaiyan turned the spanner a wee bit more than necessary, the screw gave way, leaving a hole at the head-end of the rocket. The other side of the hole was exposed to the propellant. This meant the test could not be conducted.

The way out was to drill a hole to pluck out the broken part of the screw and seal the part. This means that the engine has to be tested without a transducer, and hence the pressure of the engine cannot be gauged during the test. After all, it was only a static test and not a flight test. But the danger of this option was not in the performance of the engine during the test, but the possibility of an explosion during the drilling which produces sparks. If a spark goes through the hole and if, by another stroke of bad luck, it gets in touch with the propellant, the engine and the test facility would be pulverised, not to speak of what would happen to the people around.

Call it foolhardiness of age or the overenthusiasm of a scientist to impress the chairman, I decided to take the risk. Later I realised the irony. I was fixing a problem that resulted from a worker's overconfidence with a solution that stemmed from my overconfidence. In all fairness, Thankaiyan's was a mishap; mine an invitation to disaster.

For now, however, it was payback time for Thankaiyan.

'You are going to drill out the screw and seal the part,' I told him.

Thankaiyan nodded.

'You know the consequences, don't you?'

He nodded again.

'Don't worry, if something goes wrong, you will not die alone. I stay here with you.'

I am not sure if it was any reassurance, but Thankaiyan later told me that he saw in my eyes a determination that he dared not question.

I summoned the security chief and instructed him to evacuate the place, basically send out all people from the vicinity of the test facility.

'If anyone comes into the building, you will go out forever,' I told the security chief. 'Don't let in any visitor, even if he says he is the chairman of ISRO.'

Thankaiyan and I got to work, he deftly drilling, and I quenching the spot with wet cotton to minimise, if not prevent, sparks. The job was done in an hour, and the engine was test-ready, minus the transducer.

Menon came as scheduled. We fired the engine. The test was a success.

SEP wouldn't have allowed any such adventure. Here, protocol was supreme and the different teams worked in tandem. Egos never interfered with coordination, at least not in the open. But the best of protocols have holes; and a natural corollary to this are mistakes that often result from human carelessness. What else explains the failure of a test that was finally attributed to a worker leaving cotton waste in a rocket part? The protocol was to plug all the orifices—and there are some 500 of them—of the rocket engine every day after work. This is to prevent any impurity from getting into the feeder lines or the combustion chamber. A worker, while covering these openings with cotton, used lesser quantity at one place, and the cotton slipped in. Nobody checked before the engine was taken for test firing.

The ISRO team took copious notes of such mistakes and of high-tech lessons we learned. While the daily meetings were meant for discussing what each team worked on, the team leaders were asked to present problems they did not have answers to, at the weekly meetings. Not that all unanswered questions meant inefficiency of the engine—the engine may work fine even if you do not know how a certain material would react if the operating pressure goes up beyond a point—but finding the answers was crucial to the know-why. Questions led to analysis and eventually answers. Some answers came fast, some others took weeks, if not months, of probing and prodding.

One such question that remained unanswered till the end was the unusually high tolerance band of Viking's gas generator temperature. For a gas generator with an operating pressure of 600 degrees Celsius, the tolerance band of plus-or-minus 50 degrees Celsius was unusual, we thought. In engineering, an ideal product should have zero tolerance, which means it works as designed, to the point. In this case, the high temperature tolerance of the gas chamber meant fluctuations through other systems including the pump and combustion chamber.

We asked SEP engineers why the tolerance band was set so high.

'Can't it be around plus-or-minus 10 degrees Celsius?'

There was no answer.

Later we understood that Arianne Space, too, had raised this question to SEP, which said it was not worth studying and correcting the tolerance band since it would delay the project and incur higher costs. Since it was generally accepted that the situation did not pose a real threat to the system, it was left at that.

We noted down all the points that we did not understand and discussed. We documented all these discussions and sent them regularly to a backup team of about twenty engineers in India, headed by T P Rangamani. The backup team fired back questions at us, and this served as a double brainstorm.

Sending these documents was not easy. I requested the Indian embassy in Paris to allot a diplomatic bag for us to send the documents to India. A diplomatic bag was immune to scanning or that is what we were made to understand. The embassy wanted to know what was so secretive about the documents that came from our workplace.

'There was nothing secretive,' I reasoned, 'but these are meant only for our scientists.' Contradictory it might have sounded, but ambassador R D Sathe agreed. Still there was a problem. The diplomatic bags were dispatched to India from Paris only once a week, so I have to store the documents for six days before depositing them at the embassy.

I persuaded the Indian embassy in Paris to allot a locker to store the documents that came from Vernon every day. Only my office assistant Unni, draughtsman Muthusamy and I knew about the diplomatic channel.

What went in those bags were, again, know-how. For the know-why, we put a team back home to design a prototype based on the documents and drawings. These included details of every system, subsystem and sub-subsystem; applied mechanics that went into their making; and details of materials to be used. This is a basic practice in engineering to develop something based on a design, without directly copying from the original, and see at the end of it how much the prototype is close to the original.

Every spacefaring nation has taken either of the two paths: borrowing basics from another country and developing on them or starting from scratch and developing its own rockets. Both involves trial and error for decades; the latter route takes longer than the former. Germany was clearly a pioneer, with geniuses like von Braun developing the V2 rocket that Hitler had used to fire across the English Channel. The US mostly developed its own systems. China got its basics from the Russians, who are clearly the leaders even today when it comes to efficiency, though today's Russia is a pale shadow of the erstwhile USSR.

India, though helped generously by the Russians, was developing its first liquid propulsion engine with the help from France. India can take pride in having developed an indigenous cryogenic engine, but we owe a lot to the Russians who parted with seven engines. But again, we could not work with the Russians as we did it with the French. They might have agreed for the Viking-Vikas contract purely for business reasons, and we designed a contract that with a barter system of 'technology for man hours' to hook them, but we owe a lot to the French. *Merci beaucoup!*

In three years, the Viking-Vikas engine was almost ready. And we were confident of reproducing a Viking (Vikas for us) back home. However, as per the contract, ISRO had to provide seventy-five man years to SEP, and our men came and left in batches up to 1980, some of them working on other projects at SEP.

Having briefed to him about the progress our team had made, Dhawan in early 1978 asked me if I needed to stay back in France longer or come back. I had a five-year mandate in France, but with the know-how and know-why we had acquired, I was eager to get back to India and start work on Vikas. There was still no project to develop the engine, but I had charted out my agenda. One, to identify a place to set up a facility for liquid propulsion and start working on Vikas. Two, to get Vikas into the PSLV that has been on the drawing board before I left for Vernon. PSLV, again, was not yet a project, but I know the launch vehicle should be powered by a liquid propulsion engine.

I didn't share these plans yet with Dhawan, but told him that it's time for me to get back to Trivandrum. A Chandran, who took over the three-tonne engine from where I left at the Sriharikota test site, now replaced me at Vernon. I packed my bags in March 1978.

CHAPTER 17

IN VIYYUR JAIL, RIPPER FOR COMPANY

'Did you count the number of bars on the cell gate?'

After a sleepless night, terrified of the rats, I waited for the jail staff to open the cell. Through the night I had kept my ears open to hear for any approaching rodent. Not that I could do anything—I did not have anything in my hand to even shoo them away. At day break I searched for the nuisance and found them huddled in a corner.

When the jailor came to ask us to get ready to leave for Viyyur Central Prison, the only question in my mind was if the cell there would be as bad as this. After a couple of hours drive from Ernakulam we reached the Central Prison, a much bigger place. We were herded to a section of the prison, which I later realised was the high-security zone. It had twenty-four cells in a row.

Each cell had a toilet in a corner, without much of an enclosure separating the shit hole from the rest of the space. The cells on this corridor were numbered one totwenty-four. As we passed the second cell, the inmate shouted in Malayalam: 'Saare...avanmaar ningaleyum kurukkiyo?' (Sir, those guys have trapped you too).

It would be a while before I realise that this prisoner was Ripper, a serial killer who used a hammer to break the skull of his victims. Kerala had seen a couple of such 'Rippers', and I do not remember this man's real name. He was about 5'3" tall. He looked malnourished, but had great energy when he spoke, his volume always high. He had escaped from the Poojapura Central Jail in Trivandrum, before being caught and brought here. Ripper, during my stay in Viyyur prison became friendly, even sympathetic to me.

The cells were about 7 ft wide and 10 ft long, with the toilet in the far right corner as you entered it. The gate of each cell had eight wrought iron bars. I was given cell number six. My neighbours were S K Sharma in cell number five and Sasikumar on cell number seven. Chandrasekhar was given cell eight, something he bitterly complained about since his numerologist-astrologer had told him that eight is an unlucky number for him.

'Something bad is going to happen to me,' Chandrasekhar told me the next morning when we were let out of the cell for a bath in the open.

I have been a believer in God throughout my life, but never bothered about such numerological nonsense. Moreover, when you are falsely implicated in a case and are trying to find ways to prove your innocence, the number of your cell is the least significant of concerns. I wanted to ask him what worse can happen to him, and me, than what we were going through. I stopped myself and said, with my tongue firmly in cheek, 'I too think so. You may be hanged.'

We were allowed to step out only when all the other prisoners were locked in their cells. There was an open space where we could take bath from a few cement tanks filled with water. Slowly resuming small talk with Sasi, I would pull Chandra's leg occasionally reminding him of his ominous cell number eight.

I told Sasi about the number of bars on the gates; that I had been playing mathematical games with the bars during free time. Number eight, like any number for that matter, has some specialties. It is the first number which is neither prime nor semi-prime. It is the first number of the form p^3, p being an integer greater than 1. It is the base of the octal number system used in computers, it is also the number of vertices a cube has. For Chandra, however, it was just a bad number.

One day out on the verandah with Sasi, Chandra and Sharma, I said, 'By the way, Chandra,' did you count the number of bars on the cell gate?'

'No, why?' Chandra was all curious.

'Oh, nothing, I was just wondering if the number is good it might offset the bad things that your cell number eight brings.'

Chandra immediately ran to his cell and started counting. When he came back pale, we kept discussing the weather, each one trying hard to suppress a laugh. These were some harmless fun we had at the expense of Chandra, but I had felt bad about the man who, like me, was jailed for no fault of his.

My first impression of Chandrasekhar, the Glavkosmos representative, was not very pleasant. It was during the cryogenic deliberations with the Russians that Chandrasekhar first became close to me. While on a flight to Moscow, he was accompanying us to a meeting with the Russian space agency.

I was quietly sipping on my whiskey when he came to me and started small talk. I politely asked him to leave me alone, but the Glavkosmos agent was too keen to entertain me with his antics.

'I can give you company for a drink or two,' he said.

'Can you get lost?' I retorted.

Later, he was made to stand outside the meeting hall as we discussed details of the cryogenic contract with the Glavkosmos higher-ups. Chandrasekhar did not nurse a grudge. Here now, seeing him getting paranoid about the number of iron bars on his cell gate, I felt pity for the man who was used to having four drinks a day, not more than one each at a five-star hotel in Bangalore where he lived.

My thoughts were often broken by noise made by Ripper. He was occasionally taken along the corridor, his legs chained. He would stop by my cell, mostly to foul-mouth policemen.

'These buggers think they can keep me in these chains,' he said one day, pointing to the metal shackles across his ankles. 'I have broken many jails and these guys know I can do it again. I am just being nice to them.'

This man had an inherent hate for the khaki-clad.

Ripper told me that he was getting daily updates about the ISRO spy case, and that he knew we were innocent. I doubted if he followed the case; he would have been speaking out of his hatred for the system.

In one of our last interactions, Ripper said, 'Sorry sir, I can't be of much help to you, but I am sure you will soon walk free.'

HOME NOT SWEET

'It may remain a dream; it may not take off at all.'

Problems arising out of internal politics, and the continuing stepmother treatment to liquid propulsion system, awaited me in India. I anticipated them, but did not allow them to weigh me down. In fact, before I packed my bags for India in March 1978, I had set my agenda to identifying a place and get infrastructure for a liquid propulsion centre; get project approval for Vikas, the liquid engine; get into the Polar Satellite Launch Vehicle (PSLV) project, which Dhawan had outlined by making Vikas a part of it.

Even as Kalam's SLV project was on stream, Dhawan had initiated planning for a PSLV and a GSLV (Geosynchronous Satellite Launch Vehicle). While PSLV and GSLV were still in the ideation stage, clearance had been given for a project parallel to SLV, the Augmented Satellite Launch Vehicle (ASLV). M S R Dev, the ASLV project director, was an efficient scientist, a PhD from the US. But the vehicle was aerodynamically jinxed so much that every time it was test-launched it plunged into the sea. In ISRO, ASLV soon came to be known as 'Always Sea-Loving Vehicle'.

That was a cruel joke, given the effort Dev and his team had put into the ASLV project. Today, with six-dimensional trajectory analysis software, we are able to accurately predict flight load, trajectory, overflying countries, areas of debris fall and much more.

With these modern tools, we now foresee problems through simulation, and prevent them before the launch. Back in the late 1970s, we were not good at 6D trajectory analysis, and it was all trial and error. ASLV may not be a shining showpiece in the ISRO brochures today, but our success with PSLV and future vehicles owes a lot to this sea lover, which taught us how not to make a rocket.

Space Science & Technology Centre had by now taken shape and, a year after Sarabhai's death in 1971, it was renamed Vikram Sarabhai Space Centre. The centre had several groups working under it: a propellant group headed by Vasant R Gowarikar; a propulsion group with A E Muthunayagam as the head; an aerodynamics group under Y Janardhana Rao; a satellite group under U R Rao; a structures group headed by L Amba Rao; a control, guidance and instrumentation group with S C Gupta at the head; and a systems engineering group under D S Rane. M K Mukherjee headed the materials and quality control group and also general administration. Kalam, heading the SLV-3 project, reported to TERLS director Murthy. Muthunayagam had the additional responsibility of the mechanical engineering group. I reported to him, in the propulsion group.

Relations between various heads were far from cordial; some had a cold war, some others fought openly. Some of the bitter fights were between propulsion group head Muthunayagam, my immediate boss, and propellant group head Gowarikar. Both had ambitions to be the director of VSSC first, and then the ISRO chairman. While Gowarikar became the VSSC director in 1979, neither could reach the top post in ISRO for their own records of partisanship and infighting.

Gowarikar and Muthunayagam never saw eye-to-eye; and this affected me. I can think of no reason for Gowarikar's dislike for me other than that I worked with Muthunayagam, and that my hard work often brought laurels to my boss. Some said Gowarikar was also not amused that I had direct access to the ISRO chairman—something I enjoyed with both Sarabhai and Dhawan. I could not care less, and all I could tell myself was that I had never done anything to appease the bosses and, in fact, my straight forward nature, which irked many others, had endeared me to Sarabhai and Dhawan.

The Gowarikar-Muthunayagam tug-of-war had a history to it. In his experimenting style, Sarabhai had allowed everyone to do anything. While many utilized this freedom with caution and a sense of responsibility, some like Muthunayagam exploited it to fight ego battles. As the propulsion group head, Muthunayagam's brief was to develop propulsion systems with the propellant developed and delivered by the propellant group headed by Gowarikar.

Muthunayagam exceeded his brief, and started developing propellants on his own. His reason, that Gowarikar's group was not delivering good propellants, and that he was forced to experiment with his own, though with ample reason, infuriated Gowarikar. All these, for the record, were solid propellants for the minion Rohini-75, which did virtually nothing but rise to the sky for a few kilometers and plunged into the Arabian Sea. Satellite launches were still a distant dream, and my occasional prodding for liquid propulsion was seen as an ambition bordering on absurdity.

Gowrikar's group was not sitting idle; they were trying to develop several high-energy propellants, but just could not get them right. Taking this as a reason, and evidently to belittle Gowarikar, Muthunayagam told me that our group has to acquire cordite, a low-energy propellant made by the Cordite Factory at Aravankadu in the Nilgiris, to test-fire Rohini.

Amidst these efforts, one man felt like a king—M R Kurup, head of the Rocket Propellant Plant. Kurup's team was making PVC-based propellant for Centaur rockets supplied by the French as part of a deal Sarabhai struck in the late 1960s. The French were supplying the rockets and the technology to make PVC-based propellant, till India could make its own. So, Kurup was delivering something which was being handed out by the French, while the groups headed by Gowarikar and Muthunayagam were struggling to develop an indigenous technology to make propellants.

As part of the Centaur deal, Eswar Das was in charge of fabrication, and Abdul Kalam's job was to integrate and marry the payloads made by Physical Research Laboratory, Ahmedabad with the rocket. With nothing much to do on this front, Kalam, who always enjoyed a free hand, started working on a rocket, which he called D1. When he told me about the experiment, which was nothing more than the existing Rohini rocket, with the same 75 mm diameter, Kalam said he needed to do something to keep him occupied.

'Why the name D1?' I asked. 'Have you made A1, B1 and C1?'

Kalam smiled.

'It's an abbreviation for Dreamer1,' he said. 'It may remain a dream; it may not take off at all.'

Kalam was right. This dreamer never took off.

Though Gowarikar saw me as a Muthunayagam man, I was not interested in their politics, much less take sides. My focus was on getting the liquid propulsion Vikas engine into the PSLV project, which was now being configured on paper.

Any rocket is configured top-down. That is, you first decide on the mass of the payload and the orbit it has to be launched into; then you work out permutations and combinations of the stages of the rocket that would take the mass to the desired altitude. Teams would do mathematical calculations and simulations with various configurations to arrive at the best option.

The same was being done simultaneously for PSLV and GSLV. S Srinivasan headed the PSLV planning group, Ratnaraj Jayamani was in charge of GSLV planning. GSLV, which needed a cryogenic engine appeared a less immediate reality than PSLV, and I saw in PSLV the right opportunity to incorporate the liquid Vikas engine.

By virtue of being the deputy director of the propulsion group, I participated in the PSLV planning group presentations and discussions. The group worked out hundreds of configurations, toying with different ideas from a single-stage rocket to a four-stage rocket in different combinations of solid propulsion engines. Not one of the configurations had a liquid engine in it.

Whenever I spoke of trying out a liquid stage, there were either smirks or silence. But I did not give up. I would present scientific facts that showed the supremacy of liquid engines over solid, like the clean cut-off of the stage after burning. A liquid engine can burn for a much longer duration than a solid engine; a liquid engine can be cut off and re-ignited, while a solid engine once ignited has no control over, and has to burn out on its own.

Then there is the case of energy levels, called specific impulse in rocket science. A solid propulsion engine has a maximum specific impulse of 240 seconds, while a liquid engine has up to 295 seconds. A cryogenic engine has a specific impulse of more than 460 seconds. A higher specific impulse or energy level meant the need for lesser fuel or more payload mass to orbit. While solid has its uses in the first stage, I argued, to generate the initial thrust, but in a second or upper stage, a liquid engine is more efficient as it has lower acceleration and lower vibration than a solid engine.

When I put forward such scientific facts that none could contest, the group would hear me out, but at the end of it would carry on with simulations of the solid-only configurations as if my arguments were anything but a radio commercial of a toy that came during the break of an adult talk show. When I continued to press, the proponents of solid-only rocket, who constituted a vast majority of the system then, harped on the fact that we did not have a liquid engine, and it would be foolhardy to try out something in PSLV.

At one such meeting, many kept asking, 'Where is the liquid?' I kept insisting that we can make one. Even Kalam did not appear convinced with my arguments. It is another matter that less than six years later, when we successfully ground-tested the Vikas liquid propulsion engine in Vernon in 1985, Kalam, who had moved to the Defence Research and Development Organisation (DRDO), was the first one to congratulate me.

When an overwhelming majority in the PSLV group dismissed the probability of using a liquid engine, the reality was that my team, working with the French in Vernon for more than three years, had learnt the technology. But then, without a project approval, the Vikas engine would not be part of PSLV. To get such an approval, I knew, I had to play another game, which I already did.

It was a Herculean task to procure materials to make the engine, as suppliers to SEP, Vernon, where we learnt to make the engine, would not give them in small numbers. Again, my personal rapport with people like SEP commercial director Rene Morin, and my good old friend Kanwal Grover helped.

After using several contacts and pulling many strings through old contacts, which my team members in Vernon had been diligently cultivating, we procured almost everything, but 'O' rings, the specialised rubber joints made by a company called Le Joint Francais, remained elusive.

With his incredible contacts in France, Kanwar, who is better known in India for his vineyards than his invaluable contribution to India's space programme, managed to get them. It still remains a mystery how he collected the few 'O' rings from the French company; Kanwal told me that he casually carried them in his suitcase during one of his many monthly flights from France to India.

By 1981, my team put together one-and-a-half Vikas engines—a full engine that was ready to be tested and, with whatever leftover material we had, we put together a turbo pump and the upper part of the engine. This, however, did not qualify us to get into PSLV, since the Vikas engine—though we had made one—was not officially a project yet. Anything that has to go into a rocket has to be approved as a project, and the product has to be tested before being incorporated into a rocket.

The one-and-a-half Vikas engine we made was out of Dhawan's discretionary funds. Without a project status, it could not be tested. Even if it is given the clearance, there was no facility in India to ground-test the engine. We had to break it down, take the parts to Vernon, France and re-assemble before testing. That was to happen more than six years later, in 1985, when India's liquid propulsion capabilities came of age.

But now the Gowarikar-Muthunayagam tussle has come to such a stage that Dhawan had to create a separate unit—the Auxiliary Propulsion Systems Unit (APSU)—to accommodate Muthunayagam, who would now report directly to the ISRO chairman. APSU would transform to become the Liquid Propulsion Systems Unit, and later what is today called the Liquid Propulsion Systems Centre.

APSU worked on small control rockets and flow components. Major liquid propulsion systems came directly under VSSC. This put me in a spot because of my sphere of work, on Vikas and other liquid propulsion systems came under VSSC. When I pointed this out to Muthungayagam, he told me to report to Gowarikar. I did not mind. I thought Gowarikar would have matured enough to forget the past and let me get on with work; after all that was the directive U R Rao had given him. I was not totally right in that assessment, but Gowarikar himself, bitter that he was with Rao becoming the ISRO chairman, was desperate to get out of ISRO and find a secretary's job in the Union government.

I had to approach Gowarikar when our engineers who were trained in Vernon started getting back to their parent groups. Vikas was still in the workshop, and the team could not be allowed to dissipate. Here Gowarikar appeared to get a vicarious pleasure on my plight.

'You only handpicked people from different groups to go to Vernon. You did not take anyone from my group and now the others are leaving. What do I do?'

I retorted that he was very much part of the committee that selected the Vernon candidates, and he could not throw his hands up.

Gowarikar argued that he cannot hold people together to continue to work on Vikas since it was not yet a project. He, however, promised to get approval for Vikas as a project. Gowarikar did nothing, and I had to battle on.

At the PSLV planning group discussions, hundreds of configurations, sans a liquid engine, continued to be analysed. Two relatively junior scientists, Dathan and K Sivan (who went on to become the VSSC director) were in charge of simulation. Months into this exercise, still no configuration measured up. Simulations showed that some couldn't go as far as planned, some others couldn't carry as heavy a payload as we wanted. Yet others, the projections showed, would fall into a foreign country.

When I realised that my arguments in favour of using a liquid engine were being consistently and collectively stonewalled, I adopted a casual approach. During one of the water cooler moments, I told Dathan and Sivan to try out a few configurations with a liquid engine.

'But that is not approved by the group,' Dathan said.

'Hey man! I am not asking you to do anything for my house,' I would tell him. 'For curiosity sake, try it out. You don't have to make an official presentation.'

Dathan agreed. And, predictably, a few of these configurations using a liquid engine showed satisfactory results in simulations. In the next group discussion, when some of the analyses were presented, and the results turned out to be as usual unsuccessful, I remarked, 'Dathan, why don't you show us the results of that liquid-inclusive configuration.'

Dathan knew he was trapped. Hesitantly, he presented the simulation results, which showed satisfactory performance of a PSLV using a liquid engine as the second stage. But my detractors wouldn't budge.

'Nobody questions the efficiency of a liquid engine,' said one. 'But we are not considering it because we don't have such an engine and we can't develop one.'

It was time to do something drastic.

I went to PSLV planning group head Srinivasan's house. He was surprised, since there was nothing we couldn't discuss in office. But I chose to corner him in his den, where he would be free to react the way he wanted to, without official civility. After all, I was going to be harsh.

After turning down a coffee, I told him, 'Srinivasan, you are at the cusp of making history for India. You have two options: one, to be remembered as the person who headed PSLV, the most successful rocket India has made. Two, as the person who destroyed Vikram Sarabhai's dream of making India a space power.'

As Srinivasan sat stunned, I continued, 'You know you can't launch a PSLV without a liquid engine, but you are scared to oppose the chorus against it. I promise you to deliver a workable liquid propulsion engine. Think about it and allow a discussion on liquid engine at the next meeting.' I walked out.

In the coming days, I frequented VSSC director Brahm Prakash's office to impress upon him the need to ground-test the Vikas engine we had developed. Brahm Prakash, amidst a bunch of squabbling scientists, walked tall and commanded respect from everyone. Everyone knew that Brahm Prakash, a metallurgist from the Masssachusetts Institute of Technology who headed the metallurgy department at IISc, had agreed to take over as the first director of VSSC in 1972 after much pleading by Dhawan himself. Dhawan respected him for his scientific insights as much for the fact that Brahm Prakash was senior to Dhawan.

If Brahm Prakash said something, even ISRO chairman Dhawan wouldn't oppose. But ground-testing of Vikas needed Dhawan's approval—and clearance from the PMO. I am not sure what was in Dhawan's mind, but he still gave the proponents of solid-only versions of PSLV a long rope. And they were to reach the end of that rope soon. In one of the planning group discussions attended by Brahm Prakash, one presentation after another turned out to be short of expectations.

One of the configurations of PSLV came close to the goal, but it was found to have high levels of instability because of the thrust.

'Hey, Dathan, can you bring down the propulsion a bit,' said Kalam.

'I can,' replied Dathan, 'but you will have to bring down the payload weight a bit.'

Kalam fell silent. Finally, Brahm Prakash stood up.

'I think we have no option but to go in for a liquid engine.'

Somewhere in my mind, Vikas smiled.

A young Nambinarayanan with the Dart payload in 1967

At RH-560 launch pad with D Easwardoss and Madhavan Nair

Assembling LP-006, India's first liquid engine rocket in the early 1970s

Working on ignitor assembly for a Rohini rocket in 1969

Nambinarayanan as a student at Princeton University in 1970

Nambinarayanan with Prime Minister Indira Gandhi at TERLS on February 2, 1968

TN Seshan gets a farewell at Vernon where he came to visit ISRO scentists developing the Vikas engine in 1977

In the control room during a test firing in Mahendragiri in 1989

At a project review meeting with French scientists in 1976

Kanwal Grover, Guiebert, Muthunayagam, TN Seshan, Sathish Dhawan, Rene Morin, Nambinarayanan and Gunasekaran at the ISRO headquarters in Bangalore during discussions on the joint development of the Viking in 1975

Meena Nambi Narayanan inaugurating the SNIAS pavilion at the Paris
Air Show in 1976

After the first ground test of Vikas engine at Vernon in December 1985

After the first ground test of Vikas engine at Vernon in December 1985

With Prime Minister PV Narasimha Rao and UR Rao at Sriharikota for the first successful launch of PSLV in 1994

With Russian scientists at USSR as part of cryogenic project, in the early 1990s

Nambinarayanan and other Indian representatives with Russian scientists at Ust–Katav in the early 1990s as part of the cryogenic project

Abdul Kalam visiting Sriharikota during the assembly of the first PSLV in 1993

With UR Rao before the first PSLV launch in 1993

CHAPTER 18

MEDIA TRIAL

'Mariam, a tuna in bed.'

The Viyyur prison was not bad. Rather, some of the people who manned the prison made it a tolerable place. There was jailor Gopalakrishnan, a friendly middle-aged man, Balakrishnan, the assistant jailor and Sivanandan, a warden.

While all these men were kind to me, Sivanandan developed a special liking for me, often consoling me and trying to cheer me up. He would update me on what newspapers have been reporting on the ISRO spy case. But this warden's second hand reporting left me only gasping for specifics. I asked him for newspapers, even if they come to me a day or two late.

It was only when Sivanandan brought a couple of newspapers that I realised that I haven't told him that I could read only English, not Malayalam. I wanted English papers. The jail did not have English papers, but Sivanandan said he would try his best, through 'proper channels'.

A couple of days later, when he brought a copy of *The New Indian Express*, there were two rectangles cut out of the paper. Sivanandan told me that the superiors had agreed to give me a copy of an English paper, but only after cutting out those stories about the ISRO spy case.

'This doesn't serve my purpose,' I complained.

'Be patient for a few days,' said Sivanandan.

After a few days newspapers started reaching me without the cuts. The stories I read were shocking because of the seriousness the case had attained by then, but those I heard about reporting by Malayalam dailies were unimaginably horrible. *Thaniniram*, a paper known for its yellow journalism, had broken the story of Mariam's arrest and followed up it with stories linking her to ISRO.

Kerala Kaumudi, whose owner M S Mani had an axe to grind with inspector general of police Raman Srivastava, jumped into the bandwagon. Soon, virtually every Malayalam newspaper was competing with each other churning out 'exclusive' stories of spies, sex and rocketry—a deadly combination that would make any B-grade movie a super hit.

Most of the Malayalam newspaper stories exposed the reporters' total ignorance of technical matters (I did not expect a general reporter to know rocket science, but if you are writing about the subject, you should know the difference between a rocket and a satellite). But when it came to Mariam Rasheeda, they all claimed to know everything from her anatomy to her bedroom behaviours.

'Mariam, a tuna in bed,' screamed a front page headline of a mainstream Malayalam paper. The report was by a chief of bureau who usually stepped in to write only 'very important stories', leaving the mundane stuff to junior reporters. A budding cartoonist in a Malayalam magazine showed me in bed with a woman spy; the caption read, 'That's liquid propulsion!'

By and large the English newspapers and magazines refused to be carried away by the vernacular sensationalism; some of the papers like *The Indian Express* of the north and *India Today* even picked holes in the theory of Kerala Police and Intelligence Bureau. One the few exceptions was V K Madhavan Kutty, a senior journalist of the *The New Indian Express*, who gleefully bought the sugar-coated tales and fired away as if he was competing with the local giants Malayala *Manorama* and *Mathrubhumi*. This journalist, however, failed in his desperate attempts to get the rest of the English media to sing his tune.

VIKAS IS IN, I AM OUT

Once Brahm Prakash was convinced about the inevitability of incorporating a liquid engine into the PSLV configuration, things moved forward, but it was not as smooth as I wanted it to be.

The simulation team ran several tests, and quite a few turned out to be promising, especially a three-stage vehicle with the Vikas engine as the second stage and the first and third stage with solid propulsion. This continues to be the configuration of PSLV, which has had thirty-five consecutive successful launches till 22 June 2016. The ISRO workhorse, as PSLV has come to be known, has launched more than 100 satellites, a little more than half of them for foreign countries.

When the engine was approved as part of PSLV in 1979, such a stupendous success was not even in the dreams of many scientists. I consider it a matter of luck, too, as Brahm Prakash got the Vikas engine project as the second stage of PSLV approved just before he retired. What's more, I was made the project director of the second stage. But before that, I had to pass another hurdle—and demolish yet another one.

It was still 1979, the year of SLV-3's first flight, which was a failure. The rocket was successfully launched the next year. Brahm Prakash who was on his last leg as the VSSC director, formed two committees—one to assess the level of acquisition of the Viking engine and the other to see if a semi-cryogenic engine was doable. The first panel was headed by Kalam, the second by Kurup—both hardcore solid propulsion fans. I had my reasons to believe that the 'solid' guys had influenced Brahm Prakash to put in place these committees as a last impediment to Vikas.

I voiced my concern to Brahm Prakash.

'You don't worry,' he told me. 'They wouldn't dare tell me wrong things about your engine.'

'Indeed,' I told Brahm Prakash. 'But my worry is that they wouldn't tell you the right things either.'

Brahm Prakash asked me to drop my aggression and cooperate with the committees.

Kalam called division heads and other senior scientists for periodic analysis of the feasibility of Vikas, where I, as the person who headed the project, had to be present. The initial meetings did not progress beyond the skepticism of whether we have mastered the liquid propulsion technology. And one day, I stood up.

'How are you going to find out if we have acquired the technology,' I asked the gathering of mostly solid propulsion enthusiasts. 'One way is to cross examine me on what my team did for five years in Vernon. And, to do that, you should be experts in liquid propulsion.'

I might have sounded, as usual, haughty, but my intention was not to run down anyone, leave alone Kalam, who despite his love for solid propulsion, did not fail to see the merits of dedication and hard work.

'Now, let me explain what we did,' I continued. 'And you can shoot your questions.'

For the next hour or so I addressed the meeting, virtually like a lecturer in an engineering classroom. Now I called my team heads, one by one, to give details of what and how we learned about the technology, fabrication and assembly procedure, besides the drawings, documents and experiment reports we have.

Mohana Prasad started with the turbo pump. After each session by a team leader, there were questions. My team had ready answers for everything, but it irritated me that many of the queries were basic stuff, which have already been circulated as a document to everyone at the meeting. When there seemed to be no end to mundane clarifications, I interfered.

'Gentlemen, you seem to be having a good education here, but does anyone have a question that tests more than our memory power?' I said.

It was not a pleasant interjection.

Coming out of that meeting, Kalam threw his hand around my shoulder.

'Buddy,' he said, 'this is a learning process for all of us, don't get agitated.'

'Kalam,' I replied, 'I can't be as diplomatic as you. You know there are many people here who will find a hundred reasons to reject the Vikas engine without knowing a thing about it.'

'Wait for the report,' said Kalam, smiling. And he walked away.

The committee gave a report that said something to this effect: it appears that the technology relating to fabrication and realisation of a liquid propulsion engine has been achieved by the team to a great extent. However, only when we make a prototype would we know the exact level of expertise the team has acquired.

It was not a bad report, but I still argued what was the need for such a committee when all it could say is that it has to be done to be believed. I, however, turned this ambiguity in the report to my advantage: Now that the committee has found that ultimate validation will come only from fabricating, we need to build a prototype of Vikas.

The second committee, headed by Kurup and with E V S Namboodiri as the member secretary, made haste to report that making a semi-cryogenic engine was easy. How wrong were they! It is indeed easier to handle the fuel (petroleum) for a semi-cryogenic than that of a cryogenic, which has liquid hydrogen as the fuel, but making a semi-cryogenic was not easy—at least in the late 1970s when the committee was formed.

When the committee recommended that the fuel for the 'easy' semi-cryogenic engine could be RP1, a petroleum fuel the Americans were using, I confronted them with a bit of history. A section of engineers in the US Army, I told them, was scared of handling unsymmetrical dimethylhydrazine (UDMH), which was then used in liquid propulsion engines, as the chemical was a known carcinogen and was not easy to store, transport or handle. So, they tried to shift to JP1, a petroleum-derived kerosene-like semi-cryogenic fuel (JP stands for NASA's Jet Propulsion Lab attached to California Institute of Technology).

The Americans found inconsistency in the performance of engines, with unclean combustion. Tests revealed that the behaviour of the fuel varied because it came from different oil wells. With each well, the sulphur and carbon content in the fuel varied. They refined the process several times, leading to products christened JP2, JP3 up to JP10. This final product called JP10 was renamed as RP1, the fuel Kurup and Namboodiri had now found to be the panacea for India's propulsion problems.

I asked them if we are able to get petroleum from the same well and keep the consistency intact; if we had the time for all that as PSLV was on the drawing board. There were no convincing answers. I advocated development of a full cryogenic engine first, then a semi-cryogenic.

And that is the exact path ISRO took much later—not because I had suggested that, but because that's how the trial and error scientific method led us.

Brahm Prakash was convinced of my argument and gave the final nod to make the Vikas engine.

As Brahm Prakash was nearing retirement, the power struggle between Gowarikar and Muthunayagam intensified. Going by their academic background and experience, both were eligible for the post. But their history of playing politics was too well-known in the organisation, and that was a big negative when it came to vying for the top post at the country's premier space centre.

This meant that some deserving candidates were rejected. And one of the victims of this treatment happened to be my son-in-law S Arunan when ISRO selected a team of six scientists in 1993 to visit Russia to study the prospects of cryogenic technology acquisition. A young mechanical engineer with an impeccable track record, Arunan was among the applicants. And I happened to be the member secretary of the selection panel chaired by Muthunayagam.

When Arunan came for the interview, I disclosed my conflict of interest and said I would stay away from the interview of this candidate. The rest of the panel selected Arunan, but Muthunayagam obviously wanted another candidate in his place. After the shortlist was made, Muthunayagam came to me.

'Arunan has been selected on merit,' he said.

'Good,' I said.

'See Nambi, people may say that he was selected because you were part of the selection panel.'

'But I was not part of his selection.'

'That only we know. Others may use this to tarnish your image.'

I laughed.

'I am not bothered about my image since I have not favoured anyone,' I said. Muthunayagam now went to ISRO chairman U R Rao who soon called me. I repeated what I told Muthunayagam.

'I leave the decision to you,' I told Rao. 'But I think it is unfair that someone is denied what he deserves just because he happens to be my son–in–law.'

I don't know what transpired at the ISRO headquarters, but Arunan's name was replaced with that of D P Sudhakar, another fine scientist.

The writing was on the wall: if Arunan continued under Muthunayagam, he would not attain his career trajectory. I advised him to shift out of LPSC. Arunan moved to VSSC under B N Suresh. Three years later, he got a transfer to the ISRO Satellite Applications Centre (ISAC), Bangalore, then headed by Aravamudan. Though a move forced by circumstances, this proved good for Arunan who went on to become the project director of India's first Mars Mission Mangalyaan in 2013.

By now it was crystal clear that be it in recruitment, promotion or just being nice, Muthunayagam had his blatant likes—in fact he appeared to be proud of them. That proved to be his undoing. Gowarikar took over as the VSSC director from Brahm Prakash in May 1972.

That marked the beginning of another round of power tussle between the two men, and I was caught in the crossfire. I never approved of Muthunayagam's ways, but there was no escaping Gowarikar's barbs as I continued to report to Muthunayagam and delivered for the team, which had by now graduated to a propulsion unit, just short of being a separate centre. Gowarikar, anyway, was not favourably inclined to my ideas of developing a liquid propulsion system and had consistently tried to puncture the Vernon project—something that he failed to do.

Some colleagues would warn me that Gowarikar would get my scalp—by hook or crook.

'One wrong step and he will fix you,' said a colleague.

I told him I was not scared since I am not party to any wrongdoing. This warning rang in my mind later when Gowarikar, then VSSC director, insisted that I head a committee that decided on recruitment of drivers. I said I was too busy with my work and could not spare time for such matters. Later, I was told that a driver was appointed out of turn, and had I been the head of the committee, I would have been answerable.

Another incident that reminded me to tread cautiously happened when I was heading another such committee to recruit some casual workers. One day I was surprised to see a VSSC driver at my door. He had come with a request: a woman relative of his had applied for a casual job in VSSC. I, as a member of the recruitment panel, should help her get the job.

I told him I will consider her if she fits the job. Thanking me, the driver fished out a long cover from his trousers pocket and placed it on the drawing room table.

'A small token of appreciation, sir,' he said.

I looked at the cover and saw a bundle of currency notes in it. I started shivering in anger.

'Take the bloody cover and run, you scoundrel,' I shouted. Hearing this, my wife came down the stairs from the floor above. The driver was still there, muttering something. I moved towards the telephone in the corner of the drawing room.

'You take that trash and leave now, or I call the police,' I said.

He picked up the cover and ran, I chased him till out of the gate. As the driver turned the corner, I noticed three or four men in a jeep. It was a trap.

I have been careful since then. A few casual workers have come home, some with fish and some with fruits; I scared them away.

Muthunayagam told Dhawan bluntly that he would not report to Gowarikar. Dhawan was in a fix. He couldn't let such a senior person go; neither could he reverse the appointment of Gowarikar, who was by no means inferior to Muthunayagam.

Dhawan finally found a way out by creating an Auxiliary Propulsion Systems Unit (APSU), and made Muthunayagam its director. This was the precursor to the Liquid Propulsion Systems Unit (LPSU), which in turn developed into today's Liquid Propulsion Systems Centre (LPSC) at Valiyamala, Thiruvananthapuram. APSU was a notch below the status of an ISRO centre, but the unit director would report directly to the ISRO chairman.

I became part of APSU—and later LPSU—and was working on the Vikas engine. Though it was not yet approved as a project, Dhawan had sanctioned Rs 1 crore from his discretionary fund. While we were putting together the 'one-and-a-half' engine using original material used by SEP, I was working on indigenisation of materials. For I knew we were lucky to have friends like Rene Morin who went out of the way to get me crucial materials and spares from SEP suppliers, this wouldn't be possible every time we wanted to put together a liquid propulsion engine. As for the first piece, I didn't want to experiment with indigenous parts as a failure of a ground test, I knew, would ground Vikas forever.

Rockets have a lot of aluminium alloys. In its purest form, aluminium is not difficult to make, but developing the alloys, with specific ratios that imparted properties to withstand high pressure and temperature, was a tough job. In this case, we needed an alloy called LM-6. While many Indian laboratories at that time were not confident of developing a new material, leave alone for rocketry that was for many still a lofty idea, the Regional Research Laboratory in Pappanamcode, Trivandrum sounded enthusiastic. Given the specifications, the lab did deliver some material, which wasn't bad, but not the best.

A bigger challenge was developing the equivalent of an alloy that the Americans called HS-25 (Hayne's Satellite alloy), and the French called KC-20WN, used to make the combustion chamber nozzle of the liquid propulsion engine. Such is the versatility of this material that a nozzle of 1 mm thickness withstands the great pressure and temperature as the rocket fires away for several minutes. HS-25 also offered great workability, which means it can be made into peculiar shapes without inflicting stress points on the material. This made HS-25 ideal for the bell-shaped nozzle used by the Viking engine at high altitude. While a conical nozzle can be made in a conventional lathe using other alloys, it takes a versatile material like HS-25 to make into a bell shape by using a pressure mechanism to flow it.

After scanning details of the best among Indian centres that can develop high-end hardware, I zeroed in on Mishra Dhatu Nigam Limited (MIDHANI). As a government unit with ample facilities to give it a shot, MIDHANI fitted our bill, but the bureaucracy there was stifling. With the inherent inertia of any Indian public sector unit, the MIDHANI top brass just refused to play ball.

The other option was ISRO's own metallurgy team headed by M K Mukherjee and Sarkar as his deputy. Sarkar started working on finding an equivalent for a material called Shell-407 for control rockets.

Shell-407 was a brand supplied by the American company Shell, and the real material content remained undisclosed to ISRO. When injected with hydrozine, this material decomposes, releasing a gas that gives thrust for course correction of the spacecraft. In another example of how the US systematically stymied ISRO's efforts in rocketry, just when the metallurgy team was experimenting with Shell-407, the company, which was providing the same material to NASA, kept on increasing the price for India and, finally, stopped supplying it.

They said it had been classified as strategic material. Any scientist of the times knew that only those materials used in missiles and nuclear devices were categorised as 'strategic', and nobody – the Americans included – was using Shell-407 for missiles or nuclear devices.

This was the same tactics the US had employed to stop the USSR from transferring the cryogenic engine technology to India in the early 1990s. The US argued that cryogenic engines fell under technology for missiles. This was far from the truth. No country, including the US, has a missile with a cryogenic engine.

But already under the strain of the impending fall of the Soviet Union, the Russian facilities buckled under American pressure and changed the contract to just sell seven cryogenic engines, and not transfer the technology. That this delayed India's cryogenic programme by at least fifteen years is another tale.

So, to make HS-25, I had nowhere to go, but MIDHANI, Hyderabad. I understood that Abdul Kalam, who had by now developed SLV-3, had asked MIDHANI to deliver another material called maraging steel. This alloy, which can withstand high temperature and pressure, also has some characteristics that qualify it to be used in the first stage of PSLV boosters.

Already struggling to deliver maraging steel, MIDHANI said it would be impossible to develop the equivalent of HS-25. But I wouldn't give up. After several rounds of cajoling, I used my last weapon: threat. I conveyed it to the MIDHANI brass that India's space programme was a pet project of the prime minister and, as a government body like ISRO, MIDHANI was duty-bound to deliver the material. Any complaint to the PMO would be taken so seriously that the MIDHANI honchos can expect adverse remarks on the service records.

That made the MIDHANI heads consider the proposal, but they still needed a vigorous push. It was here that I became close to my

ISRO colleague Sasikumar, who would later be a co-accused with me in the 'ISRO spy case'. Sasi, working with Kalam, was liaising with MIDHANI for maraging steel, and had established some rapport with the MIDHANI men. I requested him to use his connections to push for HS-25 too.

Sasi succeeded in convincing some of them, and put me on to some crucial guys. It wasn't easy, but after several months of pushing and prodding, they agreed to work on it. For MIDHANI it should have been a great realisation of its strengths and capabilities when it delivered the material. The company continues to be the sole supplier of maraging steel for Indian PSLVs and the HS-25 equivalent for ISRO's rockets.

Some other things—like the silica phenolic material used for making the throat of the nozzle—we had to do it with the resources at our disposal at VSSC. The throat, the connecting part between the combustion chamber and the upper part of the nozzle would experience the highest temperature during the firing, and this needed the composite material. REPLACE, a facility of VSSC in Vattiyoorkavu in Trivandrum, was asked to do this. REPLACE was an offshoot of a group working on fibre glass and composites used for making rocket nose cones and fins.

Interacting with me on behalf of REPLACE was Rajmohan, an argumentative and efficient engineer. His team worked tirelessly on the silica phenolic throat despite repeated failures—some of which led to my chiding Rajmohan who would argue back in full vigour, before promising to overcome the challenge and deliver the material.

After the Mahendragiri facility became operational—soon after the Vikas engine was successfully ground-tested at Vernon—we tested the throat by firing the engine several times. Most of the time, after half a minute, the throat would be ejected out of the nozzle. This became so frequent a failure that some at the test site would mock: 'It is forty seconds already. Why has the throat not come out?'

Rajmohan just would not give up. After having developed the material that can withstand the high temperature, when the throat was still not a success, the failure analysis team concluded that it was being pushed out because of its seating—a kind of groove or ridge on which the throat rested—which was giving way due to charring during the firing of the engine. In a few months, Rajmohan's team found the answer, and delivered the silica phenolic throat, which was used in the first flight of PSLV in 1993.

All this while, the Gowarikar-Muthunayagam war raged on. As the head of APSU, which worked on small control rockets and flow components, Muthunayagam did not have to report to Gowarikar, the VSSC director; but some of the liquid propulsion system work still came under VSSC. For this, too, Muthunayagam refused to see eye-to-eye with Gowarikar.

'You go ask him,' Muthunayagam would tell me whenever I approached him to take forward the Vikas project as part of the PSLV project.

After taking over as the VSSC director, Gowarikar had made goodwill visits to everyone, including Muthunayagam. This made me think that Gowarikar, now as the head of a prestigious institution, would have matured enough not to nurse a grudge against me. I was terribly wrong. Gowarikar opened an old chapter when I went to him with a request to retain the Vernon team so that we can develop the liquid propulsion engine without a hitch. The Vernon team, which was put together from different sections within VSSC, was by now back home and slowly disintegrating as they were called back to their previous assignments.

To my request, Gowarikar said: 'Remember, you never recruited anyone from my team (solid propulsion) when you set out for Vernon.'

I wouldn't have been surprised to hear such a thing from Gowarikar, the unit head; but when it came from Gowarikar, the VSSC director, I was a bit taken aback. Now I was convinced that Gowarikar would remain the old fox. The VSSC director was still thinking about 'his team', which was but a unit under the centre. I knew it is going to be a long haul, but with my constant nagging of Dhawan, I managed to hold on to a core team that continued with the making of the Vikas engine till it became a project and a part of PSLV.

By now my team was doing two things: putting together a Vikas engine using the original parts that went into the making of the French Viking engine; and indigenisation of materials and processes so that we can make more engines once we successfully tested the first one. Parallel to the two activities went another significant exercise: to re-decipher, analyse and plug holes in the 'Vernon Document'.

This was but a compilation of reports our team had been sending to India while working in SEP, Vernon. Right from 1975 when we landed in Vernon, this exercise had begun. Our scientists would return from work every evening to one of the apartments that served as our office for a daily discussion and review. We had charted out ten phases of the Vernon project, starting from identification of sub-systems, detailed design and materials to fabrication, assembly, testing and integration of the stage.

Starting from a system, say the gas generator, our scientists would get down to sub-systems like injectors, regulators, combustion chamber and feed lines. We would then go down to each of the three types of regulators which had sub-sub-systems, such as 'O' rings, cylinders and pistons. An 'O' ring is a single component, and the breaking-down process ends there. If the cylinder has many parts, we go further dissecting to the last part.

Our scientists meticulously noted down every such single component of the Viking-Vikas engine. As we proceeded hand-in-hand with the French scientists, whose attitude towards us changed from curiosity and indifference to camaraderie and confidence, the Vernon Document gained muscle with details of materials, their behaviour, design methodology and fabrication process.

Some parts of this exercise, though elaborate and time-consuming, were easy; but some like the manufacturing process left us at dead-ends. These unanswered questions were documented as meticulously as the rest of the understood portions. Compiling the daily reports from team members, and the papers the SEP administration gave us (all in French), I maintained three copies of the ever-expanding Vernon Document. After translating to English, one was sent to India through the diplomatic mail, and a backup team headed by T P Rangamani reviewed them, asked for clarifications, updated them and filed them away for posterity. The second one was sent raw, in French. The third one I kept. This document where we discussed in the minutest of detail every component, down to the nuts and bolts, remains a Bible for anyone working on PSLV or GSLV.

Now, as I grappled with the Gowarikar-Muthunayagam fight while continuing to develop the Vikas engine, the Vernon Document was dusted and developed upon, to plug the holes and crack the unanswered questions through indigenisation of materials and fabrication. That is where MIDHANI after much persuasion, delivered.

✸ ✸ ✸

Given that I was caught between an indifferent boss and a scheming super boss between 1979 and 1983, I considered it quite a feat to have put together the Vikas engine. Of course, this wouldn't have been possible without Dhawan having faith in me.

ISRO had by now tasted success of its first Satellite Launch Vehicle, SLV-3. For Kalam, this was the fruition of some long, hard labour and Dhawan's unflinching trust in him. The first flight of SLV-3 on 10 August 1979 was a failure. The next launch, carrying Rohini RS-1 satellite on 18 July 1980 was a success. The aftermath of these two launches were to become a subject of Kalam's speeches in the later years when he scaled new heights and went on to become the President of India.

Kalam would recollect these days in his speeches and interviews, extolling the virtues of a leader. On 10 August 1979, media from across the world had gathered at the Sriharikota spaceport for a press meet soon after the scheduled launch early morning. Moments after the rocket plunged into the Bay of Bengal due to a valve failure, Dhawan addressed the media, owning up for the failure and promising that his team would soon be successful. After the successful launch of SLV-3, however, Dhawan asked Kalam to address the press.

'Own up the team's failure, let the team take the credit for the success—that was Dhawan,' Kalam would say.

Soon Kalam became group director, aerodynamics and was moved to the ISRO headquarters as director, launch vehicles. From there, in 1982, Kalam went back to where he came from—the Defence Research and Development Organisation (DRDO) —to earn the name 'India's missile man.'

SLV-3 had another failure on 31 May 1981, and we wound up SLV-3 with another successful launch, on 17 April 1983. Now the focus was on

PSLV, and I was the project director for the second and fourth stages of the rocket. Powering the second stage would be my pet engine Vikas. Just when I was considering myself lucky, towards the end of September 1983 Gowarikar dropped a bomb.

One morning Muthunayagam called me into his room and gave me a letter. It said I have been transferred to the programme planning and evaluation group with effect from 3 October 1983. If the quality control group was then considered a dump yard, the programme planning and evaluation group was virtually a graveyard. We had learned in Vernon that such groups are vital in planning and execution of any project, but things hadn't moved forward in India, and these groups were still considered home for the inefficient and those who the bosses just didn't like.

Muthunayagam stated the obvious: Gowarikar didn't want me in the propulsion group anymore. Not surprisingly, Muthunayagam didn't protest my transfer. And I had to fight another battle for myself. I went to Gowarikar. There was no time to beat around the bush here.

'Why did you transfer me?' I asked.

Gowarikar kept a calm face. 'It's a routine thing,' he said. 'For a while we have been discussing about rotating people in different groups.'

It was a typical bureaucratic tactic. When there is no reason or logic for a decision, call it routine. There was no point arguing with this man, at least for now. I wrote to Dhawan. When there was no reply for a couple of weeks, I went to the ISRO headquarters in Bangalore.

I asked Dhawan the same question.

I knew Dhawan had always been fair to me, but he had to be fair with procedures too. He said it was the centre director's prerogative to transfer anyone.

'If you think it was unfair, you have to ask the director,' he said.

I told him I had approached Gowarikar before coming to him. 'You have to give me a reason,' I insisted.

'Listen Nambi,' Dhawan sighed. 'Again, the reason should be given by the director. Now go back to him.'

I did. But when Gowarikar refused to give a reason, in protest I went on leave.

For me, as it was for many of my colleagues, staying away from work for long was tortuous. I had taken just one day leave for my marriage.

My mother had died on a Wednesday (23 November 1966), and I was back at my desk after a couple of days. Kalam and a few colleagues who visited my house on Saturday to offer condolences didn't find me at home—I was at work.

This time I kept away from work frequently, over many months, all the while hoping that Dhawan would do something to get me back to the propulsion team. And then, to my shock, I learned that Gowarikar had got Dhawan's approval before transferring me, for which he had shown a reason. This reason remained unknown to me, but I was sure that if it had to get Dhawan's approval, it had to be serious. I couldn't do this silent protest any longer; soon I found myself at Dhawan's office.

'Sir,' I started. 'Just this: was this done with your approval?'

'Nambi, I told you, it is the director's prerogative to transfer you,' Dhawan replied.

'Sorry, that's not the answer to my question. I asked if you approved it. Give me a yes or no.'

'Yes,' Dhawan said, looking into my eyes.

'Why?'

'Well, there was a corruption charge against you.'

'What was the corruption charge?

'That I don't know.'

Dhawan explained that there was a charge against me, and that he didn't ask for details, and there was no inquiry; and that the director was well within his powers to transfer me to keep me away from such positions where the charge would get aggravated. Fair enough. It was time to get back to Gowarikar.

This time I didn't allow him to wriggle out so easily though he remained evasive. He indicated that there were some charges, he wasn't clear from who, and that there was corruption in the procurement of some furniture for ISRO's Mahendragiri ground testing facility, which came under the Liquid Propulsion Systems Group of which I was the deputy director.

Gowarikar wouldn't give me more details, but as I started speaking to more people involved in the purchase of furniture, the plot started becoming clearer to me.

As the chairman of the purchase committee for the Mahendragiri project, I had placed orders with Godrej for some furniture for the new facility. ISRO had a rate contract with Godrej, which meant the company had to provide us materials at a mutually agreed cost through the year. This purchase came under the rate contract.

Two months after the orders were placed, the local distributor, a man called Chittaranjan Das, came to me complaining that our stores department was not taking delivery of the furniture. Das said the consignment was taking up space in his godown, and he was losing money.

When I inquired with the store manager, he said since buildings were not yet ready at Mahendragiri, we could not take delivery.

'But that is being unfair to the distributor,' I said, ordering that the papers are cleared and delivery taken immediately.

Das later told me that the store manager approached him with the offer to take delivery of the furniture if paid a bribe. The distributor told the manager that he knew me personally and he would report this to me. Knowing my temper, the manager knew he would lose his job.

In his desperation, the store manager told P M Nair, the administrative head, that I was fast-tracking delivery of furniture because I had taken a bribe from the distributor.

Nair, who had a grudge against me from a previous incident when I exposed his mishandling of an ISRO drivers' strike, readily forwarded the complaint to Gowarikar, who in turn looked at me as his number one enemy Muthunayagam's deputy. Gowarikar transferred me.

Now that I was clear about the conspiracy, and my conscience, I went back to Dhawan.

'Please do me a favour,' I told Dhawan. 'Order an investigation into the furniture deal. And ensure that the inquiry report is ready in a month; you can't keep me on tenterhooks any longer.'

Dhawan agreed. To begin the investigation, the first thing needed was the letter Gowarikar had written to Dhawan, and Dhawan had signed, mentioning the furniture deal as the reason for my transfer. Dhawan called Gowarikar on phone, in my presence.

'Since you have cited a probable corruption in the furniture deal as the reason for Nambi, and now that he is contesting it, it's only fair that the matter be investigated,' Dhawan told Gowarikar. 'And yes, you have to get to the bottom of it in a month.'

On the assurance that the deal would be investigated and a decision taken within a month, I got back to work, in the programme planning and evaluation group.

A month passed by, but nothing happened. I went back to Gowarikar, and again to Dhawan. This time Dhawan had no reason to hesitate. In front of me, Dhawan called Gowarikar on the phone and asked for the paper in which Gowarikar had requested my transfer citing corruption charges. Gowarikar said he had already passed on the paper to David, Dhawan's personal assistant.

I could not help but say, at this juncture, that he would not have given the paper to David.

'Are you an astrologer?' asked Dhawan.

I told him that Gowarikar was trying to shunt me without an inquiry, and hence he would not produce the paper. Dhawan called up David who soon confirmed that Gowarikar had sent no such paper.

Dhawan called Gowarikar again, this time asking him to send a copy from his files. As soon as Dhawan kept the phone down, I told him Gowarikar would not send him a copy. A couple of weeks later, Gowarikar told Dhawan that he was not able to trace the paper and needed more time.

Dhawan lost his cool. He constituted an inquiry committee headed by T N Seshan. The committee found no wrong doing on my part. Dhawan apologized to me. My intention was not to make Dhawan feel bad, but expose Gowarikar.

Having done that, I was about to tell Dhawan that I wanted nothing more and wanted to quit when Dhawan spoke.

'If you insist on going back to the propulsion team, my conscience would not permit me to deny you that.' Dhawan was a bit emotional. 'But if you remain in Trivandrum, that man (Gowarikar) will gobble you up. I will bring you to the headquarters here in Bangalore, as my advisory staff.'

I gave it a serious thought. Dhawan was right. Irrespective of where I worked in VSSC, Gowarikar would victimise me with impunity. Though my heart was in developing the liquid propulsion engine, Dhawan's offer made sense in more ways than one: I could be away from direct harm from Gowarikar, being in Dhawan's inner circle came with some advantages—including having some fun at Gowarikar's expense. I chuckled at the thought.

By making up the furniture corruption story to settle personal scores with me, and later exposing himself to Dhawan, Gowarikar was harming his own chances of rising to the top post of the ISRO chairman. Dhawan never showed anger, but I knew he detested dishonest people. And Gowarikar had painted himself into a corner.

Years later, T N Seshan told me this was one of the incidents that contributed to Dhawan forming a not so flattering opinion about Gowarikar, and later handpicking U R Rao over Gowarikar for the top post. It's another matter that Rao had all the credentials to be the ISRO chairman, and he proved his mettle, too, but Gowarikar's Machiavellian ways proved to be his own undoing. I felt no sympathy for his plight when Dhawan passed on the mantle to U R Rao in 1984.

I accepted Dhawan's offer and joined the headquarters on 29 September 1984. Dhawan surrounded himself with a few of his handpicked men who formed his secretariat. Prominent among them were Siddharth and Y S Rajan. I had known Rajan as the PRL scientist who used to visit Trivandrum on projects. It was using a vacuum pump that Rajan gave that I ran the bell jar experiment that almost killed Kalam.

Siddharth was another icon of efficiency. His questions sounded almost accusative; soon you would realise that it was his style of extracting the exact answer. During relatively free hours I would walk into Siddharth's room and share our scientific dreams. Siddharth developed a severe skin problem which made him a recluse. He would not meet anyone, but I would still spend time with him, as if he had no such problem. He underwent a rigorous therapy and was cured of the disorder.

Years later, when I was reinstated at the ISRO headquarters after being acquitted in the spy case, Siddharth came and hugged me.

'You should show them who you are,' he said. 'Make sure those fellows are punished.'

Being the chairman's advisor was a great elevation, but I was sure that I have to go back to Vikas engine. But as long I was here, with the additional responsibility to be the ISRO chairman's liaison officer, I would make life a little difficult for not just Gowarikar, but Muthunayagam too.

Sample this communication I sent to them. "The chairman desires an immediate report on the status of the binder VSSC is working on."

As for Muthunayagam, I bombarded him with questions about turbine motors.

The two men would have been gritting their teeth, but they had no option, but to send the reports that the chairman frequently 'desired' to see. And, on receiving their reports, I would seek a clarification. And another.

This went on for a few months, and I realised that I was not enjoying the game anymore. And the opportunity came to go back to Vikas engine as U R Rao took over as the ISRO chairman. 'You belong to VSSC,' Rao told me. 'Go fulfil your dream.'

Rao called up Gowarikar. 'I am sending Nambi back to VSSC. I have great faith in him. Hope you too will have.'

The message was clear: Don't meddle with me.

So here I was on 18 February 1985, back where I belonged, doing what I loved doing. Vikas was now part of the PSLV project. I was made the project director of the second and fourth stages (PS2 and PS4) of PSLV. Vikas, my team's tribute to Vikram Sarabhai, would soon roar to life.

CHAPTER 19

ANTONY WILL KILL AGAIN

'I have been praying to God to keep him alive till I get out.'

I was slowly getting used to the routine at Viyyur jail, though sleep continued to elude me. Around 6 am, we—Sasi, Chandra, Sharma and I—were let out of our cells for our bath. We were not allowed to mingle with the other prisoners, so we had to get back our cells by 6.15 am, before the others can be let out.

At 8 am, breakfast was served on the verandah—again, before or after the others had it. The food was not bad—idli, dosa or wheat balls for breakfast. Almost every day there came a banana with the breakfast. Lunch, served between 12 pm and 1 pm was mostly rice and a curry. The menu had non-vegetarian food four days a week: one day chicken, two days of fish and one day of mutton or beef.

One of the first things Sasi asked me after coming to prison was whether I was a vegetarian. I was not, but knowing that he was eyeing my share of non-vegetarian prison food, I happily offered him. After twenty-seven days in the prison, when Sasi was out on bail, many told him that he had put on weight. He promptly thanked me for all that chicken and mutton I sacrificed for him.

A few convicts were given the job to cook rice, which they did in a cauldron in the open. Some others would serve food, each one had to wash his steel plate and cup. One of the inmates who served rice was a young man, probably in his early twenties. He had no expression on his face, but his boyish face effused calm. He spoke to nobody. He appeared to be in perpetual meditation.

Dinner, which I rarely had, was served around 8 pm. I survived mostly on bananas and biscuits that some kind prison employees gave me. Antony, a convict awaiting release after a twelve-year jail term, was assigned the duty of locking each one's cell at the end of the day. After he is done with all others, he would get into his cell and lock his own cell before throwing out the key, which would be collected by a prison staff. That was the saddest thing to watch.

I was allowed to keep some books which I tried to read till 10 pm, when the lone bulb in the cell would be switched off. I had also got permission to keep a pen and a diary. I scrawled on this diary the daily happenings, my suspicions about the conspiracy that was keeping me in jail. One day a prison staff took away my diary, saying a senior officer wanted to read it. It never came back. Later I realised that they must have allowed me to keep the diary thinking that I would scribble some 'confessions' that someone was waiting for.

After lights out, I would struggle to sleep. A good three hours before dawn I would be wide awake, staring into the darkness, awaiting the first tinge of light that would creep in through the iron bars. Soon, Antony would be there to unlock the cell.

Antony must have got here when was in his early twenties. Having been a prisoner of good behavior for so many years, he was to be released in a few months. The Indian judicial system made allowances for such prisoners though they were technically sentenced for life.

Going by his demeanour, it was difficult to believe that Antony must have killed someone. Unable to resist my curiosity, one day I asked him if he did.

'Yes, I hacked him sixteen times,' he said.

'Why?'

'I was made to kill. I had no rivalry with the man I killed, but someone made me kill him.'

And then Antony shocked me.

'Sir, I am happy that I am being released soon, but I will be back after killing the man who made me a murderer.'

'Antony, you are young, you have a life ahead,' I tried to reason.

'No sir, nothing can change my resolve. I have to kill him and get back here. Nothing else matters. I have been praying to God to keep him alive till I get out.'

He said he did not want to talk anything more about himself.

THE MAKING OF MAHENDRAGIRI

'You can't have the brain in Trivandrum and the hands in Balasore.'

My transfer and the struggle before getting back to the Liquid Propulsion Systems Centre (LPSC) took away not just sixteen months from my association with the Vikas engine and PSLV project, it also came in the midst of our setting up an integrated test facility in Mahendragiri. As the LPSC deputy director, I was hands-on with the Mahendragiri project, starting before my transfer and completing ten months after my return.

The need for a facility to ground test rocket engines and stages occurred to us while putting together the 60-tonne Vikas engine in 1980; before that the largest rocket engine we made was a three-tonner. We could take the first Vikas engine to Vernon for the test, but if we were to make many more engines—which we were sure of doing—we needed an integrated test complex in India.

A ground test involves virtually as much preparation and operation as a rocket launch. Here, we would be testing different components of the engine for different durations to see if all the parameters—thrust, pressure, temperature, specific impulse and many more—are normal so that the engine performs as per our expectation.

An integrated test complex should have test facilities to test components—engine, gas generator, turbo pump—separately and together as a stage. Experimenting that we were so far with small rockets, we neither had the need nor knowledge to set up an integrated test complex. The one we had at Sriharikota was for testing solid propulsion engines of up to 3-tonne thrust. Now, with the mighty 60-tonne Vikas in the making, we needed it.

As for the knowledge, our team in Vernon had acquired the expertise to establish a test complex, though the primary assignment there was putting together the liquid propulsion engine. SEP Vernon had two test stands, one to test the single engine and another, a bigger one, to test a four-engine configuration, which continues to be the first stage of some Arianne vehicles.

We had witnessed several ground firing tests during our stay since 1974, and had closely studied their setting up and functioning. During the tests, as per the protocol, only those designated are allowed in the control room—a small building barely 50 m from the test stand. From there, we would peep through a slit of a window to see with naked eyes the mighty firing of the engine that literally shook the earth while data analysts remained glued to the computers to study the parameters of the firing.

On our return to India, we had the know-how and the 'know-why' to set up a test complex, but that was not all. Compared to the solid propulsion engine test facility called STEX in Sriharikota, a liquid engine test complex came with a much higher risk, primarily because it involved handling of chemicals like UDMH (unsymmetrical dimethyl hydrazine), which is used as the fuel for the engine, and N2O4 (nitrogen tetroxide) used as the oxidizer. UDMH is carcinogenic; N2O4 is equally toxic. In fact, workers were not allowed to deal with these chemicals for a long period—we kept changing them. And we had been wiser by an incident in which a worker fainted after leaning over a much less dangerous red fuming nitric acid (RFNA) tank.

A test complex needed huge space, and there should be no habitation within a radius of at least 3 km. And a test stand is only one part of the facility, which needs space for storing fuel and oxidizer, control rooms, data analysis centres and administrative and residential blocks. This meant hundreds of acres.

VSSC, situated in the capital city of Kerala, was ruled out. Some suggested we set up the test facility at Sriharikota, where ISRO had 26,000 acres of land. We already had the solid propellant test stand there, but I was against setting up the new facility because it didn't make safety sense to do firing at a site close to our launch pads. An accident at the test facility could jeopardize our launch facility. Such is the importance other spacefaring nations give their launch pads that they are not just supremely protected and maintained, there is always a second or third pad at a distant location. It beats me even today why India has not set up a back-up launch pad outside Sriharikota. (Both the pads now are close to each other, in Sriharikota.)

These people—evidently those who were not keen on liquid propulsion system—pushed for Sriharikota as the site so much that Dhawan was considering the suggestion. When I kept opposing, Dhawan told me that it makes sense to have it in Sriharikota because anyway there are going to be propellant storage tanks there. I told him those near the launch site would store only one and a half times the propellant needed for a launch, while a test complex will store propellant needed for maybe five tests. Also, we can't have the brain in Trivandrum and the muscle in Balasore. The facilities have to be co-located. In that case, I said, you shift the entire facility to Sriharikota. Dhawan smiled. He knew it was not possible, and would lead to much public and media outcry.

A Malayalam daily, incidentally, wrote a story saying I was trying to take away the space facility from Kerala to Andhra. That did it.

Not many know that Sriharikota itself was not ISRO's first choice for a launch pad. It was one of the few sites identified by senior ISRO scientist R M Vasagam, another being a place south of Nagapattinam. Both were in Tamil Nadu. For launching polar satellites, it was clear to us, our launch pad has to be on the eastern coast. Launching the rocket along the spin of the earth, it gave a huge advantage of cost; also by manouevring the rocket to the south after its initial eastward journey, we avoid flying over any landmass. The coastline of Kanyakumari was considered in the late 1960s, but a terrible mishandling by the government of Tamil Nadu, and a timely pitch by Andhra Pradesh, made Sriharikota happen.

Tamil Nadu Chief Minister C N Annadurai was to participate in a discussion with Sarabhai and a few scientists and officials over the identification of a site from a shortlist proposed by Vikram Sarabhai. Annadurai could not attend the meeting because of severe shoulder pain, and he deputed Mathiyazhagan, one of his ministers, for the meeting. Sarabhai was kept waiting, and after sometime, the minister was 'brought' to the meeting—with a few holding him from falling. The politician irritated Sarabhai no end with his impossible demands and incoherence. Much before the meeting got over, Sarabhai had decided Tamil Nadu is not the place to be.

Just then Andhra Pradesh made an offer virtually nobody could refuse. Take the 26,000 acre Sriharikota island, he told Sarabhai. With India's rocket launch pad coming up there, the Andhra Pradesh government must have realised that the sparsely inhabited place may see some development. There were a few fishing hamlets along the Bay of Bengal on one side of the island, which had a lagoon (Pulicat Lake) on the other side. Villagers on the inland side were also cooperative. ISRO had to lay a road across the lagoon to reach the island where now stands two launch pads and a few other facilities. Today, a rocket lifting off, spewing fire and smoke reflected on the Pulicat Lake, where migratory flamingoes come to roost is quite a sight.

Sriharikota, however, has one disadvantage. It is a cyclone-prone region. During October-November, when the northeast monsoon lashes the Andhra Pradesh and Tamil Nadu coast, planning a rocket launch is a precarious exercise. I have always felt the need for a launch pad outside Sriharikota, and this I tried hard while surveying land for the Mahendragiri project.

After Nagercoil was finalised, during one of my rounds of the district, I strayed into a couple of coastal hamlets called Panankulam and Chenankulam. The fishing hamlets together had not more than twenty-five families and a church. The sea was relatively shallow along a 10 km stretch of this place called Irukkanthurai, and hence it was not a favourite patch for fishermen. As the crow flies, it was about 15 km from the main gate of the Mahendragiri integrated test complex. It was ideal for a second launch site.

If launched from here, I calculated, a PSLV would save enough fuel to have a 30% additional payload. This is because we usually spend 30% of fuel to steer the rocket from its eastward path to a southward trajectory. It is called the dogleg manoeuvring. Imagine the tapering end of the Indian peninsula, and you get an idea of how a rocket going straight south from Nagercoil would be better than the one launched from Sriharikota which is some 750 km north. The only negative, if it is considered one, our rockets would then overfly Sri Lanka. But this would not be a problem as the island nation is a friendly country. After all, how many Chinese rockets overfly India without its permission!

I sold the alternative launch site idea to Satish Dhawan. After a preliminary survey, I told Dhawan that we may need just 3,000 acres in and around Irukkanthurai. I met the most influential person in the locality, the priest at the church. When we explained the compensation package for land acquisition, the priest and the community at large were happy. It, however, turned out to be an anticlimax when we took Dhawan to see the place. On our arrival, the villagers garlanded Dhawan and fell at his feet, pleading that they may not be moved out.

I went to the priest who, too, had suddenly had a volte face. Later I learnt that a group doing illicit brewing of liquor in Irukkanthurai had manufactured fear and opposition in the hamlets. But when the friendly priest suddenly turned against the project remains a mystery to me. Whatever be the reason, my plan for an alternative launch site was shelved.

Identifying Mahendragiri for the integrated test complex was not easy, either. I, as the deputy director of the liquid propulsion centre (by then a separate entity at Valiyamala in Trivandrum), and the leader of the Vikas engine project, wanted the facility as close to the liquid propulsion activities in Trivandrum. But, besides the space constraints, several other things proved to be impediments. For one, the high water table Kerala is known for. A leak of UDMH may seep into the water table, geologists told us. The very thought sent shivers down spines.

Soon, a committee was constituted to identify a suitable place to set up India's first integrated liquid propulsion test complex. Among the shortlisted places were Kottur, Kallada and Kannur in kerala, Tirupati, and Chandrayangutta in Andhra Pradesh, Puri and Balasore in Orissa, Mahendragiri and Vellore in Tamil Nadu, and Kutch in Gujarat.

Kutch was rejected in the initial screening for its proximity to the Pakistan border. Kallada, not too far from Trivandrum, was also taken off the list because of the presence of a dam that stored water for drinking; many other places were also ruled out because of environmental factors and proximity to thickly populated areas.

While in a few places there was opposition from environment groups and locals, ironically, in Kerala, there was a reverse argument—that I was trying to take away the proposed facility out of Kerala. Some of the Malayalam newspapers came up with the 'investigative report' that both Muthunayagam, the liquid propulsion centre chief and me, his deputy were from Tamil Nadu, and hence we wanted the project in that state. Little did they know that my father had lived in Kerala, and I did it most of my life. And most of the parts now in southern Tamil Nadu were then in Kerala, which meant my forefathers considered both the states their home. Anyway, these were things I didn't have time or inclination to educate the media about.

But when Kerala politicians echoed these arguments, I presented myself to a gathering of law makers and influential people.

'I want this as close to Trivandrum,' I said, 'not because of any love for any state, but I feel it should be close to our parent body of VSSC here.'

The audience nodded.

'Now, here are the conditions: the complex will be handling highly toxic substances and doing tests that have a nominal risk of causing explosions. We will need hundreds of acres of land, and there should be no habitation in the radius of several kilometers of the facility. And yes, there should not be any drinking water sources in the vicinity because the fuel we use is cancer causing, and there will be many more toxic substances being handled at the facility.'

I did not have to speak anymore; there was unanimity that the project can go out of Kerala.

The selection team visited all the shortlisted sites, and Balasore and Mahendragiri emerged as most favoured. Balasore was scarcely populated and comprised mostly non-agriculture land; it was secluded and safe. Mahendragiri was on the eastern foothills of the tail-end of the Western Ghats, much greener than Balasore. A place called Podigai, by a hill south of the Mahendragiri hill looked ideal for the test stand, but there were some villages which need to be evacuated. I favoured Mahendragiri for its proximity to Trivandrum. Balasore was more than 2,000 km away, Mahendragiri a little more than 100 km.

'Balasore is an ideal place for carrying out tests, but it is too far from VSSC and the propulsion centre,' I said. 'You can't have the brain in Trivandrum and the hands in Balasore.'

Today, when technology has enabled us to work in tandem sitting in different continents, this argument may sound silly, but in those days it was indeed tough to coordinate between two centres so apart. Besides the difficulty in transporting materials across the distance, testing, too, needed frequent shuttling between the two places. There are some 300 parameters that need to be monitored and communicated between the centres, and in those days the landline was the fastest mode of communication.

Some parameters, during the test, may not conform to the ideal, but it is virtually impossible to launch a rocket with all the parameters of all the systems reporting ideal performance. The accepted practice is that even if some parameters of a sub-sub-system are not accurate, and if the end system works within the margin of accuracy and consistency, the system is approved. This, however, involved much to-and-fro communication and visits by the quality control team, and paper work by the non-conformance board. So, Mahendragiri it would be.

The positive outcome of our Balasore survey was the establishment of the integrated missile test range later in 1989. Chandipur-on-sea in Balasore district is, today, India's only test launch pad from where Agni, Prithvi and all other missiles take off.

Calling it the Mahendragiri test complex is a misnomer. And this cost us some bad publicity from some overzealous environmentalists, which we will come to later. The test complex today stands by the valley of the Podigai hill, south of Mahendragiri, north of which stood the Kadukkaraithodu. The forest between Mahendragiri and Kadukkaraithodu was home to the endangered lion-tailed monkey, which became a subject for a baseless, short campaign against the test complex.

Once the ISRO board approved Mahendragiri (let's call it that, for that's the name it is known by), our job was cut out. We had to acquire some 7,000 acres, of which 600 acres were in private hands and the rest government forest land that spread across the two south Tamil Nadu districts of Tirunelveli and Kanyakumari. This was not an easy task as taking over private property was riddled with legal hassles, and getting forest land transferred meant navigating bureaucratic rigmaroles.

The Tirunelveli collector, Shanmugham, showed great interest in the project, even trekking the hills with us several times for surveys and talks with villagers. He put the revenue divisional officer and two tahsildars at my disposal. Whenever the tahsildars raised opposition, I asked them to put it on paper. Most of the times, they did not persist, as there was no case beyond some personal reasons.

The Kanyakumari officials tried to delay things. I asked one of the revenue officials why they were not as cooperative with ISRO as their Tirunelveli counterparts. He said that the district authorities were proud to have an ISRO facility, but they thought all credit would go to Tirunelveli district since the main entrance of the test complex was from Tirunelveli district, though major tracts of land fell on the Kanyakumari side. So much for bureaucratic pride!

Acquiring the forest land was not much of a problem though it involved multiple clearances, but we had to do it without offending the neighbouring villagers. There were two sections of villagers who were concerned. One was involved in destroying the forest. Entering the forest in the name of collecting fallen twigs for firewood, they had been chopping and carting away full grown trees. The other group had a more noble purpose to visit the forest. There were a couple of temples in the woods, and the villagers used to do puja once or twice a year. While we told the first group that there could be no more tree-cutting, we allowed the second group access to the temple for the puja. We would have to schedule the tests in such a way that there is no activity during the puja days, which was a small compromise we had to make to earn the goodwill of the local population.

And we got enough of it. By the entrance to the property, on the Tirunelveli side was a village called Panakudi. The MLA there, a man named Yusuf, helped us get local support. The project site was on the northeastern side of the tail end of the Western Ghats, and within the 3 km buffer radius of the proposed principal test stand stood Sivakamipuram, a village of barely fifteen families. The villagers were more than friendly. They received us with garlands and were willing to part with their land. These were poor families who were happy with what the government was offering them as compensation.

But the owner of a twenty-acre plot by the road to the project site refused to vacate. We learned that it belonged to someone close to a Congress MP. There were a few structures on the plot, and a board outside announced itself as 'Haldane Coconut Research Centre'. It was a complete farce, as nowhere in the vicinity was a coconut palm. We were convinced that the owner's intention was to hold on to the piece of land till its value peaks after the ISRO facility comes up.

This piece of land was not in the middle of our project site, but when everyone along the road to the test complex had vacated, I didn't want this one to be an exception. Moreover, if we planned an expansion later, it would prove an impediment. I told Seshan this. After a few days, Seshan got back to me, and his response surprised me.

'Leave them alone,' he said.

I have known Seshan as a relentless fighter. Here there was no illegality on the part of the land owner, but Seshan didn't want to upset someone even if it was to further the interests of ISRO and the Government of India.

Another local heavyweight who tried to stay put in the test complex vicinity was not as lucky. Kurien, a Keralite who held some fifty acres on the western side of the Ghats, had set up a waste rubber processing unit that gave out unbearable stench. He had to be moved out. Seshan, this time too, was not enthusiastic.

'Why do you want to evict the waste rubber processing plant when it is on the other side of the hill,' Seshan asked.

I told him the smell was unbearable and our workers and scientists have to wear masks at work.

'We can acquire the land if we need it, but the smell as a reason doesn't cut ice,' said Seshan.

I changed tact.

'We need the land.'

'For what?'

'For a cryogenic propulsion plant,' I lied.

'But you don't have a cryogenic engine,' Seshan retorted.

'What do we do when we have one? We can't create a hill and a valley so conducive for the plant. When we have the opportunity, we have to make the most of it. And yes, we will soon be testing cryogenic engines.'

When I finished saying this, I realised that I was not lying, only thinking aloud. It is another matter that ISRO got into cryogenics in the early 1990s with me at the helm, after a two-decade delay caused by the ISRO spy case and the following dip in scientist morale, and successfully established the liquid hydrogen plant here. We still do it in Mahendragiri.

Seshan agreed.

I knew Kurien was so influential that he would get information of any move we made at the earliest stage and would preempt acquisition. We decided to act swift and silent. Seshan got the PMO to write a confidential letter to Tamil Nadu Chief Minister M G Ramachandran (MGR) saying the land has to be annexed to the ISRO facility, and the state has to do it immediately, treating it as a matter of national importance.

'National importance.' Those words carried weight—and some immunity while taking possession of the land in what could be called Operation Thunderstorm. MGR deputed a minister to provide all support, and assigned the Armed Reserve Police to accompany the district officials for the evacuation. Paper work was done in utmost secrecy, and even the district collectors were told about the operation only hours in advance, just to get the official concurrence.

And the timing was great. The officials with the Armed Reserve Police literally stormed the property on a Friday night, so that the land owner wouldn't be able to get an official stay since the next two days were government holidays. Before Kurien could reach the spot, the gate was sealed and up came a board that announced it was a government property.

Kurien was furious. I later learned that some high-level government officials close to him drove some sense into him. There is always scope for some legal remedy, they told him, but don't forget that the operation had the blessings of none less than the Prime Minister of India. He did not pursue the case. Obviously, the rubber baron's influence did not stretch to the Prime Minister's Office.

CHAPTER 20

THE PRISON WAYS

'A spy who peddles marijuana sounds heady.'

Once in three days, I was allowed visitors, and most of the times it was either my son Shankar or my sister's husband Arunachalam. I would listen to the tidbits of news he brought from home, mostly about my wife Meena who had not uttered a word since she fainted on the day I was taken away by the Vanchiyoor Police.

'Amma had some rice today, she was looking better,' Shankar would say.

I would remain motionless, mostly silent.

As days passed, I became more conversational. Shankar would reassure me that I would soon be out on bail, and be back home. The mention of bail only told me that I was still an accused. I wondered when I would be able to prove my innocence. But now I wanted to go home and be by Meena and our children. I wanted to give them the courage, and get some from them. I missed my family.

Sivanandan and the other employees at the prison made my life slightly easier, but I wondered during my long hours of solitude how convicts spend years away from their dear ones. Am I feeling so because I have done no wrong? Do repeat offenders and serial killers like Ripper feel no remorse and feel at home in prison?

Twice a week the prison staff would come for an inspection of our cells. It was more of a formality as we had nothing to keep in our cells, not even our clothes. Whatever you had—pen, spare clothes, ornaments—we had to deposit at the prison office before moving to the cell.

But this inspection, I was told, was a serious matter. Jail breaks and attacks were not rare in Kerala prisons. There have been tales of prisoners attacking each other or jail staff; a few making good their escape by tunneling their way to the yard and scaling the wall using a rope made of prison clothes. In most of these cases, it was an open secret, there was an insider hand.

In my cell, too, once in every three days a staff came and looked around. One day I asked him in half jest if I can help him get what he was searching for.

'Yeah,' he smirked. 'It will be helpful if you can get me a knife or some poison.'

I stopped joking with these guys after Sivanandan told me the dark side of these inspections. If a prisoner played too smart, the inspectors played dirty by planting marijuana in their cells. They would soon 'retrieve' or 'seize' the contraband and make a case against the prisoner.

This tool of blackmail worked with brutal efficiency against convicts at the fag end of their sentence. Getting caught with marijuana and facing another trial under the Narcotic Drugs and Psychotropic Substances Act of 1985 would significantly prolong their release. Some like Antony were nice with the prison staff, some others like Ripper cared two hoots.

Sasi was horrified every time the inspection happened. But I realised that his fear was not totally without reason. I told him not to panic since we neither had anything to hide nor we were at loggerheads with the prison officials. And anyway, a narcotics case would do no bigger harm.

If the case against us stood, we could be sentenced to fourteen years in jail for breach of the Official Secrets Act. A ganja case would have a much lesser sentence that would run concurrently.

'A spy who peddles marijuana sounds heady,' I joked.

Sasi, however, had his reasons to be scared. The investigators had already filed a second case against Sasi, with the rest of us as the co-accused, to keep us in custody even if we got bail in the ISRO spy case. This second case accused Sasi of amassing wealth that was disproportionate to his known sources of income. The rest were accused of helping him amass that wealth.

My feelings for Sasi had seesawed repeatedly. When I got arrested I hated him for landing me in this mess. When the IB tortured me based on Sasi's confession, I was in mood to land a punch on his nose. But now, after coming to Viyyur, I had understood him, and the others, better. After all, we were all victims of a common conspiracy. I might not have agreed to 'confess' under duress, but why should I expect Sasi, Chandra and the others to have such a high endurance level?

According to the ignorant, scheming IB sleuths, Sasi and I had worked in tandem to smuggle out the rocket drawings from ISRO to hand it over to Pakistan through the Maldivian women. Some IB men's fertile imagination had given rise to even such stories where Sasi and I have gone with the Maldivian women to some ISRO facilities and on pleasure trips.

The truth was that Sasi and I started sharing even a joke, mostly at the expense of Chandra, only after being sent to Viyyur prison. Though we worked on the same campus in Trivandrum, we were never close friends.

In fact, our earlier interactions, including the first encounter, were bitter. Our paths crossed first, literally, on way to ISRO's VSSC campus in Trivandrum. I was on my scooter when the driver of a car kept honking from behind, trying to overtake me. Blame it on young age, I went full throttle ahead, not allowing the car to outrun me. On reaching the VSSC gate, I stopped the scooter and stared at the man in the car. We had a little fracas. I did not know who he was, not even the fact that he worked with VSSC.

It was a bit embarrassing when we came face to face the next time at work, but we got over it. Work brought us together briefly, now and then, but friction remained between us. When Satish Dhawan made me the chairman of a committee that would decide on the interchangeability of the segments of SLV-3, Sasi, who was junior to me, but was working in a different department, made a presentation. I found his premise weak, and opposed his suggestion.

'You are not a fabrication expert,' Sasi shot at me.

'Go tell that to Dhawan who put me in this chair.'

End of conversation. Sasi's proposal was rejected.

Common friends and colleagues told me that it was good that Sasi and I did not work in the same unit, for it would mean constant scuffles. I had a bad temper; Sasi had a knack of picking fights with just anyone. Working on different projects, however, we managed to maintain truce.

At a meeting of Viking engine after the first PSLV launch in 1993, Sasi had a difference of opinion with an IAS officer named Sengupta, who was a joint secretary at the department of space. Sengupta had suggested that Sasi would not understand the financial implication of a proposal we were discussing. Sasi lost his cool.

'Yes, I don't know the financial implication,' he said. 'And you, Mr Sengupta, don't understand a damn thing about engineering.'

Sengupta was to nurse this insult for some time to come. The next year, when police came knocking at Sasi's door after Mariyam Rasheeda's arrest in October 1994, Sengupta was instrumental in transferring Sasi to the Satellite Application Centre (SAC), Ahmedabad. This amounted to ISRO conceding that its scientist could have done something wrong. It also reflects on the poor judgment of R Kasturirangan, the ISRO chairman.

Curiously, former IB Joint Director M K Dhar, who was instrumental in propounding the ISRO spy story, mentions in his book *Open Secrets* about a 'Bangalore-based joint secretary of the department of space, who happened to be a Bengali,' visiting him to appreciate the progress of the investigation into the ISRO spy case.

It was during the indigenisation drive after the successful ground test of Vikas in 1985 that I established a functional rapport with Sasi. When we had to get a cobalt alloy made by MIDHANI in Hyderabad, I had taken help from Sasi who was already interacting the company on behalf of Abdul Kalam to get maraging steel for SLV-3, which was flown successfully in July 1980.

Though we never became close friends, I started seeing Sasi with some respect after he brought around MIDHANI to work for us. Sasi should be credited with bringing together scores of private industries to work for ISRO. Once, when getting the fourth stage engine's columbium nozzle fabricated for PSLV proved difficult, it was Sasi who came with a breakthrough. He discovered a small factory somewhere, which could do the tricky job for us. But the engineer there refused to part with the process. Finally, Sasi got it out of him, reciprocating by making the small-scale industry an ISRO sub-contractor.

Here in Viyyur prison, we were back to reminiscing our association, which went through a few highs and many lows. After a few cell inspections, Sasi's fear of being implicated in a marijuana case was fading. But every time the inspectors came, he stood in reverence, his heart in his mouth. The prison staff, too, had understood by now that we are a bunch of harmless, even meek, men not good at smuggling ganja or trying a jailbreak.

All that changed, however, suddenly with a rumour that Pakistan was planning to airdrop its commandoes in Viyyur jail to rescue me and the other accused in the ISRO spy case.

HOW ISRO TURNED A HILL GREEN

'The peacocks are gone.'

Once the land acquisition was over, we moved a few men to set up an office in Nagercoil and start the process of construction and moving machinery to Mahendragiri. D Subramanian, an instrumentation expert who was part of the Vernon team, was on the forefront of these activities. DS, as we called Subramanian, was a master of logistics management. When it came to engineering, DS's skills extended beyond his core competence of instrumentation.

While working in Vernon, he was primarily in charge of installing transducers in several systems of the rocket engine to gauge different parameters. But he surprised us all with his versatility when we were preparing for the Vikas ground test at SEP, Vernon. The SEP protocol had it that everything right from the smallest component of the engine we put together should be in conformance with what they tested on their campus.

Going by the specifications, the nozzle divergent of the engine should have a zirconium oxide coating; ours did not have it. We had seen it in Vernon how SEP would do it, but we had never done it ourselves. Giving a component a coating may sound a simple task, but making a microscopically uniform coating of the material over a flaring nozzle took some practice to perfect. It involved rotating the nozzle, and at the same time moving it forward and backward. The speed of the rotation and the lateral movement had to be accurate to ensure an even coating. DS did for us in a couple of months what the French must have taken years to perfect.

As work began on the Mahendragiri project, an English magazine published a story saying ISRO's integrated test complex would spell the end of the endangered lion-tailed monkey in Mahendragiri. It was partly our mistake identifying the place as Mahendragiri when the test stand was at Podigai, a hill south of Mahendragiri. The lion-tailed monkeys were found beyond Mahendragiri, towards the Kadukkaraithodu Hill, which was further north. I arranged a visit for the journalist from the magazine who was soon convinced that no monkey would be unhappy with our test facility.

Those who cried wolf about ISRO causing environmental degradation in Mahendragiri were soon silenced—not by any reaction from us, but by some proactive afforestation. ISRO taking over the forest land facilitated natural regeneration of the forest, now that the villagers were not entering the area. A couple of our engineers, Chandran and Thangaraj, who were passionate and knowledgeable about flora and fauna were given, besides their scientific assignment, the responsibility of overseeing an afforestation programme.

I realised there were no coconut palms in the vicinity (even though the Haldane Coconut Research Centre was very much there). In Trivandrum, we were used to coconut palms. Besides their soothing presence, they yielded a steady supply of coconuts to the VSSC canteen in Trivandrum so that they could keep the food price nominal. I wanted to replicate it in Mahendragiri, but there stood in the way a forest rule that prohibited introduction of fruit-bearing trees into forest land. Blame it on my ignorance on environmental matters, I never understood the logic that banned the introduction of only fruit-bearing trees while it did not stop planting of any other species, which could well be more invasive in nature.

There was nobody stopping me from doing the coconut planting, but just that I was aware of the rule. I decided to take the risk and assigned Thangaraj to get 5,000 coconut palms planted on the campus. More than a thousand of them grew up robust. Along with them, those from the three lakh saplings which grew to become trees formed a new canopy for the campus.

Those who have been flying down from the direction of Chennai to Trivandrum would know—if they looked at the right spot before landing—how Mahendragiri, which once looked like a patch of brown and sparse green at the tail end of the Western Ghats, is now a tuft of lush green. Dhawan, a nature lover who learned the nomenclature of virtually every tree in Mahendragiri from his botanist wife, would appreciate us every time he peeped out of the aircraft window after taking off from Trivandrum.

The greenery came with its share of animals. We were all for preserving the biodiversity, but snakes and leopards started giving us the creeps. Leopard sightings were not rare, snakes were aplenty. In the cold nights, especially when it rained, the slithery creatures took refuge in a tunnel we had dug to draw cables from the test stand to the instrumentation building, which was at an elevation, about 150 m away from the stand. There were instances of our workers pulling at a snake, mistaking it for a cable, and having a narrow escape from the hissing serpents.

Once I was travelling uphill in an open jeep with my left leg resting on the vehicle's side step. As the jeep was slowly taking a right turn, a long, black snake shot itself up from the ground. For a moment, it appeared to have been standing on its tail, its menacing hood at the level of my knee. I froze. After driving me to safety, the driver told me that it was a king cobra, probably the most venomous snake in the Western Ghats.

While discussing the increasing number of reptile encounters, someone had an idea. Why not bring in a predator that will take care of the snakes in a natural way? Peacocks, he explained, are known to keep the snake population under control. We learned that a TVS textile mill in the nearby Nanguneri town had been rearing peacocks for precisely the same reason. We decided to try it out.

We got five peacocks from the Nanguneri textile mill. Peacock being the national bird of India, it cannot be privately reared. But in this open forest, they could be brought in, but moving them from one location to another needed special permission from the union government. And ISRO had to give an undertaking that it would protect the bird from any human harm. Before setting them out in the open, we decided to keep the five peacocks in a large net enclosure. The peacocks soon became a major attraction to our scientists, workers and the occasional visitors from the government.

One morning, a worker came panting to me.

'They're gone!' he cried.

'What?' I did not understand what he meant.

'The peacocks are gone,' he repeated. 'Someone has cut open the nets and stolen the peacocks.'

I went to the enclosure. He was right, the net was damaged and someone had entered the enclosure. There were peacock feathers, suggesting some struggle. And then we saw the pug marks. A leopard had smelled out the new guests in Mahendragiri, and decided to have a sumptuous dinner. The bird we brought to prey on snakes, we realised, was the prey of leopards. The great food chain of nature.

Later we understood that the leopard could not feast on all the peacocks. It must have eaten one of them, the rest escaped into the nearby forests. Left to fend for itself, the peacocks must have adapted well. For, in a few years, peacocks, a species not seen in these parts, were often sighted. Today, visitors to Mahendragiri are likely to see the majestic bird in all its grandeur doing a rain dance. It may be debatable if the introduction of a species to a new habitat is advisable. Whatever be the ecologist's verdict, ISRO is responsible for the presence of the national bird in Mahendragiri and surroundings.

As for the leopards, we kept big cages around the campus, not to trap the animal, but for us to take shelter. The general instruction was, when you spot a leopard at close quarters, get into the cage, lock yourself from inside and wait till help comes or the leopard goes.

Dhawan was particular that no animal be harmed. Once a civet cat fell into a pit dug for erecting a pole. The ISRO chairman ensured that the animal was carefully pulled out and let out into its habitat. Dhawan's wife, a botanist, would go around the campus with our nature-lover scientist Thangaraj in tow. Her knowledge of taxonomy was so great, Thangaraj would tell me, that there was virtually no plant, shrub or tree that she couldn't name in the vicinity. For the years I have spent in Mahendragiri, my knowledge of botany remained limited to distinguishing a tulsi leaf from a curry leaf.

In replenishing groundwater in the Mahendragiri hills, too, ISRO played a pivotal part. When we started civil work here, water was a scarce commodity. There were a few rivulets north of the test complex site, but this patch remained fairly dry. Rainwater ran away with no structure to harvest it. Bore wells had to be drilled several hundreds of metres into the rocky mountain to hit water. And water we needed aplenty, not just for regular use, but also for storage near the test stand as a precaution against an accident.

One of the perennial risks at liquid propulsion engine test stands is the chance of fuel or oxidizer leak. The first thing to do in such an emergency is to flood the test stand with water. For this you needed huge quantities of water available, round the clock. But water availability and the storage system was so abysmal in Mahendragiri that if we had to flood and flush once, it would take one month to refill the huge storage tanks. If we were to stick to the protocol, no tests could be conducted till this water filling cycle is completed, and that meant colossal wastage of time and delay in rocket tests.

In fact, during one of the early tests, there was an accident at Mahendragiri—something no media could sniff out. There was a leak of N2O4 in the test stand pit. The scene was quite scary, with thick brown vapour spreading from the test stand. The team contained it, but not before some anxious hours. It was the only accident at Mahendragiri, and it gave ISRO a hands-on experience in firefighting with loads of water.

Chandran led a team to find a solution to the water problem. He surveyed the forest to understand the contours of the hills and designed a series of channels and check dams to guide and gather water in pits to replenish ground water. They built more than thirty such small check dams. Chandran's water harvesting measures showed result within a couple of years. The ground water table rose so much that a bore well need not go beyond 50 m in the hills.

As villagers come in during the *Panguni Uthiram* puja once a year, they comment on how their once depleted forest surrounding the temples have rejuvenated under ISRO's care. Rocket scientists, it seemed, were not as bad as they thought.

The north-east part of the campus, I explored and found, was the most beautiful, with lot of greenery and a few streams. I proposed we have our guest houses here. After all, it is not a sin for scientists, guests and others from the government to be in good surroundings when they visit Mahendragiri. But this was not to be, as the guests would have to pass through some 'danger zones' to reach the proposed guest house. So the lodgings came up on the south-east side, closer to the highways, where they are now.

Another of my plan that did not materialise was setting up a few wind mills on the Mahendragiri campus. This would have given us some green power self-sufficiency. Looking at the maps of the tail end of the Western Ghats, we found that there were quite a few wind corridors and passes where wind gathers speed because of the converging hills.

Here, we were sitting on some 6,000 acres with fantastic wind for at least three months. When I made the suggestion, some others said we are here to test rocket engines, not harness wind. Of course we were here to test rocket engines, but wasting a free resource did not make sense, especially when the neighbouring Aralvaymozhi Pass and Aryankavu Pass were becoming success stories in wind energy tapping. Anyway, I didn't push much. I choose my battles.

With my immediate boss Muthunayagam, I believed, some battles have to be openly fought. When I organised a *bhumi puja* for the 'groundbreaking' ceremony at Mahendragiri, Muthunayagam was not happy.

'Why a Hindu ritual?' he said.

'Why do you see it as a Hindu ritual?' I replied. 'It is just a prayer to Mother Earth. We may bring a Christian priest and a mullah, too. Let there be all kinds of rituals. A bhumi puja is a routine in virtually every big project in India, including government ones. And, mind you, I have arranged it with my money, not ISRO's.'

The puja was conducted.

The pace at which infrastructure for the Mahendragiri integrated test complex was put together displayed the efficiency of not just ISRO and many government arms, but also the inherent problems of bureaucracy. While the land acquisition and construction of the facility structures happened in record time, acquiring the first computer was a fifteen-month struggle. Overcoming all such delays, the integrated test facility was up and running about three years after the land acquisition was completed. And the first test of a gas generator was done here on 31 December 1985.

By then our first Vikas engine was successfully tested at SEP, which had two test stands, one for single engines and another for four-engine clusters (now used by Arianne). We set up the principal test stand at Mahendragiri as a virtual replica of the SEP facility, an unofficial technology transfer we managed simply through observation and copying for five years. The principal test stand was approved by the ISRO board as a single engine test facility, but just as the ground work was beginning I had a thought, 'Why not build a principal stand for testing a four-engine cluster like Arianne?'

It was not a big deal. The square foundation for the single-engine test stand, as approved, was 4m x 4m. It has to be increased to 5m x 5m. We knew how to build the cluster test stand as much as this one. The difference in cost was estimated to be around Rs 1 crore; not too big an amount. I told this to Dhawan, who thought it was unnecessary at this stage since we were still experimenting with our first engine, and a cluster engine configuration for our rockets was an idea light years away.

'Let's first learn to walk,' Dhawan said. 'After that we will run.'

Nobody argues with Dhawan. I kept silent, but the thought of upgrading the principal test stand was tickling me. I have worked around bureaucratic barricades and have bent a few rules when I was convinced they were standing in the way of better results. This I did, also, when I was convinced that my visionary bosses like Sarabhai and Dhawan, who had no axe to grind, would soon see reason in the exceptions to the rule and approve of them.

Now I was planning to get the foundation laid for an unapproved cluster-engine test stand, with the confidence that I can convince the chairman sooner than later. After all, once the foundation is laid at 4m x 4m, the approval for a bigger test stand would be of no use.

I was just in time when R D John, the chief engineer of construction, was doing the foundation layout on the ground. I casually told John to make it 5m x 5m.

'But the approved plan is 4m x 4m,' said John.

'Yes, but don't worry, I will get approval for 5m x 5m.'

John wasn't convinced. He said the change would entail an additional expense of Rs 1 crore, and that I have to get a note approving the change.

Getting Rs 1 crore, I calculated, was not a big deal. I could put it under 'unforeseen expenses' or do some re-appropriation of fund since I was convinced that a four-engine test pad would be an asset for future. And I was sure that I could explain things to Dhawan later. I convinced John to do the ground markings as I wanted, assuring him that I would get the note soon.

Incidentally, on the day the marking pegs were driven into ground at the test site, Dhawan was in Trivandrum, and his flight back to Bangalore was cancelled. Not one to relax, the ISRO chairman said he would use the time to visit Mahendragiri to see the progress of the upcoming integrated test complex.

I was happy to receive Dhawan at Mahendragiri and take him around. And soon we came to the test stand site where the marking pegs were in place. It did not strike me that I was showing to Dhawan something which I had altered not just without his permission, but also despite him telling me not to do it. It was another matter that I was confident of bringing him around sooner than later. Anyway, it was unlikely that Dhawan would remember the dimensions we discussed and, even if he did, he would be able to make out from the peg markings if it was 4m x 4m or 5m x 5m.

I was wrong. Just when he had turned to leave after inspecting the site when Dhawan paused for a moment, as if in hesitation, and asked John, 'What's the dimension of the test stand?

'5m x 5m,' replied John.

Now Dhawan turned to me.

'Nambi, I thought we had decided on 4m x 4m.'

I tried to explain things, but Dhawan cut me short.

'Who is the ISRO chairman?' Dhawan was rarely so curt.

'You, sir,' I replied.

'Then do as I tell you.'

There was no more discussion. The stand was built with a 4m x 4m basement, for single engine test, and this continues to be the facility to date.

Years later, after Dhawan had retired and when U R Rao was the ISRO chairman, I happened to be in a meeting where Dhawan was also present. It has been the custom at ISRO to have its former chairmen and some retired scientists in planning meetings. This one was to discuss configurations of the then proposed GSLV, and when the topic of ground testing came up, someone spoke about a cluster of engines, and the fact that we did not have a facility to test such a cluster.

Colonel Pant, a retired director of Sriharikota Range (SHAR), was quick to raise the question why a multiple-engine stand was not planned when Mahendragiri was being set up. It showed the shortsightedness of the team, he said. Several others echoed the argument blaming the LPSC team for not thinking ahead. Some participants, who were evidently not my fans, got a vicarious pleasure in rubbing it in. I kept silent for I did not want to blame anyone, much less Dhawan, who I considered the tallest figure in Indian space science.

When there seemed to be no end to the chorus, Rao stood up.

'Mr Nambi, may I ask you out of purely academic curiosity why you did not consider building a test stand for testing a multiple-engine configuration?

Before the question ended, there stood Dhawan with his hand raised. And there was pin-drop silence.

'Nambi had the foresight,' he said. 'He wanted to build a test stand for testing a four-engine cluster. It was I who stopped him. I was wrong.'

Dhawan could have kept silent and let me take the blame, for I would have never blamed anyone. But that was the integrity of the man. When Dhawan had completed his speech, there were no more questions on the subject. I did not feel proud of what Dhawan had said about my foresight. I felt sad that Dhawan had to own it up.

CHAPTER 21

THE PAK COMMANDO JOKE

'They got intelligence inputs.'

So, here was the most ridiculous of rumours, which only the Kerala police may lap up: a Pakistani commando force was going to storm the Viyyur Jail or airdrop troops to rescue the accused in the ISRO spy case. Evidently someone who wanted to buttress the Pakistan angle of the ISRO spy case had a fertile imagination. And there was this ready regiment of blockheads eager to buy the story.

We were not aware of the rumour, but were surprised to see a sudden flurry of unusual activities in the prison. Our cells were given an extra check and we were patted down. Battalions of policemen were brought in to guard our cells, and an extra ring of security was thrown around the block. Senior officers paced the corridors up and down. The jail superintendent's phone kept ringing. Guards suspiciously looked at us from a safe distance, occasionally whispering at each other. This vigil continued through the night, and the next morning.

When things were back to normal that afternoon, I asked Sivanandan what it was all about.

'Shh...' the assistant jailor gestured me to speak in a low voice. 'They got intelligence inputs that Pakistanis will be storming the jail to rescue you guys.'

I roared with laughter. Sivanandan ran away.

TESTING THE VIKAS ENGINE

'I can't make the pack smaller, you make the aircraft door big.'

By the time I got back from the ISRO headquarters in a reverse transfer that U R Rao gifted me as soon as he took over as the ISRO chairman in February 1985, work on the integrated test complex at Mahendragiri was in full swing. By the year end we expected to do the first test, if not of a fully-assembled engine or a stage, at least a component of the Vikas engine. But, with the engine incorporated into the PSLV project as part of the second stage, we could not wait for the Mahendragiri facility to get ready to test Vikas.

An option was to test the engine at SEP Vernon. I had discussed this with Dhawan, who was in agreement. U R Rao, the new chairman, was also keen that the engine should be ground-tested at the earliest. Dhawan asked me who other than SEP had the test facility. I did my homework and found DFVLR, a German space agency had the ground test equipment. German scientist Dadieu already had a rapport with India, thanks to his friendship with Sarabhai since the 1960s. We wrote to DFVLR, which said it could do another test, the high altitude test, after we get the engine tested at SEP.

High altitude test is done on the ground with simulated conditions of the upper atmosphere, where the pressure and temperature are different from that of the ground. This was crucial to test the efficacy and the structural integrity of the Vikas engine nozzle, which could behave differently at high altitudes.

Dhawan constituted a committee comprising PSLV project director S Srinivasan, aerodynamics group head T S Prahlad and I to go into the need for a high altitude test. I argued that a high altitude test was avoidable, as it would take more time and money, and it was anyway not necessary because we were using the same nozzle the SEP has been using in Viking. And Viking was already a much tested engine for several Arianne flights.

The others insisted on the test, citing the golden rule in ISRO that no piece of a rocket should be flown without a ground test. Many may still call me a man in haste, but I was in no mood to let some rules stand in the way of speedy incorporation of Vikas into the PSLV. I reiterated that the nozzle was made with the same configuration and materials under the same operating conditions by the same company (Volvo) as that of SEP. In fact, Volvo had supplied three nozzles that could well have been in any Arianne vehicle.

When the others still stuck to the rule book insisting on a test, I played a wild card. 'Why don't you consider the first flight as a high altitude test? Only that you are not doing it in Germany, you are doing it in upper atmosphere, under real conditions.'

There was a momentary silence. It worked.

Now, as I pushed for an early ground test at SEP, I had very little opposition unlike in the previous years. VSSC director Gowarikkar, who was terribly upset with U R Rao's elevation as the ISRO chairman, was now making himself sparse at work as a gesture of protest.

When I returned from Bangalore to my old job at the Liquid Propulsion Systems Centre in Trivandrum with the additional responsibility as the project director of the second and fourth stages of PSLV, Gowarikkar was in a pensive mood. I had little sympathy for him, for I believed U R Rao deserved the post of the chairman much more than anyone else in the organisation, leave alone Gowarikkar. Moreover, I remained sore that Gowarikkar was instrumental in shunting me out of liquid propulsion systems by cooking up the 'furniture scam'. So I was not expecting him to call me and give a sympathetic talk.

'I have caused you much trouble,' he said.

I silently listened, staring at him. He walked towards me and held both my hands in his.

'Nambi, I didn't mean to harm you when I opposed your ideas. Everyone makes mistakes; I, too, have. We all learn from our mistakes. You are a bright promise for ISRO and India.'

I just murmured, 'Okay,' and left the room. I felt happy, not because Gowarikkar, who had created several stumbling blocks to my liquid propulsion plans, apologised to me, but because he told me that I was doing the right thing by pushing the liquid propulsion system. So, have I forgiven him for transferring me when the Vikas project was nearing completion? No. Call me mean if you want. Nothing; no confession, no apology could dilute my resolve to get the Vikas engine tested and running.

SEP agreed to ground-test the engine, but before signing the test contract, a team from the French agency would inspect the engine, the records and the processes followed. This would include perusal of instruction records, non-conformance reports and approvals by various boards.

Record keeping was not one of ISRO's high points, but thanks to our Vernon exposure, the Vikas team had meticulously documented every step and preserved all papers. The SEP team stayed in Trivandrum for two weeks, and were convinced about our work. Later, some of the French scientists told us that they were surprised at our efficiency and speed in which we put together the Vikas engine.

We had collaborated with them in Vernon and had showcased our skills, but it appeared there were still some who found it hard to believe that Indians could actually put together a liquid propulsion engine. Once convinced, the French had other plans for ISRO, which had already delivered, to SEP's satisfaction, pressure transducers for their rocket engines. A scientist told me that now SEP considered outsourcing the manufacturing of its Viking engines to ISRO. But the European Space Agency regulation states that 90% of the cost of any space science project should be spent within the member countries.

ISRO signed the contract with SEP for ground-testing Vikas. We were to pay Rs 1 crore to SEP, and Rs 60 lakhs would go towards propellant cost. We had to take care of the packaging and transport of the engine to France and back, and bear the other expenses of the Indian team in Vernon.

On the technology side, this was a big test for me. During the initial stages of negotiating the test contract, months before U R Rao took over as the ISRO chairman, Dhawan had called me.

'How confident are you about the test results?

'100 per cent,' I lied.

'But there should be a failure probability.' Dhawan would not let me go so easily.

'Zero per cent,' I replied.

Dhawan smiled.

I knew if the test failed, I had to go. I had decided on this. With my experience and the Princeton trophy of a course certificate, a job abroad was an easy proposition. But working in a foreign country did not excite me. One option was to teach. I loved teaching. But running away was not done, especially since I had come all this way.

There are a thousand reasons a ground test can fail, and often it happens because of something we had not foreseen. But, in this case, a failure would have meant that I had misguided my colleagues including the ISRO chairman, who had immense faith in me. Despite my options outside ISRO, I realised, now I had to stay put to prove a point.

Now, preparations were in full swing to transport the engine to France. It was not an easy job. There were parts huge and small, from the turbo pump in one piece to tiny nuts and bolts.

I was worried about the packing, after the experience of returning from Vernon. Our household articles were professionally packed and shipped back to India, but many of them reached India mangled. Our teams ensured that no such thing would happen with the engine parts. With prescribed metal clamps, felt, buffers and cushions to hold the pieces in place without damage, we packed them all into twenty-one boxes.

Air India was to fly the engine to Paris, but since there was no direct flight from Trivandrum, the boxes were to be loaded in Trivandrum, unloaded in Mumbai where they would be loaded again into another flight that goes to Paris. DS was to make the arrangements with Air India.

When the boxes finally reached the Trivandrum airport, one of them was found to be just the size of the door of the aircraft's cargo hold. It would fit in there at the door, but couldn't be pushed inside without damaging the beading. The brilliant space scientists realised that they had never bothered to check the size of the aircraft's door before packing the engine!

The airline officials asked our man to repack the box, and they would take it the next day.

'I can't make the pack smaller, you make the aircraft door big,' he told them.

The airline removed the beading of the door to take the box in and refit the beading before take-off.

An eleven-member team including some from the old Vernon team left for Paris in early December, 1985. Besides me, the old members included P R Sadasivam who later worked on PSLV, H R S Mani, Narendranath and the inimitable Anandan who had a matchless skill in hand-sealing joints. Some joints have to be hand-sealed using a material that one has to apply with the palm. As per the protocol this was a fitter's job, but nobody could get the seal as perfect as Anandan. So much was our dependency on him that Anandan was worried that he would end up being a fitter. Annamma John from the quality control was the only woman member of the team. One not from the previous Vernon team was N K Gupta, an IISc alumnus and an expert in turbo pumps. We also took along Sukumaran Nair, our ace fitter who went on to assemble all the engines till the first flight of PSLV in 1993.

A shock awaited us in France. When the cargo reached Paris, three of the twenty-one boxes were missing. Air India traced them to Copenhagen where the cargo had to be reloaded. The missing boxes came four days later. SEP had given us a ten-day window period for the test. This is because the test has to be carried out only on a windy day to make sure that the flare and fumes dissipate faster. Also, the wind should be blowing from Vernon town towards the test facility, so that the flames don't leap out of the campus. The facility set up in the mid-1940s did not have the 3 km uninhabited buffer zone around the test facility.

The engine was to be fired for the full duration of 180 seconds. Computers were fed with the tolerable limits of various parameters for the system to shut down automatically if something crossed the prescribed threshold. Though we had indigenised many parts of the engine, for this test I decided to use everything—to the last bolt and bearing—that SEP used in Viking, the French equivalent of Vikas.

It was not so much because I did not trust those parts we had developed—just that I did not want to give any of my detractors to start the chorus against liquid propulsion again. If Vikas failed the test, a failure analysis committee will pinpoint the reason, which would mostly be associated with a part. Then I could always argue that the part was the same that is tested and used by SEP, and that their engines are working. We could replace the part and test again.

Having mounted the engine on to the test stand, every day we would load the propellant into the tank and await the wind, in the right direction. For a few days this continued, the conditions not being favourable. By 3:30 pm the propellant will be unloaded. This exercise would take an hour and a half, and by 5 pm the French scientists would religiously close shop and go home.

As we awaited the test, ISRO chemical engineer P Sudarshan, who had earlier opposed to the Vernon test, made a visit. Seeing the struggle we were going through, he wrote back to ISRO an appreciation letter on our efforts.

'I hadn't quite understood this,' he told me.

Finally, there came the perfect day. There was strong wind blowing from the direction of Vernon town. It was so cold that we had to wear multiple layers of clothing. It was 12 December 1985, my 44th birthday.

Vikas stood on the stand, ready to be tested. Along an arc a few hundred meters away, there was the instrumentation room, a control room and a store. We were to sit in one of the rooms. During the many tests I have witnessed at PF2, the test stand in Vernon, scientists would sit in one of the rooms, peering into consoles, monitoring the performance of various parameters of the engine being tested. I preferred to stand in the open, something that the security protocol does not allow, and gaze at the fire that the engine spewed, listening to the roar of machine that man had made to send his creations to yonder skies. The trembling of the ground as the test stand held back the engine that the liquid propulsion sought to lift was pure frisson. Experiencing all these when Vikas shows the fire in its belly, I thought, would be an emotional upheaval for me.

But none of this happened. I managed to stay put in the open as the countdown was being announced through a public address system. During the first sixty seconds of the firing, I was in a trance, not realizing that the ignition happened perfectly and Vikas was going through the rituals as expected. Then I saw the metal turning red hot and the flame a steady blast. At ninety seconds, I relaxed. After the hundredth second, it was an interplay of anticipation and apprehension. At the end of 180 seconds, when the firing ended, there was deadpan silence. And then a roar of applause and cheers by the team that now poured out of the control room and instrumentation room.

Among the revelers was Kanwal Grover, the long-time friend of Indian space science. Once it sank in, colleagues had different reactions. Sadasivam said he felt as if the test was over in no time; Narendranath said it was an eternity for him. Anandan and Sukumaran Nair were speechless. I shook Nair. All he could utter was, 'Sir, sir...' He had tears in his eyes.

I asked the SEP scientists if I could place a call to India. They obliged. When the line crackled to life, I heard the voice 'Rao speaking.'

I told the ISRO chairman that the test has been a textbook success.

'Great, Nambi,' Rao said. 'Give every Frenchman there a treat. And send us some photographs.'

I informed the ISRO Technical Liaison Unit (ITLV) attached to the Indian Consulate in Paris. Mathur, the officer, asked something I should have asked Rao, but forgot in the euphoria, 'Who would foot the bill for the party?'

The Government of India's budget for the Vikas test had definitely not taken into account the need for uncorking a bottle of champagne. Mathur checked with the ambassador who knew little about ISRO, and nothing about the significance of the Vikas test. When everyone was staring at each other, all wondering what to do, there came our perennial saviour, Kanwal Grover.

If anyone had doubts about Grover's interest in getting the deal done, one must have been convinced of his patriotism by his very presence here. Taking commission was a perfectly legal and professional thing in France and many other space-faring countries, but India still frowns at people who facilitate path-breaking partnerships. We call them middlemen, a word often uttered with disdain. It was perfectly legit for Grover to have taken a commission from SEP for the Viking-Vikas deal, it remains unknown to me if he ever saw this as a business opportunity.

Now, as we stood wondering about the thanksgiving, Grover spoke: 'I have a request, Mr Nambi. If you permit me, I will have the pleasure of getting some champagne for all of us.'

I was embarrassed. Here was this man who was neither bound by duty nor lured by any personal benefit offering to host the celebration of our success—something that our organisation or the government should be doing. Before I could gather my thoughts, H R S Mani intervened.

'For good things in life,' Mani told Grover, 'you don't need permission.'

Everyone laughed. And champagne flowed. Grover remembered the day at Windsor Manor in Bangalore when SEP head Souffle had almost called off the deal, and I had asked Grover to employ his marketing skills to win the contract for India. I remembered the day I had first met Grover, at Le Lido in Paris, where he sponsored a bottle of champagne for all the 2,000 guests of the evening. This man had passion.

That evening, back at Hotel Meridian in Paris where we stayed, I flashed a thumbs up to the lobby manager as I walked past him to my room. Over the days of 'waiting for the Vernon wind,' we had struck a friendship. After returning disappointed for many days, today he got the message. He called me on the intercom.

'Felicitations,' he said, and offered to send some champagne.

I thanked him and said no to the champagne. 'We had enough of it,' I said. 'But if you insist, we don't mind some whiskey.'

We binged, egging each other on to have some more liquid propulsion. N K Gupta, the turbo pump man, was a teetotaler. He laughed at our drunken antics, we secretly decided to get him drunk. When Gupta said he would not have anything intoxicating, Mani said with a poker face, 'How sad, Gupta. That means you can have only champagne, not whiskey.'

'Why, doesn't champagne give you a high? Now Gupta was curious.

'How silly,' Mani continued. 'Did you see how many champagne bottles we drank at Vernon? It's just the taste.'

With some encouragement from others to not waste an opportunity to taste the elixir from pinot noir in its homeland, Gupta agreed to take a sip. Someone quickly filled a glass with the white sparkling wine and added a dash of whiskey to it before extending it to Gupta. Hesitantly, he took a sip. Then two. And more.

I don't think Gupta was naïve enough to think champagne is only as good as a soft drink, but clearly he did not expect the sleight of hand that infused the whiskey into his wine glass. Gupta was soon flying. While the rest of us laughed and made merry, Gupta was getting increasingly worried about what the alcoholic concoction was doing to him.

'My head is spinning,' Gupta shouted.

'Now, that's what a turbo pump feels like,' someone shouted back.

Everyone was roaring with laughter.

The next day, as we were nursing a hangover, Gupta said he did not remember anything that happened after he had that champagne.

We looked at each other. Then I spoke, 'Are you serious, Gupta?'

'Not a thing.'

'Don't you remember dancing in the lobby?'

'What?'

That was almost a shriek from the modest and taciturn Gupta.

'The dance wasn't bad,' chipped in someone else. 'But people started staring only when you removed the shirt.'

Now Gupta was getting worked up.

'You mean I removed my shirt and danced in the lobby? Hey, c'mon guys, tell me you are kidding.'

Amidst bursts of laughter each one contributed his bit, one saying Gupta removed his trousers too; another wondering why he tried to wear his socks on his ears.

Gupta said he felt like burying his head somewhere. We told him we will help him do that, but only after reaching India.

We were ready to pack up.

CHAPTER 22

MARIAM SPEAKS TO ME

'I am sorry'

At the end of our judicial custody we were taken to a court for extension of remand. This was done twice during my twenty-six-day stay in Viyyur prison. These trips to the court were an excursion of sorts. Besides getting to see the world outside the prison walls, we also got *vada*, *bajji* and tea, which were not available in the jail. Not that we were entitled to these snacks, it was thanks to sympathetic policemen who did not have the heart to have them without giving us.

It was during one such outing that Mariam Rasheeda spoke to me for the first time. My anger for the women and my other co-accused had abated, but still I was in no mood to look at the women whose background I knew little about.

'I am sorry.' Those were her first words.

Not interested in a conversation, I kept silent. She continued, in broken English, that she was innocent and knew that I too was.

'So why are you sorry?' I said.

'They beat me, threatened me. And I had to say bad things about you.'

She was referring to her confession statement before officials of the Kerala Police and the IB. They tried several threats, and finally she gave in when they said they would harm her daughter. The interrogators tutored her to say that I had passed on drawings of rockets to her for money, and this was video recorded.

Mariam said when they showed her my photograph she could not recognise me.

'They told me your name and asked me to utter it, but I couldn't get it right. They made me try many times, but your name was still a tongue-twister for me. So one of them wrote your name on a paper, in big letters and held it above the video camera. I was asked to read out from the paper.'

This, Mariam had told CBI earlier. To verify her statement, CBI officers watched the video several times and found that when Mariam was to say my name her eyes hovered above the camera lens. This statement and a similar one by Fauziyya were to be rejected by the CBI and the courts later.

Mariam was weeping as she narrated her ordeal at the hands of the Kerala police and later the IB officials. In between she kept saying 'sorry'. For the first time, I felt sad for the woman.

A woman constable, who was listening to our conversation, could not contain her curiosity.

'So, this spy case is not real?

'The case is real, and that's why you are taking me to a court now,' I said. 'But the theory of spying is imagination.'

'Tell me in simple terms, sir. Did you or did you not give rocket secrets to Pakistan?'

'No.'

She felt relieved with the piece of information.

There was another constable, a young man, who wanted to sit next to me, both the times we were taken to the court. He, unlike the woman constable, had no confusion over the ISRO spy case.

'I have been following this case from the day Mariam Rasheeda was arrested,' he said. 'And every passing day I was getting increasingly convinced that it is a fake case.'

During the second outing for remand extension, I asked about his background. He said he was a postgraduate in arts, but had to hide his MA degree to get the job of a constable since he was overqualified for the job.

Visiting me in the jail, my son Sankar told me that we too should move for bail through a big name lawyer, preferably M N Sukumaran Nair. He had charged Rs 1 lakh for Sasi.

I did not have that kind of money. My brother-in-law Arunachalam said they would borrow money to pay the lawyer. I told Shankar to get money from my colleague Mohana Prasad, who was also my neighbour or from Isaac, another friend. But I told them not to hire an expensive lawyer. Shankar and Arunachalam came one day with news.

Sankar insisted that we move through advocate Nair. I agreed, but with the condition that we would not pay the lawyer Rs 1 lakh. Nair finally got me bail, and charged only Rs 25,000. When Sasi came to know of this later, he was cribbing about the lawyer having charged him four times what he took from me. I asked Sasi if he was unhappy that he paid more or because I paid less.

After fifty days in captivity, including twenty-seven days in prison, I was to be released on bail on 19 January 1995.

IN THE PSLV WORKSHOP

'We are making a rocket, and the Americans are not happy about it.'

We returned from Vernon jubilant after the Vikas ground test, but there was no time to waste in celebration. The team plunged into work, now that our task was cut out. We had to put together an engine for the first PSLV flight, which was planned in another five years.

PSLV, then finalised as a four-stage rocket, would have Vikas, the sixty-tonne thrust liquid engine powering the second stage. The first and third stages were of solid propulsion, the fourth was to have another liquid engine of almost one-tenth the thrust of Vikas.

This smaller engine was developed by a team headed by K Sivaramakrishnan Nair and C G Balan who did some remarkable, yet not so celebrated work. Though small, this engine that worked on the regenerative cooling technique had its own intricacies that include use of fuel also as a coolant. One of the big challenges for Nair and Balan was to ensure a uniform cooling passage. They achieved it with such great precision that the fourth stage has been a success consistently since the second flight of PSLV in 1994.

CHAPTER 22: Mariam Speaks to Me

The commitment of virtually every team member was inspiring in itself. Such was the dedication of Kuppuraj, our engineer, who worked on the turbo pump that even while battling a terminal disease, he insisted on coming to work. When I tried to advise him against working, he said, 'Sir, have you already written me off?' He did not live to see the PSLV fly.

Vikas was a bigger engine with greater complexities. Here we were, having put together the engine and ground tested it, asked to do it again for a real flight of India's first Polar Satellite Launch Vehicle (PSLV). And this meant much more than reassembling the engine and mounting it on the rocket. An engine was the core of a stage (and PSLV had four stages), but there were many other components that constituted a stage. There were the tankages that supplied the fuel, oxidiser and water to the engine; the gas bottles that held the gas to pressurise the tankages; and complicated fluid circuits, valves and regulators.

A maze of cables and pipelines had to interconnect several parts of the engine. Some had to be fitted into interstages, the buffer between two stages of a rocket; others had to be systematically packed and into the cylinder that is the body of the rocket. We were waking up to a challenge we knew from the day we landed in Vernon in 1974. The contract covered only the making of the engine that included the thrust chamber, the gas generator and the turbo pump. All the rest of the stage—tankages, inter-stage structures, thrust frame, fill-and-drain systems, pressurisation systems, pogo and splash, overflow systems, gymbal activation system and much more—we had to develop on our own. Without these subsystems a flying rocket would remain a grounded dream.

I was reminded of a golden opportunity we wasted in getting the scope of the contract expanded to cover the stage technology. Dhawan, the man of impeccable integrity, had spoiled it. The year was 1975, and Airbus, the new challenge to the American Boeing had just had its first commercial flight.

Sud Aviation, which later became Aerospatiale with the merger of Nord Aviation in 1970, was leading the consortium that made Airbus. The genesis was the annual Paris Air Show of 1965, where aviation industry giants across Europe floated the idea of making an alternative to Boeing, which then had the monopoly of the passenger aircraft sector.

By 1967, Airbus A300 was ready with a plan of synergy among the European sisters: Sud Aviation (France) would make the cockpit, flight control and the lower centre section of the fusealage; Hawker Siddeley (UK) the wings; Deutsche Airbus (Germany) the front and rear parts of the fuselage; Fokker-VFW (Dutch) the flaps and spoilers; and a Spanish company the horizontal tailplane. Rolls-Royce would make the engine.

Despite politics and financial concerns by participant governments, Airbus became a reality within five years. A300 made its maiden flight in 1972, and a slightly modified version, (A300B2) was in service by 1974. The consortium badly needed orders from countries outside Europe, and India was looking for a small new fleet of seven or so aircraft for Indian Airlines.

Then Prime Minister Indira Gandhi had appointed Satish Dhawan, the ISRO chairman, as the committee to choose between Airbus and Boeing. It was around this time that Aerospatiale technical head Delvel approached me. He was pretty straight forward with the proposal, 'You get me the Indian contract for Airbus, I will get you the technology from SEP that is not covered under your Viking contract.'

It was an offer too difficult to refuse, but I could only tell Dhawan who knew better than me how the stage technology transfer would immensely benefit India, and speed up the PSLV project. I knew Dhawan would make his selection between Boeing and Airbus purely on the merit of the aircraft, and would not allow the French promise of technology transfer of systems outside the Viking contract to interfere with his decision.

So I put it forward to Dhawan thus, 'If, after the due process—with no influence from anyone whatsoever—you select Airbus, would you allow me to strike a barter deal with the French, saying Airbus was selected expecting the French to include in the Viking contract the stage engineering technology?' Dhawan said no.

'These are two different matters, Mr Nambi,' he said. 'And don't waste your time waiting for my decision on the aircraft; you go ahead with your job of making the rocket engine.'

Finally, Dhawan selected Airbus, and I am sure he remained untouched or unmindful of the fact that he just let go of an opportunity to get associated Viking technology without much toil. It is another matter that we learned and developed all these associated stage technology, though at the cost of more time and energy.

Almost ten years later, here we were after the successful ground test of Vikas, with the mandate to put together the 'flying' engine, and second stage for PSLV. During our stay in Vernon, some of the team members had learned quite a bit on these subsystems though it fell outside the purview of the contract, but now we were called to demonstrate and deliver.

We sat down to identify the tasks. The first crucial decision was to not use any indigenous parts in the first flight. In other words, we would fabricate bigger parts with the same materials and processes that went into the making of Viking by the French, or use smaller parts like fasteners and bearings fabricated by the original SEP suppliers. This was to minimise risks and focus on our technological mastery over putting together the engine than on fabrication. Our other acquired skills, including those material development and fabrication could be put to test after three successful flights of PSLV, it was decided.

I got my colleague G Krishnamurthy, a mechanical engineer specialized in fabrication, to compile a materials manual. This involved making a list of materials used in Viking/Vikas, with details of their Indian and American equivalents. This would be an exhaustive list that would include the chemical composition and physical properties of the materials, including their tensile strength, durability and fatigue, besides expected behaviour under varying conditions.

One of the crucial parts was the contour nozzle. After convincing a committee to use this French-made nozzle without subjecting it to a high-altitude test, we had managed to get three nozzles from Volvo, Sweden, thanks to old friends in France.

Most of the nozzles have a convergent part, a divergent part and a neck that attaches the two. The gas generated in the combustion chamber gets expanded in the nozzle to convert pressure into kinetic energy that would lift the rocket. Nozzles are designed keeping in mind the pressure generated by the combustion and the atmospheric pressure outside.

Here was a small hitch. The atmospheric pressure drops as the altitude goes up. This means a nozzle that works fine at sea level may not optimally utilize the pressure generated at a high altitude where the atmospheric pressure is low. A PSLV has four stages and hence needs four nozzles for the four stages; each one is designed to work optimally for its entire flight duration. Often, fixed diameter nozzles result in waste of pressure and underperformance.

The Vikas engine nozzle is a versatile piece of engineering. Unlike the nozzle of the first-stage engine, which has a conical divergent part, this one is bell-shaped. While the other nozzles are more or less of the same thickness, the bell-shaped nozzle is also of tapering thickness, which means it is thickest (about 5mm) at the neck end and progressively becomes thin to be the thinnest (about 1.5mm) at the divergent end. It is designed to bring down the weight without compromising on the performance at high altitude where the pressure dips drastically.

The special design entails special processes. While a normal, conical nozzle is easy to make, using the roll-and-weld method, the Vikas engine nozzle is made using what we call the 'flow technique'. In simple terms, it means the nozzle is made by making the alloy flow, while high-precision machines 'pull and mould' it into the bell-jar shape with tapering thickness. To make it simpler, think about a potter's wheel, only replace the clay with alloy and the potter's hands with the high-precision machines.

To get the nozzle right, the machines, method and the material— in this case a cobalt alloy that the French called KC-20WN, and the Americans HS-25—all have to perfect. We had got Indian public sector units like MIDHANI and some private players to work on materials like KC-20WN. But these would not be used for the first few flights; we used material procured from the original suppliers of SEP and got some of the systems, like the combustion chamber, here.

Next, we had to get the tankages for the fuel and oxidiser. We approached Air Liquide, an American company that supplied tankages to SEP. Air Liquide, France, made four of them for us, and they were to be shipped two each per flight. Each flight cost Rs 30 lakh, which put the transportation cost at Rs 60 lakh. When I made an inspection at the factory only one tankage was fabricated, three remained to be made. It raised many eyebrows when I asked the only tankage ready, to be flown down immediately.

To many, it made no sense as it meant there would be at least three trips as a flight cannot carry more than two, and this would send the transportation cost up to Rs 90 lakh. I had my reasons, but this was not the time to explain. So, I got the first one immediately, the second and third in another flight, and the last in a third flight. It did cost Rs 30 lakh more, and the comptroller and auditor general did make an issue out of this.

I was not much bothered about these bean counters, for I had explained the reason to the ISRO chairman and the few people who mattered. Dhawan explained the matter to the Indian Prime Minister and got the additional expenditure ratified. Now, here was the reason. I feared an embargo due to American pressure.

Not many know I had just beaten an embargo while getting the gas bottles from another American company. The bottles, which hold the gas that gives the initial pressure to move the fuel and oxidiser into the combustion chamber, are made of a titanium alloy. The difficult part of making the bottles is machining of the alloy from a thickness of 12 mm to the required 1.5 mm–2 mm thickness.

The US manufacturer was to ship sixteen hemispheres, which we were to be put together into eight gas bottles. Just when we were awaiting the cargo at Madras port, we got a call from the manufacturer saying he had been asked to freeze the delivery since his government felt that the material fell under the Missile Technology Control Regime. The supplier had dispatched the cargo, but he would be asking the Indian port authorities not to release it; he would compensate us as per the contract.

I flew to Madras. I told the port officer that the consignment is of great national importance, but he said he was helpless as he just got a message that it should be sent back without delivering it to ISRO.

'What if you haven't got that message?' I said.

'But I have got the message.'

'Have you acknowledged the receipt of the message?'

'Not yet.'

'Listen,' I pulled my chair forward. 'This consignment is of supreme importance to the nation.

We are making a rocket, and the Americans are not happy about it. Listen to what I say, and I will get you the endorsement from the highest office in this country if that comes to that. Just release the consignment and say you got the message late.'

It was not as difficult as I thought. He agreed. I soon left with the consignment to Trivandum, from where it would be taken to the fabrication centre.

It was against this background that I hastened to ship out the first tankage made by Air Liquide, though it meant additional expenditure since two tankages could have been transported home at the same cost. Dhawan understood my urgency, stood by me and, when the CAG pointed a finger at ISRO, he got the PMO to endorse what we had done.

* * *

As the procurement and fabrication of the hardware went on, a team headed by R Natarajan was working on liquid propellants and storage systems. Natarajan, a chemical engineer who continues to research at VIT University, Vellore now, had spent four months in Vernon in 1977. This period, between April and July that year, gave him valuable lessons in not just development of propellants, but their transport, filling and storage.

Initially his team did some basic experiments with aniline and furfural alcohol made from rice husk collected from a mill in Nagercoil. Mixed with furfural, aniline caught fire. Then it moved on to bigger fuels like red-fuming nitric acid (RFNA), which we used for smaller rockets.

Vikas needed the more complicated unsymmetrical dimethylhydrazine (UDMH). In those days, the Soviet Union was using RFNA, along with aniline, to fire its missiles. RFNA, which comprised 84% nitric acid 13% nitrogen tetroxide and about 2% water, is a highly poisonous chemical, with a threshold limit value of 5ppm (parts per million). This meant exposure to 5ppm of RFNA can be dangerous, even fatal. UDMH is a carcinogen with a much lesser threshold limit value—2ppm.

Besides trying out different chemical reactions to optimally produce the propellants, the team was mastering the tricky pipeline layouts, tank layouts and mitigation, in case of a leak in a pipeline or a breach in a tank.

For the first ground test of Vikas at Vernon, SEP had provided UDMH and the oxidiser which cost 60% of our Rs 1 crore budget for the test. While we saved some of the fuel and oxidiser we had imported for the first flight, our team developed UDMH and N2O4 (nitrogen tetroxide) for several ground tests in Mahendragiri before the launch. This was a result of great toil, starting from textbooks to trials and errors before success.

For N2O4, they tried treating lead nitrate with lead monoxide (a lethal chemical when exposed in nitric acid). A pilot plant was set up for this at VSSC, Trivandrum. As for UDMH, there were two teams at work. One under Natarajan using the chloramine process, and the other under Gowarikkar using the dimethyl urea process.

In the laboratory, both the processes were found to be successful, and now we wanted to scale up either of the two. Presented with the option, VSSC director Brahm Prakash appointed a selection committee headed by Indian Petrochemical Corporation Limited (IPCL) chairman S Varadarajan. Indian Drugs and Pharmaceuticals Limited (IDPL), Hyderabad, the largest public sector pharma company, was appointed the external observer, and the prospective manufacturer of the chemical, once the process was selected.

The committee selected Gowarikkar's process, and appointed Natarajan as the manager who would set up and monitor of the dimethyl urea pilot plant at the IDPL facility.

CHAPTER 23

A REALISATION OF LOVE

'I will be your body guard.'

I got bail. It was fifty days since I was arrested. The jail authorities anticipated trouble from the public when I was to step out, on 19 January 1995. People were angry at the 'traitors', and they would vent their anger primarily at me, an officer said with a clearly put on concern. I said there would be no such trouble, and if at all anything happened I knew how to protect myself.

When Sankar came to take me home along with my relative G Subramanian, I was surprised to find an old friend accompanying them. It was John George, the fitter. After being fired for his fracas with a colleague on the work floor, John had come to me for help. I was helpless as Seshan, the administrative head, had got presidential sanction to sack John who would then have not even legal remedy. I had thought that John would hate me for not protecting his job; after all he had been seen as my right hand man even as he flexed his muscles to extract work from others.

John said he losing the job was his own making; though he was upset with me for not being able to reinstate him, he now thought that it was time to stand by me.

'I heard some people may create nuisance to you when you come out of the prison,' John said as I was collecting my meagre belongings from the prison superintendent. 'I will be your body guard till you reach home.'

239

CHAPTER 23: A Realisation of Love

The prison officials assigned a constable to accompany and deposit me at my house in Trivandrum. The constable got into the car with us. After a couple of hours into the journey, he asked me if he could get down and go home. I said yes, but he was scared that he would attract punishment if his superiors came to know that he had not accompanied me till I reached home. I said not a soul will know that he got down here. The constable thanked me profusely. I thanked him for leaving; I had had enough of the police company.

Most of the journey passed in silence occasionally broken by Sankar asking me if I wanted a tea or something. I sat blank, staring out of the window, at the passing trees and traffic. As the car reached Trivandrum, memories of the past fifty days came rushing to me. Right from the first night at the Vanchiyoor Police Station to the Latex Guest House, and the Pallipuram camp before the CBI took me to Chennai and then to the Viyyur prison in Kerala.

I realised the gravity of the case I was implicated in; I could get several years of imprisonment for violation of the Official Secrets Act, besides other penalties under the Indian Penal Code. I was not so much worried about the problems I may face in such long incarceration; suddenly my thoughts were on how my family would be without me. I had never missed my family so much as I did in the last fifty days. I also realised now that I had not been a good father or a husband. Pursuing my passion in rocket engineering, which now appeared to me as an act in selfishness, I had ignored my dear ones.

Now, a rare personal conversation with Vikram Sarabhai in August 1969 rang in my mind. Our son Sankar was born on 9 February 1969. I wanted to spend more time at home, but chose not to lose focus at work. It was the time Sarabhai was warming up to the idea of sending me to Princeton to study. In August that year I left for Princeton. While flying to the US, it so happened that Vikram Sarabhai was travelling on the same flight, Air India's *Annapoorna 707*.

Seeing me on board, Sarabhai moved from the business class to an economy seat next to mine. He was reading a book, but in between he would chat with me. On learning I was a new father, Sarabhai congratulated me.

Suddenly he fell silent. Then, as if pronouncing the result of an intense introspection, he said in a barely audible voice, 'I was not a good father...never a good husband,' he said. 'They put up with me because they don't have a choice.'

Those words continue to ring in my mind for two reasons. One, was one of the rare occasions when I had seen Sarabhai, the cheerful man who always linked everything he spoke to the nation's growth, being pensive and philosophical. Two, today I believe that I have not done justice to my family, as a husband or a father. And I have nobody to blame for this than me.

My son wanted to be a doctor, but I never found enough time to be with him and guide him to his goal. Not that it would have ensured him a medical seat, but I neither prompted him to work hard or myself earned enough then to spend on a private medical college admission. Sankar went on to graduate in commerce and took a post-graduate degree. I helped him set up a business in LPG distribution. Today he runs a successful business, but I am yet to get rid of that prick of conscience.

My daughter Geetha was born on 24 June 1971, a year after I returned from Princeton. She did not want to be a doctor or an engineer, the two professions then considered prestigious and just every parent's matter of pride. She studied home science. She, however, did not want to confine herself to home, so she tried out a few things including garment business, but finally discovered her passion for training in Montessori schools.

It was by chance, however, that she became a teacher. I had gone with her for her daughter's admission to National Public School in Bangalore. The chairman of the school, K P Gopalakrishnan, had regards for me and readily offered a seat for my granddaughter Shruthi, who later went on to become a doctor. He advised Geetha to do a Montessori teaching course, and here she found her calling.

Geetha had been writing letters to me when I was in jail. Through them she tried to infuse courage. These came as a solace to me in a different way. I realised that my daughter was strong enough to console me, so she should be able to keep my wife and son strong too.

The car appeared to have slowed down. And I could not wait to see my daughter.

PSLV TAKES SHAPE

'I will cancel the order.'

Even as we kept sourcing materials from abroad to put together the Vikas engine for the first PSLV flight, indigenisation efforts were on for further flights. We appeared to be well on our way to self-sufficiency when it came to UDMH fuel that our team was now producing at the Andhra Sugar facility. But development of some materials, especially alloys like HS-25 used for making the bell-shaped nozzle of Vikas, was proving tricky.

Getting MIDHANI on board helped us rope in other big public sector units collaborate with ISRO for the Vikas project. Hindustan Aeronautics Limited (HAL), Bangalore took up the job of fabricating the thrust frame, tankages and inter-stage structures. We still had a lot of components of the engine to be made.

One of the early challenges of rocketry the world over faced was the rocket's tendency to spin on its axis. This was kept under check through a roll control system. The changes in direction were to be effected by a process called gimballing, wherein the nozzle moves to change the direction of the thrust, and thereby that of the rocket.

A team led by ISRO's components group head Sreedharan Das along with ISRO engineers E S Joseph, Radhakrishnan, Baby T Mathew, Ram Jogi and Thomas Jayakumar laboured to perfect the flow components of the control system. This included the Group Organ de Commande (GOC), essentially a plate that holds together several valves and regulators, which they developed at the Pressure Transducer Unit (PTU) in Bangalore. PTU, where we made transducers for the French with their technology at lower cost, was a spinoff of the Vikas-Viking barter deal, something which proved to be a bonus for us.

For the engine to be part of the first PSLV flight, we continued to source parts from the original suppliers of SEP, Vernon. A French company called Le Joint de Francis supplied 'O' rings; Simmonds made fasteners. 'Make in India' became an official slogan of the government only in September 2014 after Narendra Modi became the Indian Prime Minister, but our Vikas indigenisation drive saw some of the foreign manufacturers making components for our rocket engine as early as in the 1980s, in India. One such was SNFE India Pvt Ltd, the Indian arm of a French company that made bearings.

Separate teams worked on fill-and-drain systems, pressurisation of tanks, gimbal actuator, roll control system and 'pogo and sloshing' control (to prevent the fuel and oxidiser from sloshing in the tank to create instability). Precision was the catchphrase and motto, for a minor mass difference or structural deviation can send the rocket haywire. One of the crucial aspects here was balancing the turbo pump assembly. BHEL, Bhopal did a good job with this.

We were also working on mock-ups, the making of models and assembling them to get a hang of handling components. It gave us a feel of what kind of space is needed, how the cranes need to be manoeuvred to move a component and stack it on another on the work floor.

This is when my colleague P S Krishnamoorthy brought P Ravindra Reddy, an engineer-entrepreneur from Hyderabad to meet me. Reddy was the founder chairman of MTAR Technologies, which was already doing some work for the Department of Atomic Energy.

Krishnamoorthy told me that Vikram Sarabhai had a good opinion of Reddy who started off with a small workshop in Hyderabad's Bala Nagar industrial area and expanded his factory systematically, with a passion for indigenisation. What is more, he was an engineer. That was an impressive introduction, but I had to convince myself of Reddy's abilities before I gave some orders. When he came to meet me in my office, there was a drawing of a turbine wheel on my table.

'Can you make a model of this?' I asked him.

Reddy took the drawing and studied it carefully for a few minutes. I knew it was a tough job, fabricating a model from a mere drawing. It may take a few months even if you got every reading right.

'It's just a drawing,' Reddy said.

I nodded.

'What if I need clarifications during fabrication?'

'Ask any of our engineers,' I said. 'They will give you the answers you need.'

Reddy did not ask any more questions, and left with a copy of the drawing.

A month later, Ravindra Reddy walked into my office again, this time with a giftwrap. It contained a beautiful one-to-one model of the turbine wheel that was just a drawing on my table a month ago. It was the first scale model of a part of the Vikas engine. I was impressed.

'You must have spent a lot of man hours and money on this,' I said appreciatively.

'Yes, but we did it not for money; only to show you that we can do it.'

This was one of the first lessons for ISRO that private participation should not just be allowed in the space programme, but encouraged actively to achieve our goals. While government institutions viewed private enterprises with skepticism, the base of our socialist bias being the notion that profit making is a sin, what went unacknowledged were not just the skills and efficiency of at least a section of private companies, but also their sense of belonging and the yearning for contribution for the nation's growth. First Andhra Sugars led by Thimmayya that set up our rocket fuel facility, and now MTAR Technologies were shining examples of this.

Years later, the fabricators of the ISRO spy case were to drag in the name of Ravindra Reddy, along with that of former Prime Minister P V Narasimha Rao's son Prabhakar Rao, exposing a conspiracy to stall India's leap to space. All that, however, would become clear to me only after my own incarceration and eventual acquittal.

The crafty tales of a foreign agency's collaborators in India's IB fly in the face of the commitment and delivery of Reddy's company towards Indian space and nuclear science. MTAR, which also made the solid propellant machining facilities, was soon to become one of the most reliable partners of ISRO. MTAR, along with Godrej, continues to make almost the entire Vikas engine for PSLV which has had more than thirty consecutively successful flight including the moon and mars missions.

When Ravindra Reddy passed away in January 2016, MTAR noted in a press release that the Department of Atomic Energy had fully trusted the company as it acquired the capabilities of building a nuclear reactor entirely on its own. Reddy, who served on the board of ISRO's commercial arm Antrix Corporation (Ratan Tata and Adi Godrej were among the other members), won the Prime Minister's Defence Technology Absorption Award in 2004.

It was not always big industrialists like Reddy who vied for ISRO contracts. I would give just anyone the chance to collaborate. An example was Alwar Metal Industries, which was nothing more than a workshop at Aryasala in Trivandrum when we gave it a contract in the early 1970s.

It was to make a pyro valve for the three-tonne liquid engine that we were developing for the second stage of the Rohini-560 rocket. The contraption was to work thus—a charge when fired would generate high pressure that punctures a diaphragm, allowing the liquid fuel to flow in on direction. Once this flow is established, the valve would remain open.

Tenders were called from big companies including Larsen & Toubro which quoted Rs 9,000 per piece. Responding to a newspaper advertisement, Alwar Metal Industries also filed a bid. Quoting a little more than Rs 300 a piece, it was the lowest bid. I was astonished how they could make the pyro valve for so less. I asked the company owner to meet me.

Alwar, a 60-something man, said, 'Don't worry about the quality of the valve, you may test it and if rejected, don't pay me a rupee.'

I asked him to make a few samples. Alwar delivered the samples which, when tested, worked as good as the ones supplied by Larsen & Toubro. I asked Alwar how he managed to keep the cost so low.

'We have very skilled workers and good machinery,' he said. 'We keep the overheads very low and take a nominal profit. Hence the low cost.'

I made some inquiries about the man and his company, and was delighted to learn that this was a perfect example of an efficient small-scale industry. Alwar made a small profit, which he shared with his workers. He ensured the well-being of his employee's families, including their children's education. There was no strike at his factory. He once won the President's medal for the best employer.

When it came to such a project as PSLV, however, smaller players like Alwar could not deliver crucial components, and we had to go with the big guys. ISRO shared a good rapport and goodwill with the collaborating companies, especially those in the private sector. There were occasions when a few corporate executives played tricks, and one had to make things unpleasant to get the goods delivered. And I never hesitated to do this, irrespective of the structure and stature of the company.

That happened with Larsen & Toubro (L&T), a valued collaborator of ISRO. L&T was to fabricate the gas bottles using the titanium alloy that we imported from a US manufacturer—the same ones I had to virtually smuggle out of Chennai port after the US authorities put an embargo on the supply when the consignment was on its way. Some of my colleagues had told me that there were some technical difficulties in the fabrication, but the exact reason was not told. As the deadline neared, I inquired, and the company denied any such problem and promised to deliver the gas bottles soon.

When our engineers again raised the suspicion that L&T may not be doing anything about the gas bottles, I decided to go to the company's factory in Mumbai for a status assessment. On the work floor I found the titanium alloy mounted on the machine—a sign of work in progress. A colleague was still skeptical. He said they must have mounted the alloy because they knew I was visiting.

This proved right. I returned unannounced the next day and found that the alloy has been removed from the machinery. The previous day was stage managed. I took it as a personal insult and demanded to see the top man. The floor managers kept apologising, but I would settle for nothing less than an explanation from the CEO. I was taken to him.

'What's your problem?' I confronted him. 'Is there a difficulty in fabricating the gas bottles? If so tell me, I will solve the problem for you. Why should you do a drama with us?'

He was apologetic, but I insisted on a solution. He had none.

'I will cancel the order,' I said.

'You can't do that, we are such a big establishment.' The CEO's tone had changed.

That sounded almost like a counter threat. And I was only too happy to prove him wrong.

'Okay, either this contract will be scrapped or I will not remain the project director of the second stage of PSLV.'

I left in a huff and headed straight to the ISRO chairman's office in Bangalore.

'I am cancelling the L&T contract for gas bottles,' I told the chairman. My unspoken message was this, 'The order should stand cancelled no matter what the company represented to the chairman.'

Soon the L&T honchos were shaking their heads in disbelief when the ISRO order cancelling the contract reached their headquarters. The company's representatives now came pleading to me. I politely told them that if I needed their services I would let them know. Later, we got the hemispheres for the gas bottles fabricated by another company.

Back at the ISRO work floor, I continued to be a taskmaster. By now some from the Vernon team that had closely worked together on Vikas-Viking, had been sent back to other units; I got some of them back. And there were a few who I wanted to weed out, either because of lack of urgency or skills. I was soon left with a committed group of scientists, engineers and workers who shared a vision, goal and pride.

I ensured that such people got their due share of rewards, mostly timely promotion. ISRO scientists and engineers—at least the ones with no adverse remarks on their annual confidential reports—were eligible for a promotion every three years. But in many cases the promotion was delayed or denied due to bureaucratic bungling or petty score settling. I ensured that the deserving candidates in my team got promotion without delay. This was reason enough for those who I threw out of the team to murmur that if anyone in ISRO wanted a promotion, he or she should work in Nambi's team. I laughed at the stupidity of such remarks.

I had by now earned multiple epithets—a 'bulldozer' for lethargic collaborators and co-workers; a 'blue-eyed boy' of the ISRO chairman for my jealous colleagues; and a passionate yet pushy boss for the others. On being called as any of these behind my back, I neither regaled nor riled.

As we assimilated the components and started mock assembly, the ISRO board decided to put in place the mandatory non-conformance committee and the waiver committee. The non-conformance committee was essentially a quality control mechanism. It would study every component for its structural and behavioural aberration. In a rocket, every component and function has a margin within which they can vary. The conformance committee would look into the degree of variation and decide if it conforms to the standards and set margins. But being on the border or even outside the margin, in some cases, may not be a sole reason for rejection. In other words, if a variation is not significant enough to adversely affect the overall performance of the component, sub-system or the system, the waiver committee would waive off the variation and accept it.

Here I made a demand, which many found unreasonable, even impossible. I would head both the non-conformance committee and the waiver committee. Not that I did not anticipate opposition to this seemingly outrageous demand. Traditionally, and rightly so, the two committees are headed by different people. After all, what's the point in the same person presiding over a fault-finding panel and overruling the fault by virtue of heading a panel of appeal?

Well, here was my point. The committees, no doubt, had their utility, but they also smacked of bureaucracy. Going by our experience with the development of much smaller engines and systems, committees, even while ensuring quality of the work, have delayed projects. Vikas is a project on fast-track, something that has to be completed on a war-footing, so that PSLV lifts off by at least 1992. India could not wait to launch its first big rocket using a liquid propulsion engine.

Part two of my argument also did not go down well with some colleagues, but it stems from a level of ultimate confidence. I, as the head of the team that developed the Vikas-Viking engine in collaboration with the French, know better than anyone the systems and sub-systems here. I know the margins of error and how much of it would be tolerable for a successful project. Yes, you can suspect that this being my project I might manipulate some of the readings and waive off the margins. Let me tell anyone who has such suspicion that this is my baby, I will do nothing to make it fail. Well, if it fails, haul me up, hunt me down. But for now, please let me get on with the work.

There were protests, but Satish Dhawan again came as my saviour. 'The project has its urgency,' he said. 'And let Nambi be accountable for this.'

I was not done with it. I wanted this arrangement of a single person heading both the committees as an exception, not a rule. I told Dhawan that this should be considered as a special case since we were in development stage which cannot be delayed. Once the rocket flies and we get into the production mode, the non-conformance committee and the waiver committee should be headed by different people. Dhawan frowned, then smiled.

CHAPTER 24

MEENA WAITS FOR ME

'Never again call me to an exhibition of wine.'

As the car turned to West Fort, my neighbourhood where old buildings of the Travancore royalty's remnants stood their ground amidst mushrooming modern architecture, my thoughts were on my wife. Shankar, during his visits to the jail, had been giving me tidbits of information about her—that she was mostly silent and barely eating. She was a typical homemaker, the mother of my children, with virtually no social life.

She seldom complained about my long hours at work. She once laughed when someone, during a water shortage at home, commented that I was so obsessed with liquid propulsion in ISRO's rockets that I have forgotten about the faulty water tank that fed our modest kitchen at home.

She stood by me through the travails and tantrums that work pressure brought upon me.

Meenakshi Ammal, my wife, was born as the second of the thirteen children of her parents. Her father, Ramaswamy, did coir business and had properties at Chalai in Trivandrum, where my family also owned land. The families were related, and when the proposal came sometime in 1967, I went to meet her. I liked her simplicity and readily agreed for the marriage.

The previous year was one of high and low for me, with my joining TERLS in September 1966 and my mother dying in November. Meena and I got married at a simple ceremony on 8 September 1967, attended by my extended family and a few colleagues that included APJ Abdul Kalam. There was not much of a honeymoon. I got back to work two days after the wedding.

Meena is an orthodox Indian Hindu wife. Her daily outings were to temples, and she had a fixed weekly schedule: Srikanteswaram on Monday, Attukal Devi Temple on Tuesday and Friday, Srivaraham Temple on Thursday and Sri Padmanabha Swami Temple on Saturday. When we had children, we would go to the movies, once in a couple of months, the four of us on my scooter.

I would take her on tours to Indian cities once in a while. Her first travel abroad was to France when I led the ISRO team to Vernon for the Viking-Vikas joint venture in September 1974. We had gone to France with both our children, but having found good education in English medium hard to come by in Vernon, we send back our son Sankar to India in 1975 (Kalam was kind enough to take him back during one of his visits) and daughter Geetha the next year when my wife went on a six-months break to India. Our children started schooling in Trivandrum, staying with my elder sister till we returned in 1978.

Meena had a wonderful time in Veron, the women of our fifty-plus scientists forming a virtual commune in the French town of St Marcel. She also mingled with the local residents and vendors who came to sell their wares, picking up smatterings of French.

On weekends we drove to Paris and other parts of France in an 800cc Fiat car that I had bought secondhand for 500 Francs. My successor Chandran inherited this antique piece of automobile when I returned to India in early 1978, leaving the team to complete the work. During the yearly vacations we travelled across Europe.

One of the things she could never stand was alcohol. I kept telling her that wine was to the French what water was to us Indians, but she would just not give up her stand against the spirit. She knew we men had a few drinks at the parties, and she did not make an issue out of it till I kept her out of drinking.

Once, during an Aerospace exhibition, we as a couple were invited to inaugurate a pavilion. While fine French wine was being passed around, I whispered to Meena, 'Don't say no, it will be impolite. Just pretend that you are taking a sip.'

Poor Meena tried to do as directed, but could not stand the smell. An understanding host walked up to her and took away the wine glass.

'Never again,' she said, 'call me to an exhibition of wine.'

After our return to India, Meena settled back to her routine of temple visits. The only places she went, other than temples, was the houses of my sisters and hers. She was very fond of her youngest sister Usha who was younger to her by more than fifteen years. This sister would be a pillar of strength and consolation for Meena when my arrest and incarceration left her a complete wreck.

I woke up from my thoughts as the car, now taking me home from jail fifty days after the arrest, turned the last curve to my house. I asked Shankar what time it was.

'Eleven-thirty,' he said.

CRYOGENICS AND THE CHILLING EFFECT

'It's the best drink we've made, but it cannot be bottled.'

We were still in the late 1980s and the development of PSLV, which would be launched successfully only on 15 October 1994, after the first failure on 20 September 1993, was set to put India in the club of nations capable of launching its own geosynchronous satellites. But the game was already shifting to heavy satellite launches. And for this, India had to develop its Geosynchronous Satellite Launch Vehicle (GSLV) which needed a cryogenic upper stage engine.

India's cryogenic dream was born as early as in 1972 when two ISRO scientists Kanaka Rao and Mathew were asked to draw up an action plan, under Gowarikar. But nothing much happened, after Muthunayagam got this group merged into the propulsion group that he headed.

The leadership brought into the propulsion group a few more scientists, all PhDs. They included Kanaka Rao, Mathew, M N Nagarajan, B C Pillai, R S Bhute and Agarwal. I was not a PhD, though my Princeton degree kept me in good stead whenever someone sought to put academic background before ground performance, and they thought they could overwhelm me with this new breed of spin doctors.

M N Nagarajan was one of the most argumentative, sometimes impressive, one. Noticing that he had been critical of virtually every idea we discussed in meetings, I suggested that he try out something new.

'What's that?'

'Ion propulsion,' I said. 'Some call it electronic propulsion.'

From my interactions in Vernon, I knew the French were working on electronic propulsion, and by now it was in an advanced stage. Little was known about the technology outside those labs working on it, all we knew was that ions or sub-atomic electric charge was being used for propulsion, which meant a small engine to power a big payload.

I had a gut feeling that electronic propulsion in the long run could be used for interplanetary travel, but I did not foresee its use in satellite launches. To study more, I arranged a visit for Nagarajan and another scientist, S Ramnath (brother of S Chandrasekhar who won the Nobel Prize in 1995), to SEP, France. They stayed in the Vernon facility for a couple of months and returned with some basic lessons.

'Now what,' Nagarajan asked me.

I said it was now his baby, I just opened a door for him. It was for him to decide where to go.

He was not clear where to take his electronic propulsion lessons. And he had a point. Electronic propulsion had no application in any of the projects we were working on. It was like the early years of my fight for a liquid propulsion engine.

Electronic propulsion was, and continues to be, a system of the future. For now, with Nagarajan not showing willingness to toil over a technology of uncertain application, we rested the plan. Many felt it was too far ahead of our times. This, today I feel, was a clear lack of vision, as much as Dhawan's refusal to take the French offer of the HM-7 cryogenic engine in the mid-1970s. Having developed electronic propulsion to an advanced stage, the French have now saved up to 1.5 tonnes on payload.

R S Bhute, another of the Muthunayagam recruits, made himself appear to be a man of mysteries. Asked by colleagues what he was working on, Bhute would squint, James Bond-like, and say, 'Some chemicals.'

He often reminded me of an old man I had met in a nineteenth century tavern of a whiskey maker in Scotland in the early 1970s. The tavern, which doubled up as a dining place, served unlimited drinks and food for ten pounds. They also had this custom of designating, every night, the guest who had come from the farthest place their chief guest who got everything free. Having come from India, I was the lucky chap.

The old man who hailed from the original family or the distillers, served me a drink, which he said was special. It was a mellow form of a whiskey, with a great taste. I asked for its name. He did not have one. I asked why they were not selling it.

'It's the best drink we've made, but it cannot be bottled. It's just not stable,' the old man said.

Bhute was not half as articulate as the old man in the Scotland tavern. One day he announced that he had come up with a new liquid propellant.

'What's that?' everyone wanted to know.

'I can't tell you.'

Nobody ever again asked Bhute about his alchemy. None of the new recruits were able to come up with a game-changing idea or project. Soon they left, one by one.

The cryogenic plan remained in cold storage till the early 1990s, but for some sporadic work done by small teams in ISRO. By 1991, when PSLV was in advanced stages of development, GSLV studies were also gaining pace, with three versions of the launch vehicle—Mark I, Mark II and Mark III—being on the drawing board. Still we did not have a cryogenic engine. We had to buy the technology from one of them. This was easier said than done, for buying technology doesn't happen overnight.

Those who had the technology and engines were the USSR, the US, France, Japan and China. Even if one of them were to sell us, making our own engine and stage, it would take us several years of training under the guidance of the technology seller. The perennial truth in rocket science: getting all the blueprints and even a few pieces of finished engines do not enable one to put together a rocket engine. You need the 'know-why' beyond the know-how. So the only option would be to strike a deal with a country that has the technology to buy a few engines and also get a technology transfer with long-term collaboration for development.

While discussions were on to speed up cryogenic acquisition, that day in 1975 crossed my mind, when I was at the Paris, at Le Bourget Airport for the Aerospace Exhibition. Among the rocket engines on display was a Russian engine labelled RD-100. In one glance I knew it was a cryogenic engine, but something told me it was not RD-100.

'They've got the label wrong,' I had told my accompanying scientist Mohana Prasad. Just when we were walking away after searching for a Russian scientist who could clarify our doubt, an elderly man approached us. We had seen him at a distance; he appeared to be more of a helper. Even Russian scientists were not very conversant in English, so we had not bothered to consult this man in wrinkled clothes.

'Now, gentleman, what makes you think it's not an RD-100?' he said.

Prasad and I looked at each other in surprise before I replied.

'Because it doesn't look like one.'

'It is indeed an RD-100,' he said in English.

I disagreed.

'Tell me why?' he insisted.

'An RD-100 has a different type of a cooling passage,' I said.

The Russian had an expression which I could not ascertain as confused or amused.

'Can we discuss this over dinner?' he said.

Over dinner that night, the Russian scientist explained that it was not an RD-100 engine. It was a cryogenic engine called RD-56, also called the KVD-1. It came from the Isayev Design Bureau of Glavkosmos, the Russian rocket-making entity.

'Don't ask me why we did not label it thus,' he said. 'We just don't want to show off.'

The 'secret,' he claimed was that the engine has a specific impulse of 461 seconds.

The specific impulse of an engine is a hallmark of its strength. The Americans had developed engines with much lower specific impulse. Russians were great engineers, but this claim of having an engine of 461 seconds sounded unbelievable.

'You must be joking,' I told him.

'Come to Russia, and I will show you,' he said.

Almost fifteen years later, now Russia beckoned.

As soon as we made inquiries with Japan in the late 1980s about their cryogenic engine LE5, the US, France and the USSR approached us. We roughly worked out that the deal should include sale of a few engines and technology transfer. The contract should be for seven years during which the foreign engineers would train us. We hoped to start making our own cryogenic engines in fifteen years.

General Dynamics Corporation of the US quoted around Rs 935 crore, which we found too steep. Aerospatiale quoted a slightly higher amount for a few engines and technology transfer by SEP Vernon. Glavkosmos of the USSR was too eager to collaborate with India, but were clueless about the money they should ask for. They finally quoted Rs 235 crore for two engines and technology transfer.

I favoured a Russian pact. This sentiment was shared by many in ISRO, and the India Government. Russians have been historically friendly to India, and India had reciprocated this camaraderie. Besides the government-to-government rapport fostered by the idea of socialism, I felt, there was something that made Russians and Indians natural allies despite stark differences in virtually everything from appearance to language and culture to cuisine.

Initially I thought I am biased towards Russians because of the instant rapport I could establish with every Russian I met, despite the language barrier. When I shared this to my colleagues during private conversations, many of them shared my view. The core reason for this feeling of brethren, however, remained unanswered.

I had met a few Russian scientists who had visited us in the late 1960s on Vikram Sarabhai's invitation. But one I could call my first Russian friend, though his name escapes me now, was a campus mate in Princeton during 1969-70. Doing a graduate programme like me, he never mixed with anyone. That was not unusual for Russians on the campus, because despite their great scientific temper, many of them were not very conversant in English.

U R Rao, too, was keen on a Russian pact. Rao had known the Russians closely from 1972 when he signed the contract to launch India's first satellite Aryabhata by the Russian rocket Kosmos-3M. Aleksandr Dunayev, the chairman of Glavkosmos, the contract company that made rocket engines for the Soviet Union, was not a stranger to India. Dunayev and the agency's administrative officer in charge of cryogenic technology Aleksey V Vasin had visited India a few times on invitation from Vikram Sarabhai.

I had seen Russia as a prospective partner years earlier. During the development of PSLV, when the parallel indigenisation drive was on, I had taken a twelve-member team from different institutes and manufacturing units from India to Russia for familiarisation. It included representatives from Godrej, MTAR, Keltech, HAL, L&T and Walchandnagar Industries. MTAR founder Ravindra Reddy, who had by then demonstrated excellence in delivering some crucial parts of India's space programme and nuclear programme, was also a part of the team. Years later, this visit would help a few Intelligence Bureau officials to drag Reddy into the infamous ISRO spy case of 1994.

For a person who was given the permission by Vikram Sarabhai to build almost an entire nuclear plant, Reddy was, too, impeccable for those IB officers who played puppets in the hands of a foreign agency to be pulled down. Later, they tried to bring in the name of former Indian Prime Minister P V Narasimha Rao's son Prabhakar Rao to link Reddy and give the case a political overtone, but all these plans came unstuck.

It was not just our personal equations with Russians that tilted us towards the Glavkosmos offer; the engine on offer was unmatched in many ways. It was KVD-1, the engine that I stumbled upon at the Aerospace Exhibition in Paris in 1975. With a specific impulse of 461 seconds, this engine was far better than any American or French cryogenic engine.

There was something mysterious about KVD-1. Imagine a country making more than 250 such engines of fine caliber and stocking them! Moreover, it was something the Russians never wanted to flaunt.

In his book *Russia in Space: The Failed Frontier?* prolific space writer Brian Harvey writes about the engine:

One of the most remarkable episodes of the Russian space programme was the emergence, out of the hangar, of a secret engine developed by the (Isayev) bureau in the 1960s. In the late 1980s, India was looking for a third-stage hydrogen-powered rocket motor able to get its satellites into 24-hour orbit.

India especially wanted to orbit Gramsat, a multipurpose telecommunications satellite, to bring educational television to the villages of rural India. Knowing it would take at least 10 to 15 years to develop the technology itself, India sought help from abroad.

The engine in question was the KVD-1, built by the Isayev design bureau. No one had heard of the engine, and the West was certain that the USSR had never been able to develop cryogenic engine technology …

The KVD-1 engine has a thrust of 7,100kg, a burn time of 800 seconds and a combustion chamber pressure of 54.6 atmospheres. It weighs 282kg, is 2.1 metres tall and has a diameter of 1.6 metres.

The KVD-1 had a turbo pump-operated engine with a single fixed thrust chamber, two gimbaled thrust engines, could operate for up to 7.5 hours and be restarted five times.

… The KVD-1 had unsurpassed thrust and capabilities that made it unmatched for years. Its specific impulse of 461 seconds was still the highest in the world by the end of century. The KVD-1 was first test-fired in June 1967 and was tested for 24,000 seconds in six starts. Five live engines were tested over the years 1974-75 (some were made even after the manned lunar programme had been cancelled). This small object was to spark off international controversy.

The KVD-1 was not a new motor – it was originally developed as part of the Soviet manned moon landing programme as far back as 1964. Under Vasili Mishin's plan, the KVD-1 would have been used to land a Soviet lunar module able to sustain a team of cosmonauts for a month. However, the KVD-1 never flew and was placed in storage.

We struck the deal with Glavkosmos. There were no prizes for guessing who will be upset about a technology transfer from Russia to India; and we expected the worst.

By early 1991, the Soviet Union, the only geopolitical counter power to the US, was on the brink of a collapse, with Russia preparing to secede from the Union. The cold war had long ended and Mikhael Gorbachev, having experimented with Perestroika and Glasnost, was throwing his hands up at the imminent disintegration of the union, while the Americans were 'rubbing their hands in glee,' as the last Soviet leader would say twenty-five years later in an interaction to the British media.

The imminent fall of the Soviet Union meant the Americans would arm-twist Russia into subservience. Besides this, I had a reason to be restless. I was to retire in 2001. I wanted to use the Russian technology to develop a cryogenic engine that can put into orbit a payload of at least two tonnes by 1999, and then upgrade it to four tonnes.

We signed the Russian deal on 18 January 1991. Under this, Glavkosmos was to give us four KVD-1 engines and transfer the technology. For this, Russian engineers were to work with us for the transfer or 'know-why' besides giving us drawings, mock-up models, instruments and materials to build the engine. There were milestones built into the contract, spelling out the instalments of transfer against payments.

Four engines from the stockpile were peanuts for the Russians, though now they were in a severe financial crisis because of the plunging rouble. We were amazed to realise that Glavkosmos had made and stocked some 252 KVD-1 engines. Here was India, gasping at the idea of developing a cryogenic engine, and there was Russia, the pioneering space super power, in whose warehouses scores of cryogenic rocket engines were gathering dust!

But that was the quintessential Russian style of mass manufacturing. After several interactions with Dunayev and his associates, I learned that the Russians had tested the KVD-1 engines and found them to be of very high specific impulse, but never flew a rocket using one of them. When I asked an engineer, he said with complete nonchalance, 'We never got to.'

I was told the engines were meant for a series of interplanetary missions that Russia was planning. Unimaginable to even the US have been the Russian leaps in space science. Soon after World War II, the Red Army having captured Berlin in 1945, the writing was on the wall: the Soviet Union is going from strength to strength in missile technology and rocketry.

That led to the setting of the cold war a couple of years later. Joseph Stalin took the the Soviet Union to a greater level of industrialization and, even after Nikita Krushchev's de-Stalinisation, Russia remained an American envy when it came to science and technology. How the Soviet Union took the US by surprise with the launch of Sputnik, the first man-made satellite, on 4 October 1957 is now part of the dramatic history of space science.

The US had announced on 2 April 1955 that it would launch a satellite in the International Geophysical Year of 1957-58. Five days later, The Soviet Union said it would also do such a thing 'in the near future'. The first satellite launch by the Soviet Union shocked the US President Dwight D Eisenhower so much that he called it the 'Sputnik moment', a term almost every American President had used to underscore the need for America to wake up to the advances of other countries.

Even as the US was struggling to catch up with the Soviet Union, Russians sent Yuri Gagarin to space on 12 April 1961. America could claim a lead only on 20 July 1969 when Apollo-11 landed Neil Amstrong and Buzz Aldrin on moon. The Soviet Union never got to send a human to the moon, though it set up space stations like the Salyuts between 1973 and 1976, and Mir which was in orbit from 1986 to 2001. After enabling an array of satellites that boosted communication, navigation and many other applications, the US-Soviet Union space race ended with the fall of the Soviet Union in 1991.

The great nation's disintegration could not have happened at a worse time for our cryogenic plans. By 1989, the Eastern Bloc of nations had, one by one, overthrown their Communist governments and, by Gorbachev's own plan, the Soviet Union was getting increasingly democratized.

By April 1990, Soviet Union had started its race towards its end, having introduced a law allowing any republic to cede from the union if two-thirds of its population so felt. Russia had started charting its own course a year earlier, electing the Congress of People's Deputies of which Boris Yeltsin became the chairman on 12 June 1990.

Russia voted for the continuation of Soviet Union in a referendum in March 1990, but Yeltsin asserted that Russian laws superseded Soviet laws. By June 1991, Boris Yeltsin was elected the president of the Russian Federation.

Gorbachev was readying for the New Union Treaty when hardcore communists attempted the August Coup. When Gorbachev emerged from a few days of house arrest, Yeltsin had emerged powerful. Many republics declared independence and went their way.

When only Kazakhstan remained, Yeltsin took control of whatever was left of the Soviet Government. On the Christmas day of 1991, Gorbachev resigned and announced the formal. The next day, the Supreme Soviet officially announced that it and Soviet Union have ceased to exist.

Now Yeltsin was the sole political power centre in Russia, but the dissolution of Soviet Union had sent Russia, and all the other republics, into a financial tailspin. First we thought it was good for us, as the rupee appreciated tremendously against the ruble. But it turned out that a weakened Russia was struggling to withstand pressure from the US to cancel the cryogenic contract with India.

We knew the US would impose sanctions if we went ahead with the contract. Since everything ISRO did was being closely watched by the US, we asked Glavkosmos to tie up with KELTEC (Kerala Hi-tech Industries Limited), a quasi-government entity under the Government of Kerala. But the US saw through this strategy. In May 1992, the US imposed sanctions on India and Russia for two years invoking Missile Technology Control Regime (MTCR) provisions.

The next one year was spent devising ways and means to preserve the contract and make Russia honour it despite severe pressure from the US. Dunayev was cooperative, and we had many exchanges. I made multiple visits to Russia. Once or twice I accompanied U R Rao, a veteran of Russian pacts, to interior Russia where hundreds toiled away in snow-covered facilities to make some of the finest pieces of space engineering, and try to find answers to the secrets of the universe.

There were two distinct groups within the Russian space community—one who believed that Russia and India are 'natural partners' and the friendship should continue at any cost; the other who did not quite question the Russia-India camaraderie, but yielded to either American threats or favours.

Dunayev was the tallest technocrat who represented the former group. He prevailed upon Russian President Boris Yeltsin to stand by the commitment to India to a large extent, but Yeltsin himself was on a shaky wicket during the systemic disintegration of the Soviet Union. Even when the Supreme Soviet of the Russian Federation, on 21 July 1993 passed a resolution saying that international contracts that come under the Missile Technology Control Regime should have its consent, Glavkosmos stood by its commitment. A media report quoted Glavkosmos: 'We shall not stop fulfilling our obligations under the contract until there is a government decision to the contrary.'

But we all saw it coming. In May 1993, the ISRO chairman's office received a call from Dunayev's secretary conveying that Russia will not be able to honour the cryogenic contract as it was signed. They wanted to make some drastic changes, and that called for some drastic action from us.

It turned out that the US had brought the Russia-India cryogenic engine pact under the Missile Technology Control Regime. This was ridiculous as cryogenic engines were not used for making missiles. Moreover, the US itself had agreed to supply us cryogenic engines; when India rejected the costly deal with General Dynamics Corporation and decided to sign the deal with the Russian Glavkosmos, transfer or cryogenic engine and technology became a threat to world peace!

Brian Harvey writes in *Russia in Space: The Failed Frontier?*

'...*In May 1992, the Bush administration announced that it was applying American sanctions on both the Indian Space Research Organisation (ISRO) and Glavkosmos for two years. The sanctions involved American non-cooperation with both agencies and the introduction of sales embargoes on India. India objected strongly to the American actions, pointing out that high-powered hydrogen-fuelled upper stages which took a long time to prepare were of little military value in attacking a neighbouring country with which they already had a land border. India also pointed out that the Americans had offered them the very same technology and had made no objections throughout the years 1988-92 when the arrangements had begun.*

'*In 1993, with the accession of Bill Clinton as president, the American attitude relented. He approved a re-opening of cooperation with ISRO and*

Glavkosmos if the Russians transferred individual engines, but not the production technology that would enable India to design its own cryogenic engines. In July 1993, after negotiations in Washington DC, Russia backed off its proposals to transfer technology to India and suspended its agreement, invoking force majeure (circumstances beyond their control), to the fury of the Indian government.'

Harvey unravels an American double game here in his book:

'The KVD-1 had now become caught up in a much bigger game— the negotiations between America and Russia for the construction of the International Space Station, Russia suggested compensation for loss of the Indian contract and the $400m paid by the United States for seven American flights to Mir may have become part of the equation.

In a revised agreement with India in January 1994, Russia agreed to transfer three, later renegotiated by the Indians to seven, KVD-1s intact, without the associated technology, for a price of $9m. The negotiations were later described as very tough, but the Indians managed to negotiate a lower price and extra engines in exchange for the loss of technology transfer. In addition, two models would be supplied to test how they would best fit the launcher shroud. India was required by the United States to agree to use the equipment purely for peaceful purposes, not to re-export it or modernize it without Russia's consent.'

Brian Harvey was not entirely wrong when he said that 'development of the Indian upper stage with Russian help had been underway for four years when the arrangements were denounced by American President George Bush as a violation of the Missile Technology Control Regime. Harvey got it wrong when he said four years, though.

In the same chapter, 'The rocket engine frontier', Harvey says rather vaguely: 'According to some American sources, the Russians transferred the production technology in any case. The appropriate documents, instruments and equipment were allegedly transferred in four shipments from Moscow to Delhi on covert flights by Ural Airlines. As a cover, they used "legitimate" transshipments of Indian aircraft technology travelling the other way to Moscow for testing in Russian wind-tunnels.'

This, again, was not entirely wrong. India did bring documents, instruments and equipment from Russia, but all of them were legitimate and abiding by the first contract India and Russia had.

But was it a covert operation?

Yes, and also perfectly legit.

Here is why.

Soon after we got information from Glavkosmos that it would not be able to honour the contract, I flew down to meet Dunayev.

He was quite open about the situation.

'It's equally disappointing for us,' he said, showing me a copy of the letter the US Secretary of State had written to the Russia Government seeking to bring the deal under the Missile Technology Control Regime.

'But they are opposed only to technology transfer,' I said.

Dunayev nodded.

'What if we remove that from the papers?

'And?'

'We will rewrite the contract, I said. 'Instead of technology transfer, you give us more engines than originally agreed upon.'

'We don't have the time.'

'How much time before you have to call off the contract?'

'A couple of months,' said Dunayev.

'That's fine, with a new contract, let's do the deal. With some continued help from you guys,' I said, 'we will try to develop the engine on our own.'

Dunayev now had that knowing smile.

Here was the strategy. The contract was written in such a way that payments would be made according to milestones of transfer of technology that included drawings and hardware. I told Dunayev that we will advance the payments and the milestones, so that the transfer process is accelerated before they formally announce cancellation of contract invoking *force majeure*. Within months we would enter into a new contract without a mention of technology transfer. For this we used Glavkosmos agent Chandrasekhar, who later became a co-accused in the ISRO spy case. I am not sure if the interrogators from the IB would be less cruel to Chandrasekhar had they known the role he played in advancement of these milestones to ensure India got the necessary cryogenics documents and hardware.

'Technology transfer' is a term often poorly understood; for some it is a red herring. Many think of it as something that can be transferred as files, models and blueprints. At least in rocket science, it is not. Blueprints and models are just two parts of a technology transfer; the bigger part comprise hands-on training and handholding by the masters.

Soon after we signed the contract in 1991, this process had begun. Soon after the meeting with Dunayev, we advanced the milestones of the contract so that much of the hardware and blueprints, estimated to fill the cargo holds of more than three flights, were formally ours though we could not get them to India soon. Bill Clinton as the US President was not as hawkish towards India as was his predecessor Bush, but the system was something even Presidents could not change.

American spies were all over Russia, trying to sniff out everything related to the India-Russia deal. Washington had reasons to believe that despite the sanctions, and the original contract being annulled, Glavkosmos may transfer the technology to ISRO. What they did not know, however, was that some of it had already happened, at least on paper. We had advanced the milestones and, technically speaking, India had owned some of the drawings and materials though it had not taken possession of. Then we signed the second contract in January 1994, while the cargo was still in Russia.

At our side, the Ministry of External Affairs had given instructions to allow ISRO to take delivery of the cargo from any Indian airport without customs inspection. This did not go down well with some Customs officers who thought it their birthright to rummage through any container that reached the Indian airports.

At the Trivandrum airport, some of them tried citing rules and insisted on inspecting the cargo. I told them touch the ISRO cargo at their own peril. If anyone found the government instructions overbearing, I suggested they take up their case with the PMO or the MEA. When they could not meddle with the cargo, they tried to spread rumours about a racket that is smuggling cavier and vodka from Moscow!

A big disappointment for us was Air India. Despite the import having clearance from the highest level, the national carrier refused to take the cargo fearing loss of business if the Americans came to know of it. Air India was making some money out of its trans-Atlantic flights, and without landing rights in the US, 'the Maharaja' would find the going tough. When the resistance from Air India was stiff, the government asked us if there was any other airline willing to bring the consignment.

Dunayev once again proved his friendship with India by offering the services of Russian Ural Airlines, a private airline. We finalised the schedule for export. Four flights of Ural Airlines would carry the consignment to India. One or two of the four flights, as per the schedule, were to have a stopover at Karachi (during my interrogation in the ISRO spy case later that year, the Intelligence Bureau, having collected some bits and pieces of this transshipment, had tried to link the Karachi stopover to an imaginary Pakistani connection).

The first flight (URL 224) from Moscow landed in Trivandrum on 23 January 1994 after a stopover in Karachi. The second flight (URL 9001) landed on 11 March 1994. The third (URL 3791) via Sharjah reached Trivandrum on 17 July 1994. The fourth and last flight carrying the cryogenic engine material was to come in December.

Before that, on 30 November 1994, the Kerala police arrested me in the fabricated ISRO spy case.

The foreign conspirators' political masters can pat themselves on the back for this achievement, for the case came at the most opportune time for them as India was at the cusp of a cryogenic leap.

Here is more from Harvey's book *Russia in Space: The Failed Frontier?*:

'The plot thickened when at the same time, in October (sic) 1994, two scientists at the Indian Liquid Propulsion Systems Centre, S Nambi Narayanan and P Sasikumaran, were arrested for 'spying for foreign countries'. Eventually the Central Bureau of Investigation admitted that the charges against S Nambi Narayanan and P Sasikumaran were false and baseless and they were freed. Later, the United States was accused of setting them up as part of a dirty tricks campaign against the sale of the KVD-1.'

So why did the Americans want to scuttle the Indian space programme? For the uninitiated, here is what J Rajasekharan Nair, author of the book *Spies from Space: The ISRO Frame-up*, wrote in *Open Magazine* in February 2013:

'*The move to sabotage Isro's cryogenic programme began on 18 January 1991, the date on which Isro signed the agreement, 800-1/50, with Glavkosmos, the Russian space agency. The agreement went against US business interests in two ways.*

'*The price quoted by Glavkosmos for the transfer of technology and supply of three cryogenic engines was Rs 235 crore, nearly 400 per cent less than what America's General Dynamics had quoted. The undercutting caused serious concern over sales of American rocket technology elsewhere. Secondly, the price-per-kg–payload fixed for the GSLV to launch satellites into geosynchronous orbit, 36,000 km from Earth, was less than half the price quoted by US vehicles. This, too, meant a market hit for America.*'

The ISRO spy case bubble burst in less than two years when the CBI called the IB's bluff, and I was reinstated in ISRO as the director, advanced technology and planning, on 1 June 1996 at the Bangalore headquarters. But the arrest and the subsequent damage the case did to ISRO scientists' morale was so bad that our cryogenic project languished for almost nineteen years. I can say with certainty that if this fabricated case was not to be, India would have launched its first GSLV using an indigenous cryogenic engine at least fifteen years earlier. In fact, I had a special interest to achieve this, as I wanted to see GSLV flying before I retire in 2001.

The dream was shattered when a police jeep from the Vanchiyoor station screeched to a halt in front of my house early in the afternoon of 30 November 1994.

CHAPTER 25

MEENA MAKES A NOISE

'I am back.'

The street which usually sleeps by 10 pm appeared to be awake. Lights were on at my place. Waiting at the gate were my neighbour and colleague Mohana Prasad and his brother-in-law Ramachandra Kurup who also worked with ISRO.

I got out of the car. Prasad came and hugged me as I stood looking at my house, a two-storied structure in white and ochre, the sweat of my brow. Prasad was crying. Retrieving myself from his grip, I walked towards my house. In the drawing room, my daughter Geetha and my two sisters were waiting. As soon as I entered the house, my sisters came to me and held my hands; Geetha stood there, just looking at me. My wife was not to be seen.

'Where's Meena?' I asked.

Geetha pointed towards the flight of stairs, indicating she was upstairs. I took the stairs that led from the drawing room to the first floor where our bedroom was. Why did Meena not wait for me at the gate or in the living room? I wondered. It was almost midnight. She usually went to bed early and was up before the sun. But whenever I came late, she would stay awake for me. Sometimes I would have had dinner with colleagues or friends and she would have been waiting with food for me. She would tuck away the rice in the fridge and go back to bed, with no murmur of protest.

As I entered the room, I saw her on the floor, with no mattress or pillow. The light was switched off, but light from the landing on the first floor streamed into the room, casting a disfigured shadow of hers on the floor.

She had her head resting on her right hand. I was not sure if she was sleeping, she was facing away from me. I did not want to wake her up if she was sleeping, but I was longing to console her, get consoled in her embrace.

I called out her name. Then a second time. Did she move?

I switched on the bedroom lamp.

'Meena,' I called again, this time loud. 'I am back.'

She turned around slowly, raised her head and stayed still, staring into my eyes. She had a strange expression, as if she was watching me doing something horrible. Then she let out a shriek that I had never heard—from a human or an animal. It ran through the house, woke up the neighbourhood and sent everyone at home rushing upstairs. It lasted a few seconds. Then she fell silent again, still staring at me.

I sat down and rested her head on my lap. I ran my fingers through her hair. I called out her name, softly.

She was silent. I felt her tears wet my thighs.

PSLV FLIES, SO DOES MY RESIGNATION LETTER

'My part worked well, the second stage.'

It may be preposterous to say the US prompted a Kerala police inspector to arrest a Maldivian woman to implicate ISRO scientists and stall India's progress in space science. The inspector, a virtually insignificant character in the drama, only had his personal motives in threatening and arresting Mariam Rasheeda. But later, when the police discovered ISRO scientist Sasikumaran's phone number in Rasheeda's diary, the US struck through their cohorts in Indian IB.

A few IB officers including its then joint directors M K Dhar and Rattan Sehgal, were only too eager to play along for obvious benefits. It so happened that when the ISRO spy case broke out, a faction within the

Congress party that was in power in Kerala, too, found it an opportunity to bring down K Karunakaran from the Chief Minister's chair. This they succeeded when A K Antony, then Oommen Chandy's leader, replaced Karunakaran in March 1995.

The false implication of inspector general of police Raman Srivastava in the case was part of the coup as the officer was believed to be close to Karunakaran. The CBI and the Supreme Court finally saw through these multiple game plans and acquitted all the accused. The CBI went to the extent of writing confidential letters to the union government and the Kerala government recommending action against the officers who implicated me and others in the case. That action is yet to be taken.

While the American game plan was specifically designed to stymie India's cryogenic programme, the timing of the ISRO spy case is significant also because of another ISRO milestone, the successful flight of the PSLV. It marked the coming of age of India's liquid propulsion system. For me it was the culmination of more than two decades of internal battles to bring in a liquid system into the heart of India's first satellite launch vehicle.

The first launch of PSLV (D1) on 20 September 1993 was a failure, but I was happy that the Viking engine that we so painstakingly developed had performed well. The second launch (PSLV-D2) was a textbook success. PSLV has had no failure since then, and it had thirty-five consecutively successful launches till June 2016. The first successful launch of PSLV was on 15 October 1994. Five days later, the Maldivian woman, Mariam Rasheeda was arrested. More than a month later, on 30 November they came for me.

The run-up to the PSLV launch was a period of uncertainty over some succession issues in ISRO. U R Rao, with whom I had an excellent rapport, was to retire in April 1994. Among the probable successors was Muthunayagam, my boss at the Liquid Propulsion Systems Centre. My experience as his deputy in LPSC had not been great. He was not amused by my proximity to the ISRO chairman right from Vikram Sarabhai, Satish Dhawan and now U R Rao. His inherent biases were not a secret; and these were to eventually cost his the chairman's post which Rao entrusted with R Kasturirangan, though he was not a patch on many others in terms of scientific or administrative skills.

The ISRO chairman, till then, was someone of tall stature, someone virtually everyone in the system looked up to. That ended with Rao. Since Kasturirangan, very ordinary people have sat on the big chair. I am not sure if ISRO would ever have as its chairman someone who will be in the league of the first three giants—Vikram Sarabhai, Satish Dhawan and U R Rao.

In 1993, as we were preparing for the PSLV launch, I made my calculations. I was now the project director of the second and fourth stages of PSLV, and also the project director of cryogenics. If U R Rao got an extension of service, which was likely, it would not be bad. If Muthunayagam becomes the chairman, which was unlikely, I would find it tough to get positions of importance; even my natural promotion as the LPSC director was doubtful.

I started working on an exit strategy. I had two immediate options. Go to the US, where I was sure to get a job in rocketry; get into some business where my engineering expertise can be put to use. A Kerala businessman named Kurien E Kalathil had approached me sometime earlier. A railway contractor then, Kurien had ambitious plans including a harbor project in Manila and shrimp farming in India. Kurien had been behind me for a sweat equity, and whenever I had tiffs with Muthunayagam I was prompted to say yes to the businessman. I kept it as a fallback option.

I used this contact, however, to get a job for my son Sankar, who had completed M. Com. Though I did not commit on a joint venture with Kurien, I helped him plan some ventures. For some of these, I offered advice and spoke to his prospective business partners abroad. For this Kurien had installed a telephone in my house in the name of my son. During the spy case, the investigators 'unearthed' the existence of this phone at my place, which had run 'huge bills' because of some international calls made.

These calls were primarily to Ron Zebel, an American expert in aqua culture who was employed by TIG with whom Kurien had struck a deal to start an aqua culture farm near Tiruchendur in south Tamil Nadu. Kurien had bought vast tracts of land for this. All this went to dogs after Kurien was dragged in for questioning in the spy case.

With the business venture with Kurien as a backup, I upped my ante in ISRO. In July 1993, a couple of months before the first launch of PSLV, I told Rao that I wanted to quit if there was no clear succession plan for LPSC, of which I was the deputy director. The logical progression of a deputy director was to become an associate director before taking over as the director.

Rao, who was on an extension as the ISRO chief, was to retire the next year. With Gowarikar having moved out of ISRO to become the secretary, science and technology, soon after Rao took over as the ISRO chairman, the contenders for the chairman post were R M Vasagam, Muthunayagam, both engineers, and R Kasturirangan, an astrophysicist. In terms of qualification and seniority, Vasagam would have been the natural choice for the post, but he was seen as too soft a person to captain the ISRO ship through the rough sea of challenges the organisation faced from within and outside.

Still I believe Vasagam, like Y Janaradhana Rao, was one of the chairmen ISRO never had. Vasagam could well be considered the father of APPLE (Ariane Passenger Payload Experiment). When the French offered a free ride for the first India-made satellite onboard its flight of the Ariane rocket using Viking engines on 16 July 1981, Vasagam was so sure about the satellite's success that he asked government agencies including Defence and Doordarshan to give their requirements so that the transponder could be programmed accordingly.

It appeared that nobody shared Vasagam's enthusiasm or confidence and the response was poor. Finally, ISRO had to make some videos of tribal dances to be telecast during the gaps between education programmes given by some agencies. Finally, when the satellite remained in orbit for its mission life of two years, though one of the solar panels failed to deploy, there were no Doordarshan programmes to be aired.

Vasagam was called, in VSSC, an 'encyclopedia of rockets', but he never projected himself. He could speak endlessly, with the minutest of details of virtually every rocket man had made. Probably the only person who came near Vasagam's knowledge about rocketry was A Chandran, my college mate and later colleague who took over the mantle of Vikas group from me when I returned from Vernon in 1978.

Vasagam never haggled for power; in fact, he refused to even seek the recognition he richly deserved. I was convinced of this handicap—some call it a quality—when Sarabhai was in Trivandrum, sometime in the late 1960s, to see a thrust pick-up system. Vasagam had developed the system, but his boss S C Gupta, who headed the control and guidance group, was explaining the system and getting all the compliments from Sarabhai.

This was something I could not tolerate. Whenever someone had tried to take the entire credit for systems I had developed I had made sure that I got my pound of flesh. But this man, Vasagam, was such a *karma yogi* that he was happy with his boss taking all the pats on his back. At one point, when Sarabhai turned to me amidst the appreciation for the thrust pick-up, I said it was all Vasagam's sweat. Gupta was not amused.

Probably it was this soft nature of Vasagam that went against him when it came to the selection of ISRO chairman. Vasagam was moved out of ISRO and made the vice-chancellor of Anna University in Tamil Nadu. He silently took up the assignment and plunged headlong into academics with a smiling face.

Meanwhile V Sudhakar, a brilliant mechanical engineer, was brought into LPSC. My senior in Abdul Kalam's group, Sudhakar was passionate about his work, but his heart was more in setting up and heading KELTEC (Kerala Hightech Industries Limited). KELTEC, a Kerala government enterprise aimed at making high-precision parts for vital sectors, was actually a brainchild of ISRO to work around the US sanctions to get the cryogenic technology transferred from Russia. Sudhakar went on to head KELTEC, which became operational in 1994.

Muthunayagam, meanwhile, was clear that he would quit if he was not made the ISRO chairman. Muthunayagam as chairman was not an ideal situation for me, but I would any day vouch he is better qualified than Kasturirangan, who Rao finally picked for the job.

When I met Rao in July 1993, my message was simple, 'I am in line to take over as LPSC director after Muthunayagam leaves. Spell out the succession plan, or I quit.'

Rao sought to buy time. He said he was not seeking an extension, but I knew he would not have said no if the government offered him one. However, he said, his retirement was due only the next year, and that I should focus on PSLV.

'Let's launch PSLV first, we will talk about this later,' he said.

I agreed.

We launched the first PSLV carrying the Indian Remote Sensing Satellite IRS-1E from Sriharikota on 20 September 1993. The first and the second stages performed well, but the launch was a failure because of the malfunctioning of the third stage.

Though the PSLV was a failure the success of the Vikas engine was special to me in another way. It was the first time the bell-shaped nozzle was being tested. In fact, when a committee debated whether an untested piece can be flown, I had successfully argued that the first flight of the rocket be considered as the high-altitude test for the nozzle since we did not have such a test facility on ground. This was a personal triumph of sorts.

Still there was no clarity on LPSC succession. I went back to Rao with my resignation letter. It was 8 November 1993.

I explained to him that my career path was not clear, that I could not hang around in uncertainty. By now Rao must have been clear that he would not get a further extension as the chairman once his tenure ends in April 1994. The proud man that he was, he would neither ask the government for one. I understood that Rao was also making moves to anoint his successor, who turned out to be Kasturirangan.

The ISRO chairman is nominated by a search committee and approved by the Indian Prime Minister, but often the outgoing chairman's word was the unwritten rule. The only chairman not recommended by the outgoing chairman was probably Satish Dhawan, and this was because of Sarabhai's untimely death on 30 December 1971.

In fact, Sarabhai had been inviting Dhawan to join the space programme and the prime minister did not look further in search of Sarabhai's successor. But since Dhawan, then the director of Indian Institute of Sciences, Bangalore was abroad, the government appointed M G K Menon as the interim chairman.

M G K Menon, who took over the reins of Tata Institute of Fundamental Research at the age of thirty-eight from Homi J Bhabha, on the latter's death in a plane crash in Mont Blanc in 1966, and remained the chairman for nine months, till September 1972. Dhawan put one condition before accepting the ISRO mantle. He would not move out of Bangalore. If Mohammed won't go to the mountain, the mountain must come to him. That is how ISRO came to be headquartered in Bangalore.

'What are you pondering over?' Rao's voice woke me up from my thoughts.

I took the resignation letter from my pocket.

'Now that the launch is over, I am quitting,' I said, handing over the letter.

'But the launch is a failure,' said Rao.

'My part worked well, the second stage.'

Rao considered this for a moment. Both of us knew that the argument was just technical, the real issue—the LPSC succession was still hanging fire.

He countered me.

'You are also the project director of the fourth stage. We haven't yet seen its success.'

He tore my resignation letter and threw it in the bin. It was the second time this had happened; the first time it was Dhawan flinging my resignation after the failure of the ground test of the three-tonne engine at Sriharikota in 1973.

'Get back to work,' Rao said in his usual soft voice. 'Fly the PSLV successfully and do whatever you want.'

I knew Rao was again buying time, keeping the LPSC succession plan in abeyance. Nevertheless, I thought I should be part of the PSLV success, which was imminent. But, by remaining non-committal on my elevation, and his own continuance in ISRO, Rao made me think if he had a Machiavellian streak in him. Rao had made the tactical move to Bangalore to head the satellite centre so that he could be close to the headquarters. Indeed he was most qualified for the ISRO chairman's job, but he was not the only one.

Y J Rao, who should be credited with developing the Sriharikota Range (SHAR) could well have become the ISRO chairman before U R Rao, but for some unfortunate incidents and a cardinal mistake on Dhawan's part. Sriharikota was identified in 1969 for setting up launch pads and some auxiliary facilities. Within two years, a Rohini (RH–125) rocket was launched from here, marking its inauguration.

When acquired from the Andhra Pradesh Government, Sriharikota, a spindle-shaped island, was mostly uninhabited, with the Bay of Bengal on one side and the Pulicat lake, actually a lagoon, on the other three. The place almost perfectly suited ISRO's requirements as it was on the east coast and not too far from the equator. Some fishing hamlets on the sea side were the only signs of human habitation there. Being a deserted place added to the safety.

From laying a road from Sullurpet, the 'mainland', to setting up the launch facility, it was a Herculean task that ISRO teams captained by Y J Rao and a few others achieved in two years. Soon after the land acquisition, Sarabhai asked the seniors to come up with proposals for the facilities that could be set up there. Gowarikar came up with the idea of a solid propellant space booster plant (SPROB); Muthunayagam wanted a static test and evaluation complex (STEX); Y J Rao proposed the Rocket Sled Facility which included aerodynamics testing and launch facilities. Sarabhai approved all the projects.

A year after the first Rohini launch from SHAR in 1971, Y J Rao took over as its director and continued there for five years. He was a natural choice as Dhawan's successor, but a coterie, which was envious of his well-deserved rise was waiting for an opportunity to pull him down. These people had raised several allegations against Y J Rao, including that he was autocratic. None of the charges stuck. The gang struck when Y J Rao transferred a woman, who was his personal assistant in Trivandrum, to SHAR.

When complaints against Y J Rao piled up, Dhawan constituted a committee to inquire. VSSC director Brahm Prakash, Gowarikar, Muthunayagam and ISRO chairman's advisor Y S Rajan were part of the committee. Later Rajan told me that the panel turned out to be a motley crowd of people, most of who had an axe to grind with Y J Rao.

Once when the discussions in the committee meeting degenerated to personal vilification of Y J Rao, Rajan walked out of it, never to return. Brahm Prakash, too, came out of the committee, calling it a 'gutter group'.

The committee submitted a report to the chairman recommending Y J Rao's transfer out of SHAR. Dhawan upheld the recommendation and transferred Y J Rao to the ISRO headquarters in Bangalore as the director, launch services. This post, occupied by Abdul Kalam for a short while before being moved to DRDL, thus came to be considered the 'exit route' from ISRO. Dhawan must have regretted the decision, and it might have been a gesture of apology when he invited Y J Rao for the first launch of SLV-3 from Sriharikota on 10 August 1979. Y J Rao did not turn up.

Within a few months of his transfer, Y J Rao quit and migrated to the US. ISRO just lost a potential chairman. Decks were cleared for U R Rao to take over from Dhawan as the ISRO chairman, though it would happen only in 1984.

This history was rankling me when U R Rao sounded evasive about giving a commitment on my elevation as the LPSC director. But when he argued that I cannot leave just when the PSLV had a failed first flight, and that I have to ensure its success, I agreed. With the first flight, I was confident of the success of the second and fourth phases, for which I was the project director, but every launch has to be considered a new venture. We got back to work, putting together the second Viking engine and the smaller fourth-stage liquid engine.

A month before Rao was to retire, on 15 March 1994, I returned to Rao, this time not with a resignation letter but a letter seeking permission to go to the US for 'higher studies for employment'. The letter implied that I wanted to leave ISRO after the successful flight of PSLV, but since Rao was on the verge of retirement, I did not want him the bitter feeling of a resignation. He understood it, and approved the request. The proposed US visit remained just a ruse.

As Muthunayagam was staying from work soon after Kasturirangan took over as the chairman, I made my demand to be elevated to the LPSC director post clear to Kasturirangan. When he remained non-committal, sometime in August 1994 I told Kasturirangan that I would be quitting after the next launch. He agreed.

The second launch of PSLV (D2) carrying Indian Remote Sensing Satellite (IRS-P2), on 15 October 1994 was a success, but not before some tense pre-launch moments. Towards the last leg of the countdown, a problem with a transducer, if my memory serves me right, was detected and the launch was put on hold. To set right the problem, the protocol was that the rocket had to be de-armed, meaning the fuel has to be drained, before anyone goes near the rocket.

This meant the launch could not happen within the window that day. I said I would go set right the problem, there was no need to de-arm the rocket. Engineers S Ramakrishnan (who later became VSSC director) and S Somanath (who later became LPSC director) accompanied me to the rocket. It is not exactly soothing to work on a rocket with close to 190 tonnes of solid and liquid fuels in its belly. We fixed the problem in a few minutes and the countdown resumed. It was a textbook launch.

I had kept my promise to Rao, though he had by now retired and R Kasturirangan had taken over—another reason that I found no point in continuing with ISRO without a clear career path. I could sense that G Madhavan Nair, my junior who was made PSLV project director, was waiting to be eased into the LPSC director's chair by the new dispensation. (He followed a smooth trajectory from there to the VSSC directorship and eventually the ISRO chairmanship).

Now that the PSLV had been flown successfully, I decided to hang my ISRO boots.

✳ ✳ ✳

Around the same time the PSLV lifted off, an inspector called Vijayan was 'inquiring' a Maldivian woman called Mariam Rasheeda who had gone to him with a request for extension of her stay. She had apparently come for medical treatment and also looking for a school admission for her friend Fauziyya Hassan's daughter.

According to media interviews later given by Mariam, the inspector made sexual advances and, when she did not yield, kept her travel documents with him and later booked her for overstay and soon spying. This was later confirmed by a court that absolved Mariam of the charges.

The inspector, having found ISRO scientist Sasikumaran's name in Rasheeda's phone directory, now got a reason to question the woman on her connection with the scientist. It turned out that Mariam had contacted Sasi through a common friend, for the treatment of her daughter. Sasi, whose wife was a doctor, offered help. I later realised that he did meet Mariam a few times with his wife.

The day after the successful launch of PSLV–D2, when I returned from Sriharikota, IB and R&AW had questioned Mariam, and Sasi had given a detailed note to the LPSC director and ISRO chairman about the police having contacted him.

I felt sad for Sasi, who was my deputy in the cryogenic project, but this episode had nothing to do with my decision to quit ISRO. After all, it was a settled issue with U R Rao the previous year that I would walk soon after the first successful launch of PSLV.

On 26 October 1994, I accompanied ISRO chairman Kasturirangan to New Delhi for a felicitation by the Indian Prime Minister for our successful PSLV launch. Four days later, on 1 November 1994, I handed over my letter requesting for voluntary retirement from ISRO, to the chairman. In the three previous instances when I had offered to resign—once when Dhawan was the chairman, and twice during the last leg of U R Rao's tenure—the chairman had thrown the paper in the dustbin and asked me to stay back. Kasturirangan did none of it—he took the letter from me.

Before Kasturirangan could process it, the Kerala Police arrested me, on 30 November 1994. Having been booked in a criminal case, my employment with ISRO stood suspended. Anything about my continuance or my resignation was in suspended animation till the case came to a logical end. The interrogators of IB later had a field day flashing my letter seeking voluntary retirement as a bid to escape the spy case.

'Here is proof that you wanted to run away before we came,' an IB officer had said.

'Please call me anything but an idiot,' I told him. 'If I had done something wrong, do you think I would submit my resignation and leave the letter as evidence in your hands?'

The IB man had not got it, but the CBI later found merit in my argument.

As for the resignation letter dated 1 November 1994, the IB chose not to read my footnote: Incidentally, you may kindly recall my discussion with you during August 1994 and my request to seek voluntary retirement after the PSLV launch. And you had kindly agreed to my request to be relieved after the launch.

The CBI later upheld this point.

But now, with my arrest, the ISRO spy case just had its big villain. What was a case of a Maldivian tourist's overstay in Trivandrum less than a month ago, had become a potboiler of spies, rocketry and two Indian space scientists who plotted to sell the nation's secret to Pakistan!

Hardly one-and-a-half month into the successful launch of its first polar satellite launch vehicle, ISRO's champagne had not cooled enough when the police came for me. The conspirators must have clinked glasses.

CHAPTER 26

A GOVERNMENT FALLS, CRACKS
SHOW IN SPY CASE

'If the buggers came, I would have shot them—or myself.'

Meena did not cry. Neither did she smile.

It did not take me long to realise that my wife had, ever since my arrest on 30 November 1994, plunged into severe depression. The cry, that animal shriek that no animal could produce, she let out when I returned home from jail on 18 January 1995 had startled me. Now I was told that that was the first time she had made any sound. Her tears were shed in silence.

During my absence, she continued to visit the temples, some times for long hours. Once, much after the Attukal Temple had closed, she remained there, putting the temple managers in a fix. After much persuasion, she allowed a person to drop her home. The only other person she went to was her youngest sister Usha who lived in their ancestral home not too far from our house. Meena would lie on Usha's lap for hours on end, wide awake, without uttering a word.

When my son and relatives visited me in the jail, the rare mention about Meena has been vague, I remembered. I knew she would be feeling terrible after my arrest, but I hoped her faith in God, her daily temple visits, her deep sense of spiritualism would help her sail through the rough seas. But she had sunk.

Not that I was in any better mental shape. Returning home and being with my folks came as a solace, but the uncertainty of my professional and personal future, and the unanswered questions about the conspirators and their intentions rankled on.

The day after I came out of jail, Muthunayagam visited me at home. I did not want to meet this man who, like the other bosses at ISRO, never spoke a word in support of their scientists who were falsely implicated and incarcerated. Muthunayagam had heard from someone that the IB officials had tried to make me name Muthunayagam and some other seniors, but I refused to play ball. Now he had come to show his gratitude.

Muthunayagam hugged me.

'You are great,' he said, crying.

I did not reply.

It was not out of any love for him. Naming Muthunayagam would be admitting to the lie that there was espionage in ISRO.

Once he was finished thanking me profusely, I said, 'If you are through with your expression of guilt, I would like to be left alone.'

Months later, when he came again to meet me, I locked myself in my room and told Meena to convey to him that I did not wish to meet him.

I led a life of a recluse, not stepping out of home. The few visitors were the inner circle of my relatives and friends. Businessman Kanwal Grover, the great friend of Indian space science who helped ISRO strike the Viking-Vikas deal, surprised me by knocking at my door a few days after I returned from jail.

'The moment I heard about it I knew someone was playing dirty,' said Grover.

'You didn't believe any of the spy tales, did you?' I was curious to know the perception of a globetrotter who would have only heard of the ISRO spy case.

'Not a word, Nambi,' he said. 'You know that I am no stranger to rockets though I am not a scientist. The whole set of allegations screamed conspiracy.'

My colleagues Mohana Prasad, Chandran and Narendranath were frequent visitors to my place. Mohana Prasad would analyse endlessly the motives of the conspirators who fabricated the spy case. Prasad, who lived next door, kept foul-mouthing the police and the IB. He said he had a licensed pistol, which he had kept loaded.

'If the buggers came, I would have shot them—or myself,' he said.

I spoke less, and mostly listened to the conversations. I was yet to fully understand what the world was calling the ISRO spy case. I gathered all the back files of dailies since my arrest and went through them. The more I read and listened, the more amused I was with the ingenuity of the Malayalam newspapers and the myriad imaginations of its journalists (The English papers, especially those reporters and editors who knew a bit about science and technology, did not buy the spicy tales dished out by the Kerala police and the IB; some even pooh-poohed the sleuths' theories).

One of the first journalists to see through the hollowness of the spy case was J Rajasekharan Nair of *Savvy* magazine. When he came to interview me, he came across as another journalist keen on giving a new spin to the spy case. After spending a few hours interviewing me, Rajasekharan Nair was convinced that the case was cooked up. He wrote a story picking holes in the Kerala Police and IB theories, but his editors found his story, which ran contrary to the popular perception difficult to believe and held it back.

Soon, India Today editor Sekhar Gupta and Asianet journalist T N Gopakumar came out with stories questioning the fundamentals of the case. This left Rajasekharan Nair frustrated as he never got credit for being the first one to puncture the IB bogey as his story, written before the others', gathered dust at the editor's desk.

But, in a land of total literacy where Malayalam papers are the self-appointed evangelists of information and intellectualism, this was the sensational ISRO spy case. Two space scientists sold India's rocket secrets to an enemy country for money and sexual favours. The spy ring with an inspector general of Kerala Police as a facilitator consisted of agents from Maldives, Pakistan and Sri Lanka.

It was an irony that while my foreign friends, mostly scientists, and people like Kanwal Grover ridiculed the spy case as a cruel joke on ISRO and me, people in Kerala swallowed it hook, line and sinker.

Charan (meaning spy) was my new name in Malayalam. I rarely stepped out, but the few times I had to, the name was mentioned in more than a whisper. Neither of the main political parties, the Congress and the CPM, dared to question the logic of the police or the

IB. Lower rung politicians, who routinely talk at wayside meetings as a pastime, ran out of politically significant matters found interest in the ISRO spy case.

Stirred they must be by one such wayside political buffoon, a group of trade unionists came with an effigy to be burned in front of my house. They came shouting slogans against the *charan*. My wife begged with me to keep silent, but I lost my cool. I opened the door and walked on to the road. The sloganeering stopped.

'Who is the *charan* here?' I shouted.

I abused their leaders and asked them to go to their puppeteers and ask them if they knew anything about what they were telling you. The group dispersed.

The Antony faction of the Congress in Kerala, led by Oommen Chandy, was going full steam with the spy tales in a bid to pull down the K Karunakaran Government.

Years later, Cherian Philip, then a Youth Congress leader and a co-conspirator of Chandy, confessed through a television interview how Chandy assigned him to link inspector general of police Raman Srivastava, considered close to the Chief Minister, with the spy case. Philip told an interview—first to journalist Rajasekharan Nair and later to Malayalam satellite channel Asianet—that he and another Congress leader were accommodated in a rented house near Trivandrum Medical College where they regularly fed Malayalam journalists with fresh fictitious tales every day.

When Philip & Co ran out of fiction, young reporters cooked up their bit about the mediators, middlemen and methods through which Sasi and I handed over rocket blueprints to Pakistan. Not to be left behind, their seniors fabricated more wonderful versions of the smuggling. One said drawings of cryogenic engines were smuggled out in fish baskets.

Out of sheer curiosity, I asked a few journalists I knew what the fish basket was all about. One of them told me that it was a clever prop, invented by a Malayalam newspaper reporter to link Kurien Kalathil, my erstwhile prospective business partner in shrimp farming that never happened. Less imaginative reporters tried their skills at voyeurism. 'If the story is not strong, make it steamy,' seemed to be the editorial dictum in many Malayalam newsrooms.

Even the closest of my people might have thought that I would be feeling relatively better after I was released from jail; only I knew what I was going through. After the initial shock and insults while in the custody of the Kerala Police and IB, I was numbed into sleep many nights while in CBI custody and later in Viyyur Jail. Now the uncertainty kept me sleepless at night; even if I got a couple of hours of disturbed sleep in the wee hours, I woke up to another dawn of ridicule.

I might have felt better if I cried, but often sadness was overtaken by anger. Then helplessness. When you swirl in such a rapid interplay of emotions, you see a black hole were your sanity appears to be heading to. And it is easy to give up.

One morning after a sleepless night, I called up Narasimhan, a senior lawyer in Trivandrum and a friend of mine.

'Can you help me write my will?' I asked.

'Why now?'

'It has to be written someday. Why not now?

'Tell me one argument I have won against you,' he joked.

He agreed to get the will ready soon.

After a few days when Narasimhan rang up, it was Geetha, my daughter, who answered the phone. When the lawyer said that my will was ready to be collected, Geetha got the message.

Soon she and my son Sankar were in front of me.

'So, you want to commit suicide?' she said.

I sat silent, my face in my palm.

While in the custody of the IB, living with insults and staring at uncertainty, I had once thought about suicide, but soon realised the folly of it. But this time it was a slow numbing process that made me wonder if it was worth the fight. I knew I was giving up, and I was preparing myself to the eventuality. I still did not know the means to my end.

'You have decided, eh?' Geetha was shouting now. 'What happened to my strong-willed Appa? I thought you will fight and prove to the world your innocence, show the world what you are, expose the people behind this conspiracy. If not any of that, just answer this. Do you want us to live as a traitor's children? Do you want your grandchildren and the coming generations to live with such a tag?'

When I lifted my face to look at Geetha, I realised that my eyes had welled up.

'I am sorry,' I said. 'I will live to ensure that.'

The last couple of months, starting with my arrest, flashed back in my mind. I had endured enough, I resolved, never again should I let myself give up in this fight. I have to prove my innocence and expose whoever is the perpetrator.

In the coming months, the CBI officers summoned me a few times to their offices in Trivandrum and Kochi. I dutifully answered more questions from them. After a couple of visits, it became clearer to me that the CBI was convinced that I was innocent. Many of their questions, I thought, were part of running multiple checks on what I had said earlier. If the CBI had to demolish the IB spy story, they had to be doubly sure of what they are going to say.

I felt a strange sense of gratitude towards the CBI. This would, however, soon be followed by a gripping rage on the IB officials. I would pause at the thought of the IB interrogation, rewind it again, ponder over my pain and resolve to teach those conspirators a lesson.

Among the accused, we three men were to sign a register at the CJM court in Ernakulam; the two Maldivian women were still in prison after the government cited new cases of national security against them. When it would be that day of the week for us to sign at the CJM court, Sasi would dutifully come to pick me up and drive to Ernakulam every week. During the journey he would repeat the tales of torture he underwent at the hands of the Kerala Police and the IB, probably to reiterate his apology for having made 'confessions' linking me.

I was by now reading the back files and case documents to understand the intricacies of the case. Layer by layer, the conspiracy was unfolding, but the bigger picture, including the international conspiracy, would emerge only later, after the CBI filed its report on 28 April 1996, and the case dragged on till the Supreme Court on 29 April 1998 put an end to the Kerala government's attempts at reopening it. My battle, however, would not end there.

The local politics behind the case, however, was clear by now. Oommen Chandy, captaining the A K Antony camp of the Congress, was well on his way to topple K Karunakaran from the Chief Minister's throne. Their trump card was the implication of IG Raman Srivastava in the ISRO spy case. During questioning, Maldivian women Mariam Rasheeda and Fauziyya Hassan had given statements about meeting a man, introduced by Chandrasekhar as 'Brigadier'. In real, the man they called Brigadier was K L Bhasin, a retired army officer who helped Fauziyya's daughter get admission to a Bangalore school.

Nicknamed in the case files a 'Coatwallah', Bhasin was mistaken for Srivastava, probably because Mariam, while trying to thwart the advances of inspector Vijayan just before her arrest, had said that she would complain about the inspector to the 'IG' whom she knew. She had meant the Brigadier, as she told reporters later. The IG in Trivandrum, meanwhile, happened to be Srivastava. Later, examination of some officers found that the IB conveniently did not take on record the fact that the Maldivian women, when showed Bhasin's photographs, had identified him as the 'Brigadier' or 'Coatwallah', who Mariam referred to as the IG.

Ironically, aiding this rival Congress team was a Leftist NGO called *Niyamavedi* that demanded the scalp of the IPS officer who was close to Karunakaran. The NGO, represented by an advocate called Nandini moved the Kerala High Court praying for a writ of mandamus directing the CBI to arrest Raman Srivastava on 13 December 1994.

When the court dismissed the petition, the NGO filed an appeal before a division bench. On 24 December 1994, the division bench asked the CBI to produce records connected with the questioning of Raman Srivastava, and asked if there was even an iota of evidence to establish a prima facie case against the IPS officer.

The investigating agency filed an affidavit on 2 January 1995, stating that 'according to the investigation conducted so far, there was no involvement of Raman Srivastava.' The next day, the court observed that it was not satisfied with the affidavit, and asked the CBI to peruse the entire records and see if the investigation was proceeding in the 'proper line'. The agency again filed for an affidavit, on 7 January 1995.

It said 'the oral and documentary evidence collected during investigation so far was inconsistent with the allegation contained in the interrogation reports of the accused persons recorded by the IB/ Kerala Police.' In other words, the CBI found no evidence of spying as claimed by the IB and the Kerala Police. On the involvement of Raman Srivastava, the CBI said 'a serious doubt had arisen with regard to the essential facts on which initial suspicion against him was created.'

The court was not happy. In its judgment of 13 January 1995, the bench said it was not in a position to approve the conclusion arrived at by the CBI that Raman Srivastava was implicated in the case for ulterior motives. The IB, the court said, which had its own investigating machinery, had said in unmistakable terms about the involvement of Raman Srivastava, but the CBI ignored this.

The CBI moved the Supreme Court, and got the adverse remarks of the Kerala high court expunged through an order dated 5 April 1995, but by then, the politicians had had their way. Though Niyamavedi's petition for Srivastava's arrest was dismissed, the high court's adverse remarks were enough to force the government's hand to suspend Srivastava. For Oommen Chandy, who was the charioteer of the Antony faction, this was the ultimate opportunity to hit at Karunakaran. His group ran a relentless campaign against Karunakaran, first accusing him of shielding a central character in the ISRO spy ring and later even implying that the espionage had the blessings of the Chief Minister. Karunakaran resigned as the Chief Minister in 16 March 1995, paving way for A K Antony.

Years later, Cherian Philip, a Youth Congress leader and a foot soldier of the Antony camp, would confess about Chandy's machinations that resulted in the suspension of an upright IPS officer.

Seventeen years later, when the Kerala high court in 2012 directed the state government to pay Rs 10 lakhs to me as an interim compensation, the episode would return to haunt both Antony and Chandy. The Karunakaran family would then demand an investigation into the 'political conspiracy behind the case and action against three officers of the Kerala Police who the CBI found to have fabricated the case. Even today, Chandy squirms in his chair when asked about the ISRO spy case. At a press conference in July 2016, Chandy was at pains trying to argue that Karunakaran's ouster in 1995 had nothing to do with the ISRO spy case, and that it was because of a difference of opinion over the selection of a Rajya Sabha candidate.

MARIAM GETS A REPRIEVE, CBI SAYS SPY CASE IS FALSE

The two Maldivian women were still in jail, as the government slapped another case of national security. When a Chief Judicial Magistrate on 14 November 1995, acquitted Mariam Rasheeda in the case of overstaying; the genesis of it all, the very foundation of the spy story was shaken.

The case in which Mariam was charged under the Foreigners Act, 1946, stated that she was staying in India beyond the ninety days that the rules permitted. Maldivians were exempted from the requirement of visa, if the stay did not exceed ninety days. For Mariam, who was on her third visit since 2 June 1994, the deadline was 14 October 1994.

According to the chargesheet, on 20 October 1994, city special branch inspector S Vijayan, while on a routine inspection of lodgings where foreigners were staying, came across details of Mariam, who was staying in Hotel Samrat, Trivandrum.

'She could not reveal the source of Indian currency which she was spending. She was also unable to give satisfactory explanation regarding her telephonic contacts from Samrat Hotel (one of the numbers found in her diary was that of ISRO scientist Sasikumaran, and this formed the first link to ISRO). Since she violated Rule 7 of the Foreigners Order, 1948 and Section 14 of the Foreigners Act, 1946, she was arrested and produced before the sub inspector of police, Vanchiyoor Police Station,' read the case file.

D Mohana Rajan, Chief Judicial Magistrate, Ernakulam, considered these points:

- Whether the accused overstayed in India as alleged by the prosecution.
- If overstayed, whether there was justifiable cause for the same.
- What, if any, is the offence committed by the accused.
- If found guilty, what is the sentence to be imposed on the accused.

Advocate B S Prasad Gandhi, appearing for Mariam Rasheeda, argued that the ninetieth day of her stay in India fell only on 17 October 1994, on which day she already had an Indian Airlines ticket to return to Male. Indian Airlines direct flights from Trivandrum were cancelled indefinitely from 4 October 1994, due to plague epidemic in India. Mariam had approached inspector Vijayan, days before she was arrested, to apprise him of her situation, but the inspector maintained 'a hostile attitude' towards her.

So she got a confirmed ticket on Air Lanka on 17 October 1994. Vijayan confiscated both these tickets, along with Mariam's passport as she was 'not amenable to his illegal demands'. (Later Mariam gave an interview to *Savvy* magazine, accusing Vijayan of seeking sexual favours from her). Without the travel documents, she could not return to the Maldives.

The prosecution now brought in samples of the bigger conspiracy theory, saying Mariam was in touch with 'an institution concerned with the defence of India and officials working in that institution.' While the inspector was making inquiries, she shifted from Hotel Samrat to a house in Trivandrum. The inspector went here and asked for Mariam's passport and other documents. Now, he found that her visa had expired on 14 October 1994.

After several cross examinations and perusal of documents, the court found many of pieces of evidence against Mariam inadmissible. What is more, it clearly pointed a finger at inspector Vijayan for the way in which he arrested Mariam. The judgment said:

'A careful scrutiny of the evidence as a whole reveals that the accused was arrested by PW2 (Vijayan) suspecting espionage activities on her ... air tickets were recovered by PW2 with his full knowledge for the purpose of arresting the accused on the ground of her overstay in India. As she had obtained air tickets for her return journey within the permissible period, there was no necessity for her to apply for extension of her stay in India. In fact she was chased by the police party consisting of PW2 and others at least from the middle of October, 1994, obstructing her from leaving India.'

The court acquitted Mariam Rasheeda.

For me, this case marked the first victory for another reason. It was during this trial that the first definite statement from the CBI came that the spy case was false.

From the judgment: 'During the course of argument, the learned senior special prosecutor submitted that in investigation the espionage case was found false and baseless and that the CBI is going to file refer report in the connected case ...'

CHAPTER 27

CBI TEARS INTO KERALA POLICE, IB

'Incoherent and full of contradictions.'

The CBI's investigation report filed before the CJM, Ernakulam on 28 April 1996 demolished the spy theory. But what made it more attractive to me was that it gave a clear picture of the theory itself. While being in the custody of IB, my tormentors' questions and actions had moved me between surprise and suspicion, but now this the 104–page document gave me the story according to them—and helped me fill in the gaps in my theory of an international conspiracy to stall India's advance in space.

The CBI report said:

'Though no independent evidence has come on record during the course of local police/crime branch investigation about the alleged espionage activities of the accused persons, yet based on the revelations allegedly made by the accused, the module that emerged regarding the espionage activities was that accused Nambi Narayanan and Sasikumaran used to pass on documents/ drawings of ISRO relating to Viking/Vikas engine technology, cryogenic engine technology and PSLV flight data/drawings, and accused Chandrasekhar, S K Sharma and Ramana Srivastava, the then IGP South Zone, Kerala, passed on secrets of Aeronautical Defence Establishments, Bangalore.

'The documents/drawings were allegedly passed on to Mohd Aslam, a Pak nuclear scientist and Mohd Pasha/Ahmed Pasha for monetary considerations... running into lakhs of US dollars was received and shared by accused Sasikumaran, Chandrasekhar, Nambi Narayanan and Raman Srivastava and that Mohiyuddin,

assistant manager of Habib Bank, Male, was one of the persons who was financing the accused.

Accused Fauziyya Hassan, Zuheira, a Maldivian national settled in Colombo, Glavkosmos chairman Aleksey Vasin and Raman Srivastava worked as conduits. Some of the important meetings were held at Hotel International Madras on 24 January 1994, in Bangalore in mid-September and on 23 September at Hotel Luciya, Trivandrum in which some of the accused as well as Zuheira and Raman Srivastava took part.'

At the onset, the report listed out the conclusions of the previous investigation by the Kerala Police Crime Branch:

1. *Mariam Rasheeda was a foreign agent collecting information about the possible coup plan against the President of the Maldives. For this purpose she was travelling frequently between Male, Colombo, Trivandrum and Bangalore, and the details of her activities were recorded in her diary.*

2. *Fauziyya Hassan was a frequent visitor to Colombo, Trivandrum, Madras and Bangalore and in June 1994 she got her daughter admitted in Baldwin Girls High School, Bangalaore.*

3. *Both Mariam Rasheeda and Fauziyya Hassan kept in constant touch with Chanrasekhar and Sasikumaran.*

4. *Chandrasekhar, Mariam Rasheeda, Fauziyya Hassan and Sasikumaran and others attended a secret meeting at Hotel International, Madras on 24 and 25 January 1994; here documents and money were exchanged.*

5. *No evidence was forthcoming to prove which were the secret documents passed on by the accused to foreign agents who were the foreign agents and what they received in return and where was the money.*

6. *There was no clear proof regarding identity of 'Brigadier' Srivastava who was allegedly present during the deals at Madras on 24 January 1994 and at Indira Nagar, Bangalore in September 1994.*

Among the other terms of reference of the CBI were S K Sharma's alleged role in getting secret documents from defence establishments in Bangalore, whether I had stashed away documents and money with some others, if the alleged meetings happened at Hotel International,

Madras and if military secrets were smuggled out, besides establishing the identity of 'Brigadier', also known as 'Coatwallah'.

The CBI report said:

'Immediately after taking over the investigation, by the CBI, all the six accused persons were thoroughly interrogated, taking the statements purported to have been made by the accused before the Kerala Police/IB to be true, but all of them denied having indulged in any espionage activity. On being confronted with the statements made by them before Kerala Police as well as IB officials, the accused took the plea that the statements were made on the suggested lines under duress.

'Though there was no complaint either from ISRO or from ADE, Bangalore about the loss of documents, the alleged revelations of the accused made before local police/intelligence officials were taken at their face value and focused investigation was carried out to find out the details and purposes of various visits accused Mariam Rasheeda and Fauziyya Hassan to India, their places of stay were verified, the persons, including the accused with whom they came in contact were examined and efforts were made to gather oral as well as documentary evidence to find out whether the accused have committed any acts which were prejudicial to the sovereignty, integrity and security of the state and violative of the Official Secrets Act, 1923.'

The report went into each aspect of the Kerala police/IB investigation, and at the end of it there was not one point that stood scrutiny of the CBI. According to the police/IB tale, there were at least three meetings – on 19 January 1994 at Hotel International, Madras; on 25 June 1994 at Army Club, Bangalore; and on 23 September 1994 at Hotel Luciya, Trivandrum— in which the transactions of money and documents happened. The CBI report presents the IB version, presented as statements of the accused, against the findings of the CBI's own investigation.

MEETING AT HOTEL INTERNATIONAL, MADRAS ON 24 JANUARY 1994

IB story:

Chandrasekhar booked five rooms at Hotel International, Madras for a secret meeting on 24 January 1994. On that day, Chandrasekhar went with Sasikumaran, Sharma and Raman Srivastava to Hotel International, Madras to meet Fauziyya, Zuheira and her boss Mehboob Pasha. Fauziyya passed on a packet, given to her by Mohiyuddin of Habib Bank, Male, on 19 January with Chandrasekhar's name on it.

Mehboob Pasha had agreed to pay $100,000 for complete drawings of cryogenic engine and flight records of PSLV. Now, Fauziyya gave $10,000 and Sasikumaran and $5,000 to Chandrasekhar. Sasikumaran handed over the PSLV flight details to Fauziyya. Also discussed were the possibility of trade in Russian tanks and setting up of a factory to make bullet-proof vests using carbon technology which Sasikumaran had developed.

CBI report:

No such meeting happened at Hotel International, Madras. Inquiries in Male, through Interpol, did not find any Mohiyuddin working in Habib Bank, Male. Interpol, Colombo, which examined Zuheira, reported that she had not visited India since June 1993.

Fauziyya Hassan was in Madras from 24 to 28 January along with two other Maldivians, for shopping for a wedding. They stayed in Hotel Pandyan, not Hotel International. She did not meet anyone.

Chandrasekhar was in Madras from 16 to 18 January with his wife to attend the wedding of a friend's daughter. The friend, S Diwakar, had arranged for their accommodation at Presidency Club.

As per the records of Liquid Propulsion Systems Centre (LPSC), Valiyamala, Sasikumaran was in his office on 24 January 1994. On this day he went to Quilon to attend the funeral of his mother-in-law Janki who died in Hospital Upasana, Quilon the previous day. He attended the funeral with his wife and was in Quilon till 4 pm. People at the funeral confirmed this.

IG Raman Srivastava, as per his tour note and the log book of his car (KL02-A 9100) was in Trivandrum on this day. Trivandrum police commissioner V R Rajivan and Major S Suresh Kumar, Commander of Republic Day parade two days later, confirmed Srivastava's presence in Trivandrum on 24 January. As per the wireless log book of the Kerala Police, Srivastava's call sign 'Rover' contacted call sign 'City Tiger' at 10:18 am on 24 January.

On January, the IG had taken his foster father R C Srivastava, who suffered a head injury, to Cosmopolitan Hospital, Trivandrum. Dr M Sambasivan of the hospital confirmed this. Hospital staff said Raman Srivastava and his family regularly visited the hospital from 22 January to 2 February 1994 when R C Srivastava died.

The presence of Raman Srivastava in Trivandrum between 22 and 24 January is firmly established by the documentary and oral evidence and as such he could not have been present in Madras on 24 January.

A scrutiny of the records of Hotel International, Madras did not indicate the booking of any room by Chandrasekhar. It did show the stay of one R S Srivastava of GIC of India, V Chandrasekhar, assistant engineer, Kerala State Electricity Board, Sudhir Lulla and Shasi Kapoor on 24 January. When examined, these people confirmed their stay in the hotel.

A Satish, assistant front office manager and Ruby Alex, bell captain of Hotel International Hotel were shown the photographs of the accused, but neither of the hospital staff could identify any of them.

S K Sharma visited ECA Club, Bangalore on 24 and 25 January as per documentary and oral evidence, and, thus, he too could not have been in Madras on 24 January.

MEETING AT CHANDRASEKHAR'S OFFICE AND ARMY CLUB, BANGALORE ON JUNE 25, 1994

IB story:
Mariam Rasheeda brought $25,000 given by Mohiyuddin through Fauziyya's daughter Nasiha and handed it over to Chandrasekhar at his office on 25 June 1994. Sharma took the women to Army Club where he introduced them to a person as Brigadier Raman Srivastava.

CBI report:
On 21 June 1994, Mariam Rasheeda and Fauziyya Hassan visited Chandrasekhar's office and were taken to the house of Thomas (husband of Baldwin School principal) by S K Sharma and his business partner Ramasrey Rai in connection with the admission of Fauziyya's daughter Zila Hamdi.

In the evening, squadron leader K L Bhasin (introduced to the women as 'Brigadier' and suspected to be IG Raman Srivastava) went to S K Sharma's house with his wife. Sharma asked Bhasin to accompany him to the Baldwin School principal's house where the two Maldivian women would be coming. After meeting the principal, Bhasin and Sharma took the Maldivian women to the Army Club as Fauziyya wanted to use the rest room. Bhasin offered the women soft drinks and the men had a few drinks.

IG Raman Srivastava had contacted City Tiger over the wireless at 6:28 pm, 10:03 pm and 11:35 pm on 23 June. The next day he contacted the sub-inspector Cantonment and City Tiger at 4:50 pm and 4:55 pm. At 7:37 pm he contacted City Tiger and again at 7:44 pm. On 26 June, Rover contacted City Tiger at 11:23 am. Thus, the presence of Srivastava in Trivandrum is established up to 7:44 pm on 24 June and in the forenoon of 26 June.

Trivandrum police commissioner Rajivan also confirmed Srivastava's wireless calls. The IG's car logs and TA bills confirm his presence in Trivandrum on these days.

MEETING AT HOTEL LUCIYA, TRIVANDRUM ON 23 SEPTEMBER 1994

IB story:
Nambi Narayanan was in touch with Zuheira since 1991, after conceiving the idea of selling the technological know-how of PSLV. By 1992, definitive proposals came from Zuheira, and the buyer was Pakistan. The deal was struck for $ 900,000.

Nambi Narayanan brought four bundles of complete drawings of PSLV after unsuccessful launch of PSLV. As per the plan, Mohammed Aslam, Abdul Haleel and Zuheira stayed in Hotel Luciya, Trivandrum. On 23 September 1994 at 9:30 am, Sasikumaran, Nambi Narayanan, Chandrasekhar, S K Sharma and Raman Srivastava met in room 108 where Zuheira was staying. Raman Srivastava took a bag containing $ 900,000 and documents were delivered to Abdul Haleel and others.

CBI report:

No person by the name Mohammed Aslam, Abdul Haleel or Zuheira stayed in Hotel Luciya between 20 and 25 September. According to Regi Varghese, then general manager of Hotel Luciya. Room 108 was occupied by an Air India employee called Naikwadi on 23 September 1994. This guest was initially allotted room 104, but he shifted to room 108 and stayed till 30 September. He was transferred to Trivandrum from Bombay for three months.

Nambi Narayanan and Sasikumaran attended office on 23 September 1994. Both of them went to LPSC in the morning in the company of fellow scientists Mohana Prasad, K Ramamurthy and V Gnana Gandhi by official car (KBU 6863). The log book of the car was signed by Sasikumaran in the morning; Gnana Gandhi signed it in the evening. The duty slip given to the drivers confirms this. The driver said he picked up the two scientists in the morning from their homes and dropped them back in the evening.

S K Sharma was present at ECA Club, Bangalore on 22 and 23 September.

Raman Srivastava was in Trivandrum on 23 September, but there was no evidence to show he visited Hotel Luciya on this day.

House search at the houses of Sasikumaran, Nambi Narayanan, Chandrasekhar and Sharma did not indicate receipt of such a huge amount. The bank accounts of all the accused as well as that of Raman Srivastava were scrutinized, but there was no indication of receipt of any huge amount.

MEETING AT INDIRA NAGAR CLUB IN MID-SEPTEMBER, 1994

IB story:

Chandrasekhar, S K Sharma, Fauziyya Hassan and Mariam Rasheeda met at Indira Nagar Club. Zuheira and 'Brigadier' came in a taxi, and called out Chandrasekhar. 'Brigadier' asked Chandrasekhar to drive them in his car, and after fifteen minutes of drive asked him to stop the car. 'Brigadier' went inside a house and brought a packet which was handed over to Zuheira.

Chandrasekhar asked Sharma to collect aerial photographs of ADE as demanded by Mohammed Pasha. Sharma collected the documents and handed over to him. He sealed these documents and got the cover delivered to Fauziyya through Sharma.

CBI report:

Zuheira did not visit India in 1994.

Raman Srivastava had attended a course at National Police Academy, Hyderabad from 5 to 9 September. There is no evidence of his visit to Bangalore after this.

S K Sharma was a member of Indira Nagar Club. A perusal of the guest list did not show the names of any of the accused. Waiters were shown photographs of the accused, but only one of them identified Chandrasekhar as someone who had been there with Sharma. Thus, investigation has not established the visit of Fauziyya or Mariam to the club.

SENDING DOCUMENTS THROUGH URAL AVIATION

IB story:

Nambi Narayanan planned to sell Vikas engine drawings to Pakistan and struck a deal with Aleksey Vasin. Nambi Narayanan used to hand over the computer charts/drawings to Raman Srivastava who used to deliver it to Ural Aviation. Aleksey paid Rs 10 lakh to Nambi Narayanan, which he shared with Sasikumaran and Raman Srivastava. One such consignment is lying at Moscow air cargo, for which a deal was struck with North Korea and Aleksey promised to pay Rs 60-70 lakh.

CBI report:

National Airport Authority deputy director PA Raghunathan confirmed that there were only three flights of Aeroflot. The first flight, URL-224, landed in Trivandrum on 23 January 1994 from Karachi and departed on 25 January 1994 for Sharjah. The second flight, URL- 9001 landed on 11 March 1994 from Ras al Khaimah and departed on 13 March 1994 for Ras al Khaimah. The third flight URL- 3791 landed on 17 July 1994 from Sharjah and left on 20 July 1994 for Bombay.

V I Samuel, assistant collector, Customs, confirmed that these three flights carried cargo meant for the Liquid Propulsion Systems Centre from Russia. No export of any kind was made through these three flights.

The Indian Embassy in Moscow communicated that Glavkosmos chairman Dunayev told the ambassador that his cryogenic man Aleksey Vasin has communicated that there was no question of his getting any confidential document from India, particularly of the French origin Viking engine which has been in use for a decade. Russia has incomparably better engines to offer.

Aleksey Vasin also told the Indian authorities that there is no question of Glavkosmos having any link with any mafia group for indulging in clandestine transaction. According to Dunayev, the Counter Intelligence Services officer was embarrassed and apologetic for having made these inquiries after he received the clarification from Vain. Dunayev said, 'Those who are initiating such inquiries did not obviously have any technical expertise, let alone any idea of the rich legacy of Indo-Russian space cooperation.'

FAUZIYYA'S VISIT TO LPSC, VALIYAMALA ON 29 SEPTEMBER 1994

IB story:

Fauziyya was taken for a picnic to a dam, and from there she went to Sasikumaran's office. On 24 September 1994, she visited Veli with Sasikumaran and took photographs of the ISRO Complex. Sasikumaran gave her ten photographs, which she sent to Mohiyuddin on 1 October 1994. Sasikumaran handed over another cover countaining four photographs of a building and five sketches. Charts. These were destroyed as police inquiries started on 13 October 1994.

Sasikumaran and Nambi Narayanan took casual leave on 23 and 24 September and took Fauziyya to LPSC at 10:30 am. Fauziyya signed the visitors register at the gate. Fauziyya took photographs of LPSC installations and they went to Aruvikkara dam.

CBI report:

Nambi Narayanan or Sasikumaran did not take any casual leave on this day; both were in office.

Ibrahim Ihzaan, a Maldivian national living in Trivandrum said he and Fauziyya had gone for a picnic to Aruvikara dam where they took some photographs, but the film was exposed.

Central Industrial Security Force at LPSC said Fauziyya had not visited the place, there was no such name in the visitors register.

INVOLVEMENT OF ALEKSEY VASIN

IB story:

Six scientists including Sasikumaran visited Russia for six months along with Chandrasekhar. In Russia, Chandrasekhar introduced Sasikumaran to Aleksey Vasin who negotiated regarding sending of Viking engine drawings. Aleksey had close links with Nambi Narayanan. Drawings of Viking engine were sold to Brazil with Aleksey's help in 1989-90. Nambi Narayanan and Aleksey received payments.

Raman Srivastava used to deliver documents through Ural Aviation to Aleksey who paid Rs 10 lakh. Aleksey also arranged two-week trips in 1991 for Sasikumaran and Nambi Narayanan to Switzerland and West Germany. Aleksey was exploring the possibility of selling Viking technology to Indonesia, Taiwan and Brazil.

Zuheria was introduced to Aleksey in March/June 1990 at Hotel Fort Manor. Nambi Narayanan met Zuheira at Hotel Pankaj in June 1991 in connection with cryogenic engine components, and payments were made by Aleksey.

CBI report:

LPSC records show that Sasikumaran did not visit Russia during 1991. Hotel Fort Manor became operational only on 21 December 1991. Hence the introduction of Zuheira with Aleksey in the hotel in March/ June 1990 is ruled out.

Zuheira did not visit Trivandrum after 1989.

Hotel Pankaj's partner D Chandrasenan Nair stated that Zuheira did not stay in the hotel in June 1991.

Records show that Sasikumaran did not take any earned leave during 1991. Nambi Narayanan visited Moscow on an official tour from 10 January to 19 January 1991. This proves that Nambi Narayanan and Sasikumaran were never on leave simultaneously for fifteen days at a stretch, and hence, they could not have gone for the alleged two-week trips.

INTRODUCTION AND MEETING WITH FAUZIYYA

IB story:

Nambi Narayanan introduced Chandrasekhar to Fauziyya Hassan at Hotel Fort Manor in March 1993. After three weeks, Chandrasekhar again met Fauziyya Hassan at Fort Manor and she showed interest in cryogenic engine. The Russian delegation was staying in the hotel in December 1993. During that period Chandrasekhar saw Fauziyya with an eight-year-old girl in the room of Nambi Narayanan. He offered to sell PSLV flight details. In the third week of December, Fauziyya conveyed approval of her boss and a deal was struck for $14,000. The relevant information was to be supplied before 15 October 1994. Fauziyya visited Trivandrum in the first week of January. Ahmed Pasha, Fauziyya's boss, confirmed the deal for $100,000.

Chandrasekhar again met Fauziyya in August 1992 and delivered twelve bundles of Vikas drawings, which were returned by Fauziyya in December 1992 stating that the user had got it from other channels.

CBI report:

Fauziyya's passport does not indicate her visit to India before January 24, 1994 and thus the alleged meetings with her before that could not have taken place.

Hotel Fort Manor records do not indicate stay of Fauziyya. No Russian delegation stayed in the hotel in December, 1993. Rather, the Russian delegation visited Trivandrum between November 29, 1993 and December 3, 1993 and stayed in Hotel Ragam Nagar and later at South Park.

ROLE OF RAVINDER REDDY, PRABHAKAR RAO

IB story:

Nambi Narayanan, in collusion with Ravinder Reddy of MTAR, Hyderabad (a contract industry of ISRO) sold technical information including cryogenics. Ravinder Reddy was related to the Chief Minister of Andhra Pradesh, and had business links with Prabhakar Rao, son of then Prime Minister P V Narasimha Rao.

CBI report:

Ravinder Reddy said he knew Nambi Narayanan and many other ISRO scientists, but his firm was given the contract for manufacture of Vikas engine after a number of discussions with the contract negotiation committee which comprised of the LPSC director and other senior officials.

Ravinder Reddy said he knew former Andhra Pradesh Chief Minister Bhaskar Reddy as a friend, but was not related to him. He denied having any business dealings with Prabhakar Rao.

SELLING OF VIKING ENGINE DRAWINGS TO ABUBAKER/ HABIBULLAH

IB story:

Habibullah, who was sent by Nambi Narayanan's classmate Abubaker, went to Nambi Narayanan's house in 1982 to purchase drawings of Viking engine for Rs 70 lakh. The deal was deferred as the telephonic conversation was overheard. On 30 January 1990, Abubaker again contacted Nambi Narayanan for purchase of the drawings. On 22 January Habibullah, Sasikumaran and Chandrasekhar discussed the deal with Nambi Narayanan at Hotel Rock Holm. The deal was sealed for Rs 1.5 crore. Drawings were to be given in three lots. Two instalments were given to Fauziyya at Thampanoor bus stand and in Hotel Luciya. The third instalment was due for 5 December 1994. Nambi Narayanan received Rs 75 lakh in US dollars from Fauziyya at Hotel Luciya at the time of handing over the last instalment.

CBI report:

Abubaker was known to Nambi Narayanan since their school days. Abubaker, an assistant director of animal husbandry department in Kanyakumari, Tamil Nadu, visited Nambi Narayanan during 1991-92 in connection with a job his son had applied for in ISRO. Nambi Narayanan said he would help Abubaker in case his son qualified the written test. The candidate did not qualify.

Abubaker denied having any knowledge about Vikas technology or any other technology relation to ISRO.

On the request of the CBI, LPSC director constituted a committee of senior scientists to ascertain if any documents had gone missing from LPSC. The committee submitted two reports, the first on 11 January 1995 and the second on 24 February 1995. According to the first report, there were 5,767 recorded documents in the cryo area. Out of which only four were found to be missing. In the non-cryo area, there were 33,436 documents, of which 529 were missing.

In the second report, the committee said the four cryo documents that were missing earlier were located and, thus, there were no missing documents. On checking and re-checking, the committee found only 254 of the non-cryo documents were missing. The committee noted that these missing documents constitute less than 1% of the total documents/drawings. They were random in nature and do not pertain to any particular system or sub-system.

The committee made the following observation: as our development is based on in-house drawings and as all the in-house drawings are available, the committee does not see any impact of some small number of drawings missing, on our programmes.

The documents/drawings are not marked as 'top secret', 'secret', 'confidential' or classified. ISRO follows an open door policy in regard to the issue of documents to the scientists. Since ISRO is a research-oriented organisation, any scientist wanting to study any document is free to go to the documentation cell and access the files.

Scientists could take copies on indent after entering the details in the documentation issue register. The fabrication division, where Sasikumaran worked, had issued 16,800 sheets. After Sasikumaran's transfer to Satellites Application Centre, Ahmedabad on 7 November 1994, all the copies of the drawings were found to be intact.

Nambi Narayanan, being a senior scientist, had access to the drawings, but at no stage any drawings/documents were found to have been issued to him. It is usual for scientists to take the documents. Drawings required for any meetings. Discussions to their houses for study purposes. In these circumstances, the allegation that Nambi Narayanan and Sasikumaran might have passed on the documents to a third party is found to be false.

TORTURE

The CBI report also noted that the accused were tortured by the Kerala Police and the IB, and recommended questioning of the officers. It said: in these circumstances, particularly in the context of allegation of torture and harassment made by the accused persons against the Kerala Police/ IB, it is imperative to examine the Kerala Police officials/IB officials.

Buttressing the point of torture, the report mentioned that I was medically checked by Dr V Sukumaran of Sri Krishna Hospital, Trivandrum in the Latex Guest House on 3 December 1994.

'Dr Sukumaran found Nambi Narayanan's legs swollen and multiple hemorrhage rashes on both the legs. He (the doctor) also observed that Nambi Narayanan was looking exhausted and tired. Nambi Narayanan stated before the CBI that he was not allowed to sleep for two days, and was kept standing.

'Similarly, Chandrasekhar, while in custody, was taken to PRS Hospital on 28 November 1994 where two sets of ECGs were taken. However, these facts of medical treatment to Nambi Narayanan and Chandrasekhar have not been reflected in the case diaries of Kerala Police which reflects adversely on the methods and intentions of the investigating officers of the Kerala Police.

'Further, Ammini Kutty Amma, SI, who was on security duty of accused Rasheeda has stated that Rasheeda was not allowed to sleep during interrogation, which continued round the clock for about a week and she (Rasheeda) was kept standing. This SI has also stated that Rasheeda was threatened by IB officers that she would be stripped naked and made to lie on ice blocks and insects would be thrown on her body. It is only after the torture and treats that Rasheeda identified the photograph of Raman Srivastava as the person who had met her and Fauziyya at Army Club, Bangalore, as desired by IB officers.

'It is significant to mention here that from 3 November 1994 to 7 November 1994 Raasheeda did not make any incriminating statement before the Kerala Police/IB and it can be inferred that it was only after her continuous harassment that she made the alleged statement.'

Inspector Vijayan, who started it all with the arrest of Mariam Rasheeda, himself admitted to the CBI that 'at the insistance of IB officers' he threatened Mariam that 'she would be stripped naked by the interrogators and crabs would be put on her body while she would be made to lie naked on ice.' He also said that the photograph of IG Raman Srivastava was shown to Rasheeda by officials of the central intelligence agencies. Vijayan sought to bail himself out by saying that IB officers asked him to go out of the room and, therefore, he had to keep out.

The CBI report, signed by deputy superintendent R S Dhankar and submitted to the Chief Judicial Magistrate, Ernakulam, wound up thus: To sum up, in view of the evidence on record, oral as well as documentary, as discussed above, the allegations of espionage are not proved and have been found to be false. It is, therefore, prayed that the report may kindly be accepted and the accused be discharged and permission be accorded to return the seized documents to the concerned.

That was not the last word from the CBI. The central investigating agency submitted two confidential reports, one each to the union government and the Kerala Government, detailing the falsehoods and pointing fingers at officers of the Kerala Police and the IB.

CBI REPORT ON THE ROLE OF IB OFFICERS

This report makes it clear at least two facts: one, the IB officers threatened and tortured the accused to extract statements, which turned out to be contradictory. Two, the Kerala Police were either kept in the dark or the state force, at this point of time, wanted to wash their hands off and blame the IB for trying to foist the spy case.

Analysing the 'unofficial' (UO) notes of the IB, the CBI report said: 'It is crystal clear that the DIB first issued UO notes to the highest functionaries in the Government of India indicating involvement of Raman Srivastava, Ravinder Reddy and others and subsequently negated its own version given in the earlier notes.'

The CBI investigation found that Ravinder Reddy had no business links with the then Prime Minister P V Narasimha Rao's son Prabhakar Rao. 'Despite the above, the DIB sent several UO notes referred to the above mentioned important functionaries, little realising that those notes from the Director, IB, would be treated as authentic and having been sent after careful verification and consequences of report being false or untrue would be serious.

Ammini Kutty, a sub-inspector on security duty of Mariam Rasheeda could not identify the IB officials who threatened Rasheeda. The SI said after threatening Rasheeda, the IB officers brought four photographs and kept Srivastava's photograph in the set and asked Rasheeda to identify the photograph (of Srivastava), which she did. 'This clearly is questionable, illegal and unprofessional method adopted by the IB officials to get Srivastava's photograph identified under pressure.'

G Babu Raj, who was part of the Kerala Police team headed by Siby Mathews, said the IB did not share the result of their interrogation of the accused with his team. When Chandrasekhar was being interrogated by the IB at Latex Guest House, Trivandrum, Babu Raj said he visited the place and found a bunch of hair lying in the bathroom and felt like vomiting. He stated that the IB had already come to the conclusion regarding the involvement of Srivastava in the espionage case even before the case was registered, and, therefore, he did not feel it necessary to verify the facts. He told the CBI that 'it was difficult on our part to digest the above conclusion of the IB, but we were helpless.'

Babu Raj said he showed Fauziyya the photograph of K L Bhasin, and she readily identified as that of the person she had seen at Army Club, Bangalore and has been referring to as 'Brigadier Srivastava'. He said he was convinced that the person whom Fauziyya had met at Bangalore along with Sharma was none other than K L Bhasin.

Siby Mathews, who was in charge of the investigation, wrote a letter to the DGP, Kerala, saying the special team has not conducted any investigation on Srivastava. 'During discussion with officers of IB at the office of DGP (Intelligence) and also with your good self, I have mentioned that without some incriminating evidence, it is highly embarrassing to inquire about the alleged role of the IGP. The officers of IB have not disclosed the grounds for the allegations against the IGP.'

MATHEW JOHN, JOINT DIRECTOR, SIB, TRIVANDRUM

Mathew John told the CBI that the IB got involved in the interrogation of Mariam Rasheeda on the request of Kerala Police. He, however, could not recollect the names of all the IB officers involved, but he named P B Sreekumar, deputy director, SIB, and some other subordinate officers.

Mathew John said he had sent a report to the IB headquarters in Delhi expressing the view that the facts disclosed by the accused persons were a mixture of half-truths and falsehood. He also stated that the involvement of Srivastava, IGP, was highlighted by the media but he did not take steps to verify the disclosures of the accused persons nor questioned Raman Srivastava in this regard. Though the name of Srivastava figured in the interrogation reports of Fauziyya and Rasheeda, the exact identity of Srivastava had not been established.

R B SREEKUMAR, DEPUTY DIRECTOR, SIB, TRIVANDRUM

Sreekumar said that whatever was stated by the accused persons were jotted down and a consolidated report was prepared in the evening. However, it was unsigned; the disclosures were not verified by the IB.

He could not identify the IB officers involved in the preparation of the video tapes. He also declined to vouch for the genuineness of the video tapes because he had not seen them. He admitted that the IB does not have the legal authority to examine the accused when they are in the custody of the police.

C M RAVINDRAN, DEPUTY DIRECTOR, SIB, BOMBAY

Ravindran said till he was in Trivandrum interrogating Rasheeda, no espionage angle came to his notice. He had prepared a report in this regard and submitted to John Mathew.

Calling the IB's bluff, the CBI report concludes:
The interrogation reports as recorded by the IB officers are incoherent and full of contradictions and do not give the exact nature of documents, which were allegedly passed on to foreign agents. Rather, they have blandly recorded that the drawings/documents of Viking engine and cryogenic engine were secreted out. Further, they failed to reconcile the statements, as the statements contradict each other on several points.

The above mentioned facts show that the aforesaid IB officials comprising the team inquiring into ISRO case acted in an unprofessional manner and were privy to the arrest of six innocent persons, thereby causing them immense mental and physical agony. The senior officers who were supervising and monitoring the inquiries under reference, particularly Mathew John, Joint Director, and P B Sreekumar failed in their duty to conduct the inquiry in an objective and fair manner. At the IB headquarters, the UO notes referred to herein above were prepared based on these interrogation reports and without verification, leading to serious complications including casting doubts on the integrity of two top ISRO scientists who were responsible for developing the PSLV project and launching our country into space.

CBI REPORT ON THE ROLE OF KERALA POLICE OFFICERS

S VIJAYAN, INSPECTOR, SPECIAL BRANCH, TRIVANDRUM

Vijayan questioned Mariam Rasheeda and Fauziyya Hassan since 14 October 1994 when they had approached him for getting permission for stay beyond ninety days. He told Mariam to get a confirmed ticket for her return. Accordingly, she purchased an Indian Airlines ticket to Male and another ticket to Colombo on Sri Lankan Airlines for 17 October 1994.

Vijayan, however, kept with him the tickets of Mariam Rasheeda unauthorisedly and on 20 October 1994 arrested her at 4:15pm and lodged a complaint with Vanchiyoor Police. This formed the basis of the case against her under the Foreigners Act. The seizure of the tickets was not shown even after the registration of the case and, thus, he caused obstruction to Mariam Rasheeda's return to Male on 17 October 1994.

Vijayan was entrusted with the police custody of Mariam Rasheeda by the magistrate, but he surrendered her custody to IB officials in contravention of the court orders and caused the IB officials alone interrogating and torturing Mariam Rasheeda. Vijayan has recorded in his several case diaries that the IB officials asked him to get out of the room and, therefore, he had to leave the room leaving the lady accused to the male officials of IB. He is, thus, liable for dereliction and abrogation of legal duties.

On 11 November 1994, Mariam Rasheeda disclosed about her contacts with accused Sasikumaran and Chandrasekhar. Inspector Vijayan took no steps to question immediately either Sasikumaran or Chandrasekhar and to confront them with Mariam Rasheeda so as to bring out the truth, especially in the context of wide media coverage from 22 October 1994 alleging espionage activities.

The basis of his deduction that Mariam Rasheeda and Fauziyya Hassan had come to India for espionage purposes has not been brought out on record by him. During investigation, he did not collect any information about any particular espionage activity committed by the accused. Despite this, he preferred to lodge a report at Vanchiyoor Police Station on 13 November 1994 that Mariam Rasheeda and Fauziyya Hassan had committed activities prejudicial to the sovereignty and integrity of the state.

The main grounds mentioned in the FIR for allegation of espionage is that Mariam Rasheeda contacted Sasikumaran several times and that she had made lot of entries in her diary, which was seized by them. Verification of these telephone calls and a translation of the diary entries would have confirmed that they had nothing to do with ISRO or espionage. Without any verification, Vijayan asked in haste to lodge an FIR on allegations of espionage. Inspector Vijayan, thus, acted in an unfair and unprofessional manner, thereby, causing avoidable harassment and suffering to the accused persons.

While Mariyam Rasheeda was in his personal custody, he allowed the IB officials to ill-treat her and even he himself threatened Mariam Rasheeda of dire consequences. In his statement, Vijayan admitted having shown the photograph of Raman Srivastava to Mariam Rasheeda. But strangely enough, he did not bring this fact on record. Nor did he bring on record the rationale of why only Raman Srivastava's photograph was shown to Mariam Rasheeda. This shows malafides and lack of professional integrity on his part.

K K JOSHWA, DSP, CB, CID, TRIVANDRUM

Joshwa was drafted in the Special Investigation Team which took over the investigation of case on 15 November 1994. That very day he was assigned the job of preparing the case records.

He recorded that both Mariam Rasheeda and Fauziyya Hassan admitted that they came to India to collect vital information for some agent of alien countries and that they contacted Sasikumaran, scientist of LPSC, and Chandrasekhar or Bangalore and others and collected valuable information and passed on the same to foreign countries. However, he did not record the statements of the accused on

16 November 1994. Neither did he mention the details of the alleged valuable information.

He took no immediate steps to recover any incriminating documents by way of conducting house searches of Sasikumaran and Chandrasekhar. It is on record that the interrogation of accused Fauziyya Hassan was videographed by IB, but the same has not been indicated in the case records in spite of the fact that the custody of the accused was with the Kerala Police.

Though it has been brought on record that the accused were interrogated by IB officials, no interrogation report whatsoever prepared by the IB was taken on record by him. Nor did he verify the allegations contained in the statements.

The accused, during questioning by the CBI, have stated that they were mentally and physically tortured during police custody as a result of which they had to make statements on suggested lines. The investigation also disclosed that accused Nambi Narayanan and Chandrasekhar were given medical treatment while in police custody on 3 December 1994 and 28 November 1994 respectively. However, the fact of medical treatment given to the accused has been suppressed from the case diaries and case records of DSP K K Joshwa.

Joshwa took no steps either to question Raman Srivastava or check the official records, which were available to ascertain the movements of Raman Srivastava. This again tantamount to dereliction of duty.

On the one hand, Kerala Police was suspecting espionage activities and, on the other hand, they delayed the conduct of house searches to recover incriminating documents, if any. This is clear from the fact that the house and office search of accused Sasikumaran at LPSC was conducted on 30 November 1994, in spite of the fact, that the accused has been arrested by them on 21 November 1994.

Similarly, though Nambi Narayanan was arrested on 30 November 1994, house search was not conducted till the case was handed over to the CBI on 4 December 1994.

The house search of Mohana Prasad (LPSC scientist) as mentioned in Siby Mathews's letter dated 16 December 1994 has not been reflected in the case records of K K Joshwa.

SIBY MATHEWS, DIG, CRIME

Siby Mathews was heading the Special Investigation Team and was, therefore, fully responsible for the conduct of investigation in the aforesaid two cases. The CBI investigation has revealed that he did not take adequate steps either in regard to the thorough interrogation of the accused persons by the Kerala Police.

In fact, he left the entire investigation to IB, surrendering his duties. He ordered indiscriminate arrest of the ISRO scientists and others without adequate evidence being on record. It is stressed that neither Siby Mathews and his team recovered any incriminating ISRO documents from the accused nor any monies alleged to have been paid to the accused by their foreign masters.

It was unprofessional on his part to have ordered indiscriminate arrests of top ISRO scientists who played a key role in successful launching of satellites in space and, thereby, caused avoidable mental and physical agony to them.

Siby Mathews sent a report to the DGP, Kerala, stating that it was embarrassing for him to conduct further investigation into the alleged role of Raman Srivastava, IGP, in this episode as even the IB had not enlightened him about the grounds on which they were suspecting Raman Srivastava's involvement. Being a senior officer, he should have verified the facts from all possible angles and conducted investigation in a professional way and, thereafter, taken a clear and firm stand on the role of Raman Srivastava. It is unfortunate that he allowed the doubts and suspicions in the mass media and the public mind to linger on without conducting proper verification.

While handling over the case records to the CBI, Siby Mathews recorded that the CBI should conduct searches of the houses and offices of Nambi Narayanan, verify investments made by the accused with Thomas Kurisinkal of Cochin, confirm the identity of 'Brigadier' also known as 'Coatwallah', ascertain the nature of secret documents alleged to have been secreted out by Mehboob Pasha/Mohiyuddin and verify with the records of Hotel International, Madras regarding the stay of accused persons on 24 January 1994.

It is important to mention that Mathews took over the charge of the cases on 15 November 1994. The case continued with him till 4 December 1994. Thus, the case remained with him for about twenty days. It is surprising that he did not take any steps at his own level to conduct investigation on the points suggested by him. Since, Mathews was based in Trivandrum there was no justification for not having the searches conducted in the official/residential premises of accused Nambi Narayanan who was arrested by the Kerala Police on 11 November 1994.

Even though accused Sasikumaran was arrested on 21 November 1994, his house search was conducted on 30 November 1994, after seven days for which there is no justification. This shows lack of professionalism on his part.

Babu Raj, SP, CB, CID, Trivandrum has clearly recorded that the person who had accompanied Rasheeda and Fauziyya to the Army Club at Bangalore in June 1994 was K L Bhasin. He, thus ruled out the possibility of Raman Srivastava's presence in the said club along with the Maldivian ladies. The case diary is presumed to have been submitted to Siby Mathews, being in charge of the team.

It is intriguing that Mathews did not take any steps to educate the media about the outcome of the investigation conducted by his team on this aspect and, thus, deliberately and intentionally allowed the rumours to float uninterrupted and, thereby, caused deep embarrassment to Raman Srivastava.

Mathews, before handing over the case to the CBI, recorded that further investigation is required to be conducted to firmly fix up the identity of 'Brigadier' or 'Coatwallah'. It is not known as to why he did not inquire into this aspect himself for twenty days when the case was being supervised by him.

It is not clear as to why Mathews did not examine Raman Srivastava in this matter. It appears that he deliberately and intentionally allowed the investigation to drift for reasons best known to him.

Siby Mathews in his statement has admitted that the photograph of K L Bhasin was collected at Bangalore and on return to Trivandrum, the photograph of Bhasin was shown to accused Fauziyya Hassan who identified the photograph of Bhasin to be of the person with whom she and Mariam Rasheeda went to a place which looked like Army Club in Bangalore. However, this fact had not been brought on record.

Siby Mathews and his team miserably failed even in conducting verification of the records of Hotel Fort Manor, Hotel Pankaj and Hotel Luciya, which were located in Trivandrum to ascertain the veracity of the statements of the accused. Similarly, he failed to get the records of Hotel International, Madras, checked up notwithstanding the fact that the investigation remained with him for twenty days.

The above facts are being brought to the notice of the competent authority for their kind consideration and for such action as deemed fit.

CHAPTER 28

FIGHT TO THE FINISH

'We've won the case.'

On 2 May 1996, the Chief Judicial Magistrate (CJM), Ernakulam accepted the CBI report discharging all the accused and proclaiming the ISRO espionage case as false. That marked the happy ending of the investigation and the beginning of a bitter legal battle.

Kerala was in the process of electing its tenth legislative assembly. The CPI (M), which had mentioned the case in its election manifesto to checkmate the Congress, was on its way to power. Leader of the opposition V S Achuthanandan had set the tone in March 1996 by filing a petition in the Kerala high court, seeking a judicial inquiry. The high court dismissed this petition on 27 May 1996.

The CBI report had sent shivers down the spine of the investigating officers as it mentioned that the agency would be sending two separate confidential reports to the union government and the Kerala Government. Kerala officers Siby Mathews, Joshua and inspector S Vijayan knew well they were in the dock.

On 7 May, inspector Vijayan filed a criminal review petition in the Kerala High Court against the CJM's order. The officers knew their political masters were changing, as the CPI (M) was riding the crest of an anti-Congress wave in Kerala. On 20 May, the CPI (M)-led Left Democratic Front replaced the Antony government, with E K Nayanar as the Chief Minister.

Siby Mathews, Joshua and Vijayan wrote separate letters to the Chief Minister seeking withdrawal of the consent given to the CBI to investigate the case. It was ridiculous to do that since the agency had already filed its report and a court had discharged the accused, but derision is often the child of desperation.

While the letters of Joshua and Vijayan were routed through the DGP, Siby Mathews showed the temerity to write directly to the Chief Minister. The Chief Minister's office forwarded this letter to the DGP, who recommended that the government may implead in Vijayan's petition for a review of the CBI's final report. 'There is scope for a thorough reinvestigation of the ISRO espionage case,' said the DGP's confidential note to the government.

Now Siby Mathews and others went to the Chief Minister and fell at his feet. I am told, they painted a picture of themselves as valiant sleuths who tried their best to protect national interest, but ended up being wronged. Their plea: a re-investigation. With the DGP, too, suggesting there was scope for such a move, Nayanar agreed.

The CBI sent its confidential report detailing the unprofessionalism of the police officers and seeking action against them on 9 June 1996. The next day the state government issued an executive order for re-investigation. It formed a special team headed by T P Senkumar, commissioner of police, Ernakulam. The team members were M Sugathan, DSP, CBCID, Thiruvananthapuram (earlier Trivandrum), T V Sasikumar, assistant commissioner of police (traffic), Thiruvananthapuram and V K Girijathan Nair, circle inspector of police, Vizhinjam, Thiruvananthapuram. C A Chaly, additional director general of police (crime) was to 'personally supervise' the investigation.

The same month, the government appointed M K Damodaran, who represented Nayanar in the case when he was served a notice as the chief editor of CPI (M) organ *Deshabhimani*, which was reporting the spy case. Kallada Sukumaran, who represented Achuthanandan while seeking a judicial inquiry into the case, was appointed the new director general of prosecution. On 27 June, the state government withdrew the consent given to the CBI to pursue the case.

While the drama of desperation was unfolding in Kerala, I was reinstated at the ISRO headquarters in Bangalore, with effect from 1 July 1996. As I entered ISRO chairman Kasturirangan's room, he stood up to receive me.

'You've been through hell, Mr Nambi,' he said.

I stood still, not showing my anger at this man and the organisation, which made no effort to tell the world the past twenty months that its scientists were clean and the allegations of smuggling out rocket secrets were laughable, if not despicable.

'You have a lot more to contribute,' Kasturirangan continued.

'I've nothing more to contribute,' I said. 'I've got more than enough for all the contribution I have made.'

He mouthed some kind words which both of us knew were hollow. About ten minutes later, I moved to my new office in the ISRO headquarters. Colleagues streamed in, many telling me in hushed tones that it was disappointing how the organisation did not stand by me in testing times. I listened to these formalities with a sense of cultivated equanimity.

The board outside my office room read 'Director, Advanced Technology & Planning'. I got down to planning my legal battle with the Government of Kerala and its minions in khaki.

The Malayalam media, which has been on an overdrive, paused and reflected. But still some of those, who were carried away from the initial days of misreporting on the case and did not bother to check the basic flaws in the allegations, fell silent. The English newspapers, which had refused to buy the spy theory right from the beginning, stood vindicated. Television channels, which lived only in the present, were just happy with the sound bytes.

Now I was mobbed by television channels. In one of the interviews to *Asianet*, I said the government's order for reinvestigation would not stand legal scrutiny. Instead, I said, it should have gone for further investigation.

I did not know then that I was giving my opponents an idea. On 8 July 1996, the government issued an erratum, changing the word 'reinvestigation' in its order to 'further investigation'.

Some groups, which had by now used the ISRO spy case for their publicity, were upset that their façade of the crusade in national interest was coming apart. One such was a group called All India Lawyers Forum that filed a criminal review petition challenging the CJM's order. A man called P A Viswambharan, who claimed to be a retired

IB man, followed suit, with Kallada Sukumaran, the director general of prosecution of the Kerala Government representing him. The Kerala High Court dismissed all these petitions. On 18 July 1996, the union government announced in Parliament that the ISRO espionage case has been closed.

But this clutch of Kerala Police Officers just could not let it end this way, for they had to now face the music. They kept repeating portions from an order of a Kerala High Court bench comprising K Sreedharan and B N Patnaik on 13 January 1995. On a writ filed by an NGO called Niyamavedi, some videos of our interrogation were produced before the court. Curiously enough, nobody knew or acknowledged the source of the videos (later it became clear that it was the IB). Watching one of the videos, a judge had prematurely observed that it was 'crystal clear' that espionage had happened.

What he didn't know was that the Maldivian women, whose 'confession' formed the basis of this observation, had told the CBI that their interrogators had held sheets of paper with names of people to be identified in the confession statement, just above the camera (My name, especially, was a tongue twister for the Maldivians). The discerning CBI officers found that the eyes of the accused where hovering above the camera while they uttered the names.

The same order, incidentally, also had some uncharitable remarks against the CBI. This, the premier investigating agency, got expunged by the Supreme Court via an order dated 5 April 1995.

Now, after the Kerala Government issued the order for further investigation, I challenged it in the Kerala High Court. Here, the bench comprising Justice K G Balakrishnan and Justice B N Patnaik gave an ambiguous order, refusing to quash the government order, but at the same time saying that the state government has no jurisdiction to file a chargesheet in the case.

The court said, 'It has been held above that the state government has no jurisdiction to file a complaint or a chargesheet in respect of the alleged offences under the IOS Act (Official Secrets Act). Of course, the state in exercise of its power under the Police Act can direct a police officer to do any further investigation. But that power, in our opinion, is circumscribed by the provisions of the IOS Act...'

This, in effect, meant that the Kerala Police could do further investigation into the spy case, but could do nothing with what the findings of the investigation!

In September 1996, Senkumar, the officer in charge of 'further investigation', moved court seeking all records from the CBI. This did not yield any result. So, the officer did something unusual—he sought permission from the CJM, Trivandrum to carry out further investigation as ordered by the government.

He highlighted that part of the Balakrishnan-Patnaik judgment that upheld the government's power to issue the order (without mentioning that the court had also said that the police cannot file a chargesheet). The CJM gave its order on 13 December 1996, permitting further investigation as ordered by the government.

It was a curious case, since the police officer, already armed with a government order, could execute it without a court's permission. So why did he go to the CJM? Well, he wanted to engage me in a longer legal tussle and delay things.

This was more so in the interest of Siby Mathews who did not want to be sacked till he got a voluntary retirement. Siby Mathews stood a fair chance of retiring as the DGP, but his desperation for an 'honourable exit' drove him to voluntary retirement. And Oommen Chandy, who came to power in 2011, posted him as the chief information commissioner of Kerala, clearly a reward for dancing to the political tunes to oust K Karunakaran from the Chief Minister's chair using the ISRO spy case.

Now that the CJM had given him a favourable order, Senkumar expected me to challenge it in the high court. I refused to fall into this trap. Instead, I went to the Supreme Court, challenging not the CJM's order that gave permission for further investigation, but the Balakrishnan-Patnaik order that upheld the government order for further investigation. I filed a special leave petition on 20 December 1996, praying for quashing of the high court order and, thereby, the Kerala Government's executive order.

The battle was now in the final stage. My co-accused Sasi, Chandra and Sharma joined in as petitioners. Having decided to fight to the finish, together we employed a battery of lawyers including Harish Salve, K

K Venugopal and T S Arunachalam. S Muralidhar, who later became a judge of the Delhi High Court, was my lawyer on record. The Kerala Government brought in Advocate General M K Damodaran, besides Shanti Bhushan who was rumoured to be charging Rs 1.25 lakh per appearance.

Salve, who later became the Solicitor General of India, was a busy lawyer. So busy that he would hold conversations with different people at the same time. Or so I thought. During a discussion about the case, I found Salve preoccupied by too many things. I was talking, and he kept humming in reply to my sentences while poring over some other papers and attending phone calls. As a scientist, I was used to people listening intently and focusing on one thing a time.

'Mr Salve, are you listening?' I said.

He looked up from the files.

'You may be good at multitasking,' I continued, 'but I demand your full attention when I am talking to you.'

I was as surprised as the lawyer was, when I finished the sentence.

Salve looked at me for a moment, then said, 'Okay. You have seven minutes of my uninterrupted attention.'

He listened in silence as I broke into a speech, capturing the essence of the case right from the sexual frustration of an inspector that led to the arrest of Maldivian woman Mariam Rasheeda to the CBI report that had exonerated the accused in the ISRO spy case. I took an extra couple of minutes to say all that, but Salve sat patiently.

During the course of the case hearing, Justice Mukerjee appeared to be having an information overload, especially after Shanti Bhushan's convoluted arguments. On one such occasion, Justice Mukerjee wondered aloud, 'What's this all about?'

At this point, Salve stood up. 'Sexual perversion of a Kerala Police Officer, your honour,' he said. And he launched himself into a compelling argument, in parts quoting verbatim from my nine-minute briefing. This man, who I thought was not listening to me during the client-lawyer meetings, was making mental notes of everything. I was in the fourth row of the visitors' gallery, on the front row were Kerala Police Officers Siby Mathews and Senkumar.

After Salve's one-hour non-stop argument and a many appearances of Muralidhar who made an equally forceful presentation of facts, I was confident of a favourable verdict from the Supreme Court. By now more than two years had passed.

The judgment was reserved sometime in early 1998, and I was in the court corridor with Sasi and others, when I noticed Siby Mathews at a distance. Senkumar brought him tea, and Mathews, visibly disturbed by the course the case had taken, told him to 'get lost'. Shanti Bhushan passed by us, then came back to tell me, 'I hope you win the case.'

The judgment came on 29 April 1998 when I was in Tenkasi in Tamil Nadu for my nephew's wedding. After the ceremony at Ilanji temple, I was having lunch with my wife Meena, our son and a few relatives when Advocate Muralidhar called.

'We've won the case,' he said.

I must have gone into a trance. I didn't register the rest of what Muralidhar was saying; he kept talking in an animated voice. Only much later, after repeatedly reading the order did it sink in that the Supreme Court has finally delivered me justice.

The order was critical of the Kerala Government. Here are some portions from Justice M K Mukherjee's judgment dated 29 April 1998:

'Even if we were to hold that the state government had the requisite power and authority to issue the impugned notification,' the court said, *'still the same would be liable to be quashed on the ground of malfide exercise of power. Eloquent proof thereof is furnished by the following facts and circumstances as appearing on the record...*

On a careful perusal of the police report submitted by the CBI on completion of the investigation (which runs into more than 100 pages) we find that it has made a detailed investigation from all possible angles before drawing the conclusion that the allegations of espionage did not stand proved and were found to be false...

If before taking up further investigation an opinion has already been formed regarding the guilt of the accused and, that too, at a stage when the commission of the offence itself is yet to be proved, it is obvious that the investigation cannot and will not be fair—and its outcome appears to be a foregone conclusion.

From the above facts and circumstances we are constrained to say that the issuance of the impugned notification does not comport with the known pattern of a responsible government bound by rule of law. This is undoubtedly a matter of concern and consternation. We say no more.

On the conclusions as above we allow thee appeals and quash the impugned notification. We direct the Government of Kerala to pay a sum of Rs 1,00,000 (Rupees one lakh) to each of the six accused-appellants as costs.'

But now, having just heard the three words 'we have won' from Advocate Muralidhar, so many things flashed through my mind— the humiliating arrest, the torturous interrogation, my tormentors who I had vowed to hunt down, my family that came back from the brink, my friends who stood by me, my career which would never be the same again …

'What happened?'

Meena was shaking me vigorously. My vision was blurred as tears roll down my cheeks.

'Tell me, what happened?' she repeated.

'We've won the case,' I said.

Meena looked at me for a moment, then swooned. I gathered her in my arms and sprinkled some water on her face. After a minute or two she regained consciousness. We wept in each other's arms.

CHAPTER 29

THE REAL CONSPIRACY

But how did I get into this mess?

That is a question I am asked by even people who have followed the ISRO spy case to its deathbed. In fact, I have asked myself this question right from my arrest to much beyond my acquittal. I started getting clues to the answers from my days of interrogation at the hands of the IB, but I got a comprehensive picture only much later. This is because the ISRO spy case was not born out of one conspiracy, but multiple ones that served different interests.

For every conspiracy there is a victim or many. The ISRO spy case is unusual in that though the conspirators were different with different motives, the victims were the same set of people. When a desperate police inspector found Sasikumaran's name in Mariam Rasheeda's diary, ISRO was dragged into it. When a master conspirator found an opportunity to slow down, if not stop, ISRO in its march to the global satellite launch market, I became a pawn.

Before we get to that crucial part, let us start at the beginning. The ISRO spy case was a lie, right from Mariam Rasheeda's arrest on 20 October 1994. Though the Maldivian woman's arrest marked the beginning of the case, the genesis of it all was a chance meeting she had with Chandrasekhar at the Trivandrum airport on 20 June 1994.

Mariam had followed her Maldivian friend Fauziyya Hassan to India. Fauziyya was in India seeking a school admission for her fourteen-year-old daughter Zila Hamdi. Mariam came for treatment for a heart condition, and explored the possibility of getting her eleven-year-old daughter Nisha, too, educated here. Much later, a CBI report that found the ISRO spy case false, mentioned that Fauziyya first came to India as an interpreter for a businessman from Sri Lanka, and Mariam had the intention of meeting her old lover, a doctor from Kozhikode.

Earlier, Mariam was an agent for the National Security Service of the Government of Maldives and was in India to gather information about some people who were believed to be planning a coup against the Government of Maumoon Abdul Gayoom.

At the airport, the customs officer extracted $100 from Mariyam. The Maldivian kept cribbing about the 'extortion' when she was overheard by a co-passenger, K Chandrasekhar, a Bangalore-based Indian representative for Russian space agency Glavkosmos. Playing the hero and trying to help the damsel in distress, Chandrasekhar quarreled with the customs officer and got back the money for Mariam.

He struck a conversation with a thankful Mariam who tried to take as much advantage of the helping hand as possible. She told him that she had a heart problem for which she needed to consult a doctor. Also, on her wish list was a school admission for her friend Fauziyya's daughter and her own daughter.

Chandrasekhar promised to deliver on everything. In Bangalore, he took Mariam to meet his friend S K Sharma who was also a labour contractor. Sharma's uncle K L Bhasin was a retired brigadier, an influential person who could be tapped for the school admission. Bhasin was later to be mistaken for or misrepresented as Kerala I G Raman Srivastava by the Intelligence Bureau. Bhasin and Sharma met Chandrasekhar and Mariam at a club in Bangalore where Sharma promised to get admission for Fauziyya's daughter. As for a doctor for Mariam, Chandrasekhar suggested the name of Sasikumaran's wife. Later Sasikumaran met Mariam.

In Bangalore, Mariam Rasheeda stayed with Fauziyya at Sara Palani's house where Fauziyya was a paying guest. As Fauziyya Hassan was having difficulty in getting admission for her daughter in a good school, and the schools were demanding high capitation fees, Fauziyya and Rasheeda met Chandrasekhar at his office on 21 June. Chandrasekhar asked S K Sharma, a labour contractor in Bangalore, for help since Sharma knew the husband of the principal of Baldwin Girls School.

A circle had been formed among the Maldivian women, Chandrasekhar, Sharma and Sasikumaran. All of them were to become accused in the spy case after inspector Vijayan bumped into Mariam in Trivandrum.

Mariam, in an interview to *Savvy Magazine*, said Vijayan made sexual advances to her after she went to inform him about the need for an extended stay in Trivandrum. She snubbed him. This was probably the reason, she alleged, that the inspector fixed her.

The CBI report on the role of certain officials of Kerala Police the investigation of ISRO espionage case says Vijayan questioned Mariam Rasheeda and Fauziyya Hassan as early as 14 October 1994, when they had approached him for getting permission for stay beyond ninety days. He told Mariam to get a confirmed ticket for her return. Accordingly, she purchased an Indian Airlines ticket to Male and another ticket to Colombo on Sri Lankan Airlines for 17 October 1994.

Vijayan, however, kept with him the tickets of Mariam Rasheeda, unauthorisedly, and on 20 October 1994 arrested her at 4:15 pm and lodged a complaint with Vanchiyoor Police Station. This formed the basis of the case against her under the Foreigners Act. The seizure of the tickets was not shown even after the registration of the case. Thus, he caused obstruction to Mariam Rasheeda's return to Male on 17 October 1994, the CBI report said.

Thaniniram evening daily reported Mariam's arrest on 20 October 1994 *Deshabhimani*, the CPI(M) mouthpiece reported it the next day, bringing in the espionage angle. Vijayan, who had discussed the 'offensive strategy' with Trivandrum city police commissioner V R Rajeevan, had by now made a valuable discovery that Mariam was a private for the Maldivian National Security Service. This was the genesis of the word 'spy' in the *Desbhabhimani* story, and later in the case itself.

The IB had already interrogated Mariam and Fauziyya, and evidently formed an opinion that spying had happened, though they had no evidence of it. In the following days, *Kerala Kaumudi* came out with an 'exclusive' linking I G Raman Srivastava with the spy ring. In his book *Spies from Space: The ISRO Frame-up*, Rajasekharan Nair explains the Malayalam daily's motive in fixing Srivastava who evicted its editor M S Mani from the office, following a court order on a family feud. This came as a shot in the arm for the 'Oommen Chandy-led Antony' faction of the Congress to hit at Chief Minister K Karunakaran. The faction constituted a crack team that kept feeding Malayalam journalists' imaginary tales of the spy case. Srivastava was suspended later, following adverse remarks by the Kerala High Court (which was later chided by the Supreme Court), and Karunakaran lost his chair. Those were two victories for two minor players who were not aware of the bigger conspiracy, which was being hatched by some foreign hands to delay, if not prevent, India from entering the commercial satellite launch market.

With Vijayan finding the names of ISRO scientist Sasikumaran in Mariam's diary, the stage was set to link the arrested women with the space organisation. As the newspapers went to town with the spy women's links with ISRO scientist Sasikumaran, ISRO made the wrong move of transferring him to Satellites Application Centre (SAC), Ahmedabad on 5 November 1994.

Behind this move was Sengupta, an IAS officer in the space department with whom Sasikumaran had a tiff earlier. In a review meeting, the bureaucrat had chided Sasikumaran, saying he did not understand administration. Sasikumaran, for his part, retorted that he as an IAS man did not understand technology. Now, with his name linked to Mariam Rasheeda, Sengupta made haste to impress upon the ISRO chairman to sign on the dotted line to transfer Sasikumaran.

On 9 November 1994 the day Sasikumaran joined SAC, Ahmedabad, Fauziyya Hassan was arrested in Bangalore and brought to Trivandrum. The next day, IB joint director M K Dhar came to Trivandrum, marking a turning point in the case. It was on this day that the IB claimed to have got the first 'confession statement' from Fauziyya about espionage. On 13 November 1994, Mariam and Fauziyya were charged with espionage.

With newspapers going overboard with spy tales, the Kerala Police held internal meetings and decided on 14 November 1994 to hand over the investigation to the CBI. But IB was against the idea. The next day the Kerala DGP constituted a Special Investigation Team (SIT) headed by DIG Sibi Mathews to investigate the case. By now IB men were torturing the accused to extract 'confessions'.

On 21 November 1994, Sasikumaran was arrested in Ahmedabad, and Chandrasekhar was picked up in Bangalore. On the same day, IB sent an unofficial (UO) note to the highest authorities in Delhi, to book the accused under Official Secrets Act and implicate Ravinder Reddy of MTAR and Prabhakar Rao in the case. These moves were to tighten the noose around ISRO, and prepare ground for my arrest.

The first indication of dragging me into the plot came on 28 November 1994, when *Kerala Kaumudi* published a false report that I was under house arrest. On this day, the IB sent another UO note recommending that Raman Srivastava may be questioned. Two days later, I was arrested.

THE PLOT

Till IB Joint Director M K Dhar flew down to Trivandrum on 10 November 1994, there was nothing to link me with the case. In fact, the first UO note the IB had sent to the higher ups said that no espionage had happened. A second UO note, sent after Dhar's visit, said spying appeared to have taken place. A third UO note, after IB could not gather any evidence to substantiate their theory, said it was all a combination of truth, half-truths and lies.

So what urged Dhar to rush to Trivandrum? It was part of his counter-intelligence operations against Pakistan, argues the IB officer in his hilarious book *Open Secrets: India's Intelligence Unveiled*. There may still be a few conspiracy theorists who would find enough masala in that book that tries in vain to argue there was indeed espionage in ISRO.

Someone made haste to arrest me. All that, later, they gave as reason was that Sasikumaran had 'confessed' that I was hand in glove with him in carting away drawings from ISRO. The CBI report, endorsed by the Chief Judicial Magistrate, Ernakulam, and later the Supreme Court, said no such thing happened. Before all, that if they did suspect that I had traded drawings for dollars, they should have raided my house and office. They did not.

Had they raided my place, as the CBI did later, they would have nothing to substantiate their claims with, and my arrest would not have made sense. So, I had to be implicated even without evidence. Someone wanted the head of the cryogenic mission arrested as part of the plot. The project had be stalled.

Curiously enough, I was arrested on 30 November 1994, the same day the Kerala Police wrote to hand over the investigation to the CBI. Once you have decided to entrust the central agency with the investigation, why not wait for them to take a decision on my arrest? From the beginning, Dhar and his colleague Ratan Sehgal were in a tearing hurry to establish espionage even though there was no evidence. Dhar's book mentions about Ratan Sehgal in the initial phase of the investigation, but Dhar took upon himself the task of being the prime fabricator of the ISRO spy case.

The timing of the implication of ISRO makes it a suspect on at least two counts. One, when Dhar came to Trivandrum, the countdown for the launch of PSLV-D2 rocket was about to begin. Even as he was questioning Mariam Rasheeda and Fauziyya Hassan, on 15 October 1994, PSLV-D2 put in orbit Indian Remote Sensing Satellite IRS-P2. It was the first successful launch of an Indian rocket that could be used for commercial satellite launches. Two, ISRO was in the process of bringing materials and drawings as part of a cryogenic technology transfer from Russia after the US imposed sanctions on Russia and India. Owing to the pressure from the US, Glavkosmos wanted to cancel the contract, but ISRO had succeeded in advancing some milestones and making payments before the new clauses kicked in.

It was quite an achievement for us to have skirted the US pressure to bring home the cryogenic consignments. We managed, much to the chagrin of the US, to get the Russian Ural Airlines to bring the voluminous documents and hardware to India. Of the four scheduled consignments from Moscow, three had landed in Trivandrum between 23 January and 17 July 1994. The last one was to come in December 1994. However, before that the ISRO spy case was fabricated.

Some people were clearly not happy also with India flying its first satellite launch vehicle; they knew India would barge into the commercial satellite launch market with high competent prices (as less as half an American launch) if it acquired cryogenic technology. Then Prime Minister P V Narasimha Rao put it mildly during a discussion in the Parliament, indicating the 'involvement of a foreign country' in thwarting the Russian cryogenic contract.

Six respectable people—Satish Dhawan, T N Seshan, U R Rao, Yash Pal, R Narasimha and S Chandrashekar—had this to say in an open letter after the Kerala Government ordered 'further investigation' in the case even after the Chief Judicial Magistrate had accepted the CBI report and absolved all the accused of the charges: 'The "espionage case" reveals that the country's space programme or for that matter other strategic programmes, may no longer be immune to outside interference.'

So, were the IB officers pawns or active foot soldiers in this interested party's international board game? It will be tough to say 'no' if you look at the systematic way in which the US imposed sanctions to scuttle the cryogenic technology transfer from Russia to India only two years earlier, and the way in which Dhar and a few other IB officers decided on the espionage angle, even before they started investigation.

American intelligence is known for penetrating a developing country's intelligence network by targeting two kinds of people: young officers and those on the verge of retirement. They believe some youngsters in crucial Indian departments can be 'cultivated', and, as they grow in their diplomatic career, can be a valuable asset for the US intelligence. India's counter intelligence strategists are well aware of this cat-and-mouse game; this is why R&AW keeps shuffling its decks, especially at the bottom.

The superannuating officers are a high-risk, instant return target. They approach such officers only after ascertaining their level of integrity, and the quantum of barter to break it. Those fishing know what an upright Indian bureaucrat or intelligence officer must have earned at the end of his service. Some of them find the promise of a slightly wealthy retired life tantalizing after a middle-class sojourn of more than three decades.

M K Dhar was to retire by the beginning of 1995, a few months after Mariam Rasheeda was arrested. It is also on record that Dhar had made some desperate attempts to get his official date of birth 'corrected' so that he could get an extension of service. When a senior officer nearing retirement is handling a sensitive case, it is usual for the government to give him an extension beyond superannuation to complete the assignment. Dhar had tried in vain to weave a story of a Pakistan conspiracy by arresting a Muslim religious leader in a northern state, but when the government was convinced of the leader's background and standing, Dhar had to eat a humble pie. It is at this juncture he saw the potential of the ISRO spy case.

In *Open Secrets*, written after the CBI indicted the IB and the Kerala Police for virtually foisting the ISRO spy case, Dhar paints himself as an Abhimanyu of sorts. After the castle of a case he built fell like nine pins, Dhar blamed virtually everyone, including then IB director D C Pathak, then CBI director Vijaya Rama Rao, and then Prime Minister P V Narasimha Rao. In the process of explaining his strategy, Dhar inadvertently makes some confessions including one that admits that the IB had interrogated the ISRO spy case accused and denied Kerala Police access to IB's tech team, which he had instructed to videograph the entire interrogation process. 'Altogether seventy-one black and white and one colour video cassettes were produced by the TechInt boys,' boasts Dhar.

Why did the IB not produce these recordings to prove that there was no torture of the accused as the CBI found? Well, Dhar blames it on his boss for not having a separate counsel for the IB, which had to move the court along with the CBI. At one place, he confesses: 'We were in no position to substantiate most of the linkages revealed during interrogation.'

Letting his frustration known that he was not able to convince the higher ups, Dhar flaunts his ignorance by implying that rockets can be duplicated using stolen and smuggled drawings thus, '... Pakistan had abiding interest in Indian rocket technology and they were themselves engaged in developing indigenous rockets with borrowed and stolen know-how.'

Those who agree with Dhar should know that if this is true, Pakistan could source these drawings from many small-scale industries, which are given the drawings of several components for fabrication. And then, there is a difference between know-how and know-why, the latter being the reason we worked in close coordination with the French for almost five years to develop the Vikas engine. If a bunch of drawings were enough, we need not have gone to Vernon to master it.

Here is an extract from the open letter signed by the country's leading scientists and administrators in space science: 'As people who have been associated with technology development in India, we have not been able to understand the logic of what is supposed to have happened in the "espionage case". Clearly the acquisition of technology by any foreign power is quite a complex process. Experience indicates that even when drawings are acquired under open technology transfer agreements, their transformation into working hardware takes time, expertise and large financial outlays.

'The Maldivian women involved, their mode of entry into India or their activities seem to be inconsistent with the aim of acquiring sensitive technology by any interested foreign power. ISRO does not classify working level documents as secret, top secret or confidential. An internal investigation carried out by ISRO has shown that there are no original drawings related to the Viking or cryogenic engines missing. In fact, in this case, even fabrication drawings which ISRO routinely passes on to industry, are not missing.'

Dhar's observations on rocketry and 'the plot' show either he was ignorant of how rocket technology is transferred or if he had some basic understanding, he was fabricating the ISRO spy case, ostensibly on someone's orders.

That the IB was penetrated by the US became clear when Dhar's colleague Ratan Sehgal was sacked as the IB joint director and charges of having nine 'unauthorized and clandestine' meetings with CIA station chief in Delhi, Timoty Long, and his deputy Susan Brown between

19 September and 31 October 1996. The investigation found that the meetings happened in Sehgal's house in Bharati Nagar and in the parking lot of Ambassador Hotel, both in Delhi. Counter intelligence officers reported evidence of Sehgal having received a 'large packet' from Ms August, a former deputy station chief of the CIA, outside Ambassador Hotel.

Sehgal was asked to face prosecution or put in his papers. He chose voluntary retirement. It is strange that the ISRO spy case started a few months after Sehgal joined the IB from the Ministry of External Affairs and ended around the same time he was chucked out of the IB.

Another interesting coincidence is that R B Sreekumar, Deputy Director, IB, Kerala unit, happened to be the CISF commandant in charge of security of ISRO's VSSC campus in Trivandrum many years earlier. It was only after my arrest, I realised that I had given enough reasons to Sreekumar to hate me. Here is one of our past encounters.

I had seen Sreekumar on the VSSC campus a few times, he came across as a silent officer doing his duty. He reported to P M Nair, the administrative head, who in turn reported to Gowarikar. There was no scope for much interaction between me and Sreekumar. VSSC was to recruit some mechanical engineers, and I was in the selection committee when one day Sreekumar walked into my room. He had a request to favourably consider the candidature of a woman. Going by selection guidelines, those who come with recommendations should be removed from the candidate list and should not be considered for the interview.

I did not follow this guideline since that may deny the job to a deserving candidate just because someone had come with a recommendation for him/her, sometimes without his/her knowledge. During such recruitment phases it was common for me to receive calls from ministers' offices and such high places with recommendations. My practice was to listen to the requests, some even bordering on 'instructions', ignore them and select the candidates on merit. And that is how I treated Sreekumar's request. Being the commandant of CISF, our prime sentinel, I listened to him courteously and told him that if the candidate is good she will make it. Sreekumar left the room. When the selection list was out, Sreekumar came to me again.

'You should've told me that you couldn't get her the job,' he said. Only then had I realised that the woman for whom he had recommended the job had not made it to the selection list. I explained to Sreekumar that as a matter of policy we just hear people out, but don't act on recommendations. Several people would also call to thank us for giving someone a job. With equal nonchalance, we listen to such responses, often not telling them that their recommendation made no difference to the prospects of the candidate who was selected purely on merit.

He raised his voice. I raised mine. In normal circumstances, I should have reported to the CISF commandant about a 'trespasser' in my office. Now, the trespasser was the CISF commandant. Even as I stood wondering who to call, Sreekumar walked to the door, but turned to me and issued this threat, 'You will pay for this.'

'Get out,' I shouted.

During my interrogation, Sreekumar would have enjoyed his petty revenge, but I am not sure if he knew about the bigger conspiracy some of his masters were privy to. Meanwhile, Siby was dancing to the tunes of Congress faction leader Oommen Chandy whose prime aim was to unseat Kerala Chief Minister K Karunakaran.

Siby, after his retirement, was rewarded by Chandy, then Chief Minister, with the post of the chief information officer in Kerala. Siby, like Sreekumar, has been pleading innocence, and blaming others for the fiasco in public. In private, however, Siby was at least once profusely apologetic to me for being part, inadvertently, according to him, of the conspiracy that ruined my career. And that was a secret meeting Siby must be trying hard to forget.

It was after much persuasion by a common friend and a popular figure that I agreed to meet Siby Mathews. The ISRO spy case was long rotting in history's dustbin after the Supreme Court had ruled in my favour and the National Human Rights Commission asked the Kerala Government to pay me compensation. I was still fighting to get punishment for the officers of the IB and the Kerala Police named in the CBI report. And Siby was worried of getting punishment not just from the government, but from God, as I was soon to realise.

Siby was with his wife at the friend's place by the time I reached there. I controlled my rage at the very sight of the officer, but kept my composure. After Siby tried to explain that he was dragged into the whole affair and had no intention to harm me, it was left to his wife to do the crucial part of the talking. She explained that her husband—and the family as a whole— is facing a 'divine punishment'.

She knew my wife Meena's daily visits to temples, and it appeared that the couple were worried that she was doing special prayers to harm Siby Mathews.

The rendezvous, that soon ended, did not get any more pleasant.

By 1998, when I came to know of Ratan Sehgal's forced exit as IB Joint Director because of his secret meetings with CIA agents, the Supreme Court had ruled in my favour, dismissing the Kerala Government's executive order for further investigation into the ISRO spy case. I could not resist the temptation to visit Arun Bhagat, the new IB director, to know if Sehgal's CIA connections had anything to do with the ISRO spy case.

As an R&AW officer then, Bhagat had interrogated me. He did not have a clear answer to my question. He said when he was involved in the ISRO investigation, he was not aware of Sehgal's dalliance with CIA officials, and hence could not comment on any correlation. My next question was point blank, 'Why did you let Sehgal take voluntary retirement, and not prosecute him?'

He said something to the effect that international relations are not drawn in black and white, and some allowances have to be made under some circumstances 'in national interest'. I got the drift, having read about how the Sehgal episode had deteriorated the Indo-US relations.

Media had reported when Indian cabinet secretary T S R Subramaniam and foreign secretary Salman Haider asked US ambassador Frank Wisner in January 1997 that CIA station chief Timothy Long and his deputy Susan Brown be removed. The US retaliated by asking two junior officers of R&AW at the Indian embassy's consular section in San Francisco and Chicago to leave the country. India, obviously had some national interest in mind not to aggravate the issue. And Sehgal got to retire, albeit unceremoniously.

I did not stop with the IB director. The next year I went to a senior minister. I had heard about the minister as being a no-nonsense man. The minister had agreed for a ten-minute meeting, but it went on for more than an hour, more because of the minister beating around the bush than having any meaningful discussion.

After explaining the course of the ISRO spy case, I raised my suspicion about Ratan Sehgal having played a role in it. I asked the minister why the government let him go.

'Let who go?' he feigned ignorance.

'Ratan Sehgal.'

'Who is Ratan Sehgal?'

I knew the game by now, but played along.

'The IB joint director who was forced to retire three years ago. And I just explained to you that he had joined IB just before the ISRO spy case was filed, and retired too soon after the case ended.'

The minister went on to quibble more before repeating the same set of words behind which the answers I sought were taking refuge: national interest.

The Union Home Ministry made an eyewash of an inquiry in late 1999 against nine IB officers including R B Sreekumar on nine counts on recommendation of the CBI. Going by the CBI's confidential report, the other names were Mathew John, Jai Prakash, John Punnen, G S Nair, C R R Nair, V K Maini, K V Thomas and C M Ravindran. After the 'investigation', the ministry dropped seven charges, and decided to conduct an 'oral inquiry' into the first two charges. These were, one, forcibly taking custody of the accused from the Kerala Police; and two, torturing at least three of the accused. Nothing came out of the 'oral inquiry'. Sreekumar went on to become DGP, Intelligence, Gujarat.

I was still exploring options to unravel the conspiracy behind the ISRO spy case when M K Dhar's book *Open Secrets: India's Intelligence Unveiled* was published in 2005. Once I read the book I realised there was no point in meeting this man who knew more than me about the conspiracy against India, but continued to be loyal to his foreign masters by clinging on to the theory of espionage.

I found Dhar's book a big bundle of 519 pages, to be precise, of self-righteousness, lies and bravado. In an attempt to give his arguments a façade of credibility, Dhar makes a suggestion. A joint investigation agency should be formed with representatives from the IB, CBI, R&AW and the ISRO to have a detailed look into the evidences and documents for arriving at a final conclusion. There is no harm if this reinvestigation is carried out silently and out of the glare of the media.

Dhar did not live to see such an investigation. He died in May 2012. Now, his suggestion is my demand. A joint investigation of all the top agencies should expose the real conspiracy and its infantrymen. I will strive to make it happen.

Till then, Mr Dhar, RIP.

EPILOGUE

In March 2001, the National Human Rights Commission (NHRC) ordered the Kerala government to pay me a compensation of Rs 10 lakhs. The government and Siby Mathews challenged this in the Kerala High Court. In 2005 Justice K M Joseph quashed the NHRC award and referred the matter back to the commission.

Siby Mathews and the government went to a division bench of the Kerala High Court with the appeal that the matter should not go back to the NHRC. The case dragged on till 2011. Justice C N Ramachandran Nair, who was hearing the case, was nearing retirement, I pleaded that at least the compensation part be cleared before the judge left.

Justice Nair set aside the single-judge bench order and upheld the compensation part, but asked the NHRC to hear out the police officers who said they were not given an opportunity to present their case.

Meanwhile, in 1999, I had filed a suit in a Thiruvananthapuram Sub Court, asking for Rs 1 crore compensation, with the Government of Kerala, Government of India and the police officers as respondents. Justice Prakasan was to give his order in March 2016. But, a few days before the scheduled last hearing, the judge was moved out of the post.

The case is pending.

Meanwhile, I am also awaiting an order from the Supreme Court which he had moved seeking action against officers of the Kerala Police named by the CBI for cooking up the ISRO spy case.

All the accused in the case have been exonerated, but nothing can compensate for what they suffered.

D Sasikumaran, having suffered enough humiliation, decided against fighting another legal battle, and lives a silent life in Thiruvananthapuram.

Epilogue

K Chandrasekhar, once a high-flying agent of the Russian space agency Glavkosmos, leads a modest life as a Reiki practitioner in Bengaluru.

SK Sharma, a former contractor of ISRO, suffered health problems after the ISRO spy case, and had to close down his steel rolling industrial unit in Bengaluru.

Mariam Rasheeda and **Fauziyya Hassan** lead a quiet life in the Maldives.